RESUMES THAT IMPRESS!
The Insider's Guide for Success

Cory J. Schulman
Author of *Resumes For Higher Paying Positions*

Best Seller Publications, LLC
Germantown, Maryland

Bestsellerpublications.com

Resumes That Impress!
The Insider's Guide for Success

Published by Best Seller Publications, LLC
Copyright © 2016
By Cory J. Schulman

Printed in the United States of America

Library of Congress Control Number: 2015914398

Schulman, Cory J.
    Resumes That Impress! The Insider's Guide for Success

ISBN: 978-0-9962344-0-5

Acknowledgements

A special thanks is reserved for Hillary Blackton, who provided thoughtful editorial feedback; Graphic Artist Anup Kumar Bhattacharya, who designed the appealing cover of *Resume That Impress!*; and to Lori Schulman, who provided insightful technical guidance. Acknowledgements are further extended to the numerous former clients who I interviewed to write the broad array of resume samples contained in this book. I also appreciate all of the polling responses and advice from family members, friends, and colleagues who offered their constructive comments for this ambitious project.

Dear Reader:

The United States' economy has grown for 8 consecutive years since the onset of the The Great Recession. Yet, millions of Americans remain out of work, underemployed, or still vulnerable to potential layoffs. So why do some job candidates wallow for months looking for a new job while others of the same caliber find new jobs with relative ease even in the worst of economic conditions?

Resumes, while not the only factor, play a pivotal role in securing your next job. An effective resume helps recruiters and employers select you amongst a large pool of competing, often equally qualified candidates. That selection can get you the all-important interview, which gives you the best chance of getting hired. The resume also possesses a post-interview influence, in that candidates are often forgotten once they leave the interview. However, your resume remains as a continued reminder of who you are and the potential you promise. Your resume may also be forwarded to a higher-up manager who may not have had the opportunity to meet you in person. Therefore, what you put in your resume is critical to getting opportunities and influencing the decision makers who preside over the hiring process.

Unfortunately, many accomplished professionals often have poorly prepared resumes that hold them back. No matter how great you may be, if you don't successfully convey that greatness in your resume, your job search will be hampered. After all, employers typically don't know you personally, so all they have to make a decision about you is what is on your resume.

Resumes That Impress! shows you how to create a potent, credible resume that enables you to effectively compete for the job you want. By using the proven techniques in this book, you can capture your greatest strengths and convert weaknesses into a positive self portrait of a successful, high achieving professional.

As the United States and the rest of the world continue to rebound from "The Great Recession," job opportunities are in the cross fire of one of the largest pools of job seekers ever. To stand out amongst the crowd, you need a powerful representation. This effort can be guided with the unique resume writing techniques detailed in this book. *Resumes That Impress!* is one of the few resume writing books that provides substantive samples and may be the only book, among the hundreds of resume writing books, that thoroughly covers how to quantify and qualify career highlights. With the strategic weapons this book provides, you will arm yourself with a better resume that can help you get the position you want, in a quicker timeframe, and for a higher salary.

Cory J. Schulman

Dedication

Resumes That Impress! is dedicated to all aspiring job seekers who want to make a difference.

Table of Contents

Look-up Guide for Samples

Resumes That Impress!
The Insider's Guide for Success

1 Introduction

Resumes That Impress! shows you how the experts write resumes. You will learn what it takes to create a substantive resume – one that increases your chances for getting the position you want, in a quicker timeframe, and for higher pay. This book also points out many myths and mistakes commonly made by job seekers of all calibers, including executives.

An effective resume not only convinces a prospective employer that you are qualified, it also convinces them that you are a better selection than other qualified applicants. The samples in this book emphasize measurable performance and qualifying statements that enable a candidate to emerge from the crowd of qualified competitors.

More than 700 resume books are sold on the market today. Although all of these guides contain samples, they are typically shallow with a great deal of filler verbiage. They often harp on the format, personal attributes, basic responsibilities, and obvious rules of the preparation process. *Resumes That Impress!* stands out by giving substantive samples and techniques to develop your job-winning resume.

2 What's Wrong With My Resume?

Most people already have a resume. But that doesn't mean they are well prepared to search and compete for a career position. Since resume preparation is one of the first steps taken and one of the pivotal phases in the employment process, this section addresses how to size up your own resume.

If your resume contains your contact information, experience, and education, it easily meets the general definition of a resume. However, it may not be an effective one, and it may even work against you.

Take a few minutes to learn some of the common mistakes, misconceptions, and issues found among most resumes. Then re-examine your own resume. You may start to think of new ways of casting your professional image that will result in more interviews and an easier time getting that higher paying, more rewarding position.

A resume should not be…
- **Too Sparse** by listing employment without elaboration

- **Written in Narrative or Third Person**

- **A Job Description** of Responsibilities

- **A Comprehensive Report** on Every Detail

- **A History** of Every Job Ever

- **A Mirror** Objectively Portraying Who You Really Are

- **A License** for Fraud or Distortion

The following bullets identify some common errors job seekers commit and typical issues that job seekers face followed by concise guidance.

2.1 Common Misconceptions: Check your resume

2.1.1   Too Sparse

A resume is not a list of past employment. Some candidates who may not feel comfortable with writing make the mistake of listing their employment background without elaborating on each past position. This bare bones approach defeats the primary purpose of the resume, which is to intrigue and persuade the prospective employer to select you.

Since employers typically don't know you, their perceptions of you are influenced by what you put or don't put on your resume. Listings of employment without elaboration suggest poor literacy and a lack of understanding of your own past. That lack of information also prevents a prospective employer from understanding the scope of your responsibilities, transferable skills, and quality of your performance.

Overall a sparse resume suggests that you either haven't accomplished much or that you don't have the capability to convey your worth to the company.

2.1.2   Not A Narrative, Third Person

Novice applicants who are unfamiliar with standard protocols of resume writing often and erroneously use narrative or third-person. Narrative is when a writer uses "I" or "my" along with varied sentence structures, including adverbial phrases. For example, a sentence that is structured in the following manner would be in narrative form.

> As a Computer Programmer, I installed, configured, and maintained a 500-node LAN running on Windows 2010. My ancillary duties included the development of a disaster recovery and emergency backup system. I also ensured security for all PCs and servers.

Standard protocols for resume writing emphasize brevity by using implied first person, which eliminates the "I" and uses strong action verbs. The information above would be conveyed in the following concise manner:

Computer Programmer
- Installed, configured, and maintained a 500-node LAN running on Windows 2010.
- Developed a disaster recovery and emergency backup system.
- Ensured security for all PCs and servers.

Use of implied third person is also an error. Third person is implied when you add an "s" at the end of the action verb. "Develop**s** a disaster recovery system." The "s" at the end of "Develops" implies "He/she develops a…." Since you do not speak in third person when referring to yourself, imply first person by omitting the "s" at the end of the verb. "Developed a disaster recovery system." is like saying "I developed a disaster recovery system."

Tense should reflect whether the bullet is an ongoing function or an action that has already taken place. If it's in the past, use past tense; if it's in the present, use present tense.

2.1.3 *Not A Job Description*

The number one misconception is that a resume references all the responsibilities performed at each previous employer. Your resume is not a job description.

A resume that simply describes responsibilities tells an employer a lot about your job, but little about how well you performed the job. An effective resume conveys how you positively impacted your previous employers and how you made a difference. You must present your accomplishments, which inevitably convey your responsibilities in addition to your effectiveness on the job.

2.1.4   A Comprehensive Report

Some job seekers fill up their resume with everything they did. A resume is not a comprehensive report on everything you did. It is a summary, a selection of key examples that constitute your qualifications. In essence, you are selectively perceiving your image by showcasing your best accomplishments that reveal your transferable skills, scope of responsibility, and positive impact on your past employers.

In many ways you withhold many elements of past jobs to purposely accentuate the aspects that are significant and relevant to the requirements of the position you are seeking. Therefore, in order to know what to write about and what to select from your background, you should know something about the hot buttons of your next position.

Think of the 90/10 percent technique. Even though as an administrative assistant, you answer the telephone 90% of the time, you should eliminate that responsibility of the job on your resume and focus on the 10% of the time that you write reports, train new employees, and coordinate logistics for meetings, so you can apply for the meeting planning position which requires writing, training, and logistical coordination skills.

If what you do most of the time does not address the requirements of the prospective position, see if what you do some of the time relates to your targeted job. Remember your resume doesn't necessarily indicate the depth of your experience. Even if you did something once, it can be legitimately put on your resume.

2.1.5   Not A History of Employment

Contrary to popular belief, a resume is not necessarily a complete history of every job you have ever had. Although a resume could consist of every job you have had, it usually doesn't. By definition, a resume is a summary of your qualifications.

If you are seeking a position as a biologist and worked as a biologist for the past two years, and had worked as a waiter prior to that, you certainly could omit the irrelevant waiter job. Most people have a number of start-up jobs or side jobs that are better left off the resume, which enables you to focus on the most significant and relevant background.

Candidates who have very short term employment experiences are also most likely better off omitting them. Positions lasting only a few months rarely promote your best interests to an employer.

Candidates who have an excessive number of positions should carefully select the ones that best represent their highest qualifications and show the greatest breadth and depth in their field of expertise. Short term or second jobs, especially ones that don't add anything to your qualifications are targets for elimination from your resume.

Candidates, who have long work histories, often stretching back 30+ years, should most likely truncate their early part of their career. Most employers don't care much about how you got to where you are; they are most interested in what you have done lately and what you are doing now. Of course, exceptions are always a consideration and therefore, you must draw a judgment as to what promotes you best and what the prospective employer probably wants to see. Often executive level positions give greater allowance for longevity because they are unlikely to take interest in someone without a life-time of experiences. In such cases, showing how you rose to the top can be an exception to the general rule and cast a compelling and decorated career.

For some candidates, every past position logically supports their career qualifications and direction. If this scenario describes your situation, then your resume may be synonymous with your career history.

The key concept here is not to junk up your resume with irrelevant information. You have latitude to choose the positions that go into your resume. However, you don't want to start omitting jobs for errant reasons. Employers will be looking for gaps. Your first line of strategy is to interpret your background so that it is striking and relevant. Use the omission strategy for positions that mar your professional image.

2.1.6   *A resume is not a mirror*

Some candidates feel compelled to write a resume that "accurately" reflects who they are. Big mistake. Your resume is not an objective assessment of who you are. It is a biased representation – one of the few times you can legitimately tout all the good things about yourself at the exclusion of anything negative. Your resume is a not a mirror; it is a marketing tool.

Your resume will probably cast an image of someone much more capable than you probably really feel about yourself. And although you may not feel comfortable about that contrast, that's the nature of a resume. Just remember, if your most legitimately decorated image can't sell you to get a position, how will a toned down version do it?

Your goal when writing your resume is not to feel comfortable with how close your image is to yourself, but rather how close you are in exciting employers to select you for an interview. Of course your touted points of interest should always be truthful. If you follow the techniques and approaches in this book, you will find ways to capture your best without needing to resort to lies. The truth is compelling in its own right, just know how to interpret it and write it in a way that is also compelling.

The worst self-inflicted abuse can be in conveying irrelevant "truths" that undermine your goals. For example, one candidate wrote on his resume his reason for leaving his employer. First you do not write reasons for leaving an employer on a resume. Secondly his reason for leaving was "Currently in litigation with employer." Yeah, let's hire this guy. Even though he is telling the truth, a prospective employer would probably conclude he is a troublemaker. The negativity of his truth presents an image that a prospective employer would most likely reject.

2.1.7   *Not a License for Fraud/Distortion*

If your accomplishments don't ring true, lack specificity, seem exaggerated, or rely on personality attributes, then your resume will lack credibility and may stick out like a sore thumb in a negative way. For example, "Achieved significant increases in revenue." This quote only makes a vague claim, which suggests that the accomplishment is made up or negligible at best. It suggests that you really don't know what the quantifiable improvement was. In other words, what is the "significant" increase in revenue? It could be 30% or 2% of revenues. Who is to say what constitutes a significant increase. Likewise, the reader doesn't know the amount of the revenues. These obvious omissions indicate an evasiveness that dissuades prospective employers from selecting your resume.

On the opposite side is exaggeration, which is also easily detected. "Achieved 300% of annual revenue goals." 300% of what? It sounds too fantastic to be legitimate.

2.1.8   *Shallowness*

Many candidates promote personality attributes, such as "highly motivated with a success-driven approach and strong people skills." While all of these qualities are important in the real world, they aren't persuasive on a resume because they are unsubstantiated claims that, frankly, could be put on any resume whether for a high-powered executive or for an entry-level clerk. Your bullets should show how you are better than the next candidate, not that you are indistinguishable from anybody else. Since anybody could write an unsubstantiated claim, it doesn't ring true with authority.

2.1.9   *Order content by frequency or sequentially*

Typically you should order your bullets in accordance to clarity, relevance, and importance. At times this ordering approach will coincide with the frequency and chronological sequence by which you perform your functions. However, more than likely they will not. The basic approach to determining the order of bullets begins with answering the primary question, "What did you do overall that addresses the requirements of your next employer and most impacted the past employer?" The first bullet will no doubt be an umbrella statement that gives the primary or totality of your impact, transferable skills, and scope of responsibility. Most of the remaining bullets will probably justify the first bullet telling in greater detail all of the things you did that enabled your success.

Example 1:

Technical Writer
- Wrote, edited, and formatted technical documents in support of a modernization contract with the U.S. Department of Justice.

Example 2:

Property Manager
- Managed $30 million of commercial and residential real property in the Washington Metropolitan region.

After the global, umbrella statement is listed, more detailed bullets – reflecting accomplishments, would follow.

2.2 Common Issues Facing Candidates

Everyone has a challenge or an issue in their pursuit for another position. For some, the issues seem insurmountable. But more than likely, what you think is a big problem, may have a simple solution. Remember, your resume is a marketing device – a flexible document that casts a carefully crafted image. You have many tools to shape that image, which can circumvent many issues indicated in the following subsections:

2.2.1 Employment Gaps

At times, you may want to eliminate an insignificant short-term position from your resume. When you do, the omission may create a few months gap in employment. A lot of times, gaps can be de-emphasized by listing the years you were employed at each position instead of using months and years.

For example, suppose you had the following jobs A through C:

Job A   October 2009 – Present
Job B   March 2009 – September 2009
Job C   January 2003 – February 2009

By omitting the short term employment "Job B" you can represent Job A and Job C seamlessly by just stating the years:

Job A   2009 – Present
Job C   2003 – 2009

2.2.2   *Divergent Career Interests*

Suppose you have been a nurse for the past 10 years. Now you are looking for a new career in journalism. You are also willing to get another nursing position. You should create different versions of your resume to address the dissimilar requirements of the two positions you are marketing.

In the case of the journalism position, your resume should cover all of the writing projects and responsibilities you did as a nurse. A nurse writes reports, may have written articles for a medical publication, researched different subject areas. All of these skills and experiences directly support the requirements for a journalism position.

For the nursing position, you would probably emphasize different aspects of your background that directly relate to nursing, such as patient management, pain management skills, etc.

Another option is to have a functional highlights section, which would have categories such as Journalism Experience, with examples of such. The highlights section would have bullet points that relate to the prospective position. These bullets could easily be replaced so to maintain relevance to the requirements of any other position sought.

2.2.3 Too Much Experience

You should remember that a resume is a summary and that you don't have to reference every project you ever laid your hands on. You can also omit higher level degrees if you feel you're not being considered because of being perceived as "over qualified." Another technique is to truncate a long history of employment, putting the focus on what you've done lately. Where to truncate varies depending on how your history of jobs lays out. For example, if you are a senior worker with 45 years of work experience, you would want to cut away the early jobs, but leave enough experience so that they know you are a seasoned professional. You probably would cut away the first 25 years and leave the past 20 years showing on your resume. However, each case is different and requires independent judgment based on how your previous jobs lay out in time and whether they effectively contribute to your qualifications. If the older jobs don't say anything more about your qualifications than what the most immediate past 20 years have already said, toss out those jobs.

Ultimately your interpretation of your background should regulate how powerful a presentation you create. If your accomplishments are too overwhelming for the audience, then don't give yourself as much credit by either omitting certain accomplishments or interpreting them and writing them in a toned down manner. One example is a self-employed candidate who is giving up his business to rejoin the employment sector. Give up on the idea of calling yourself "owner or President" Prospective employers may be turned off that you are self-employed. They may believe you are not manageable, not able to follow orders, or worse, that you may steal inside information from them such as clients and then become a competitor.

A simple initial solution is to change your title from the pompous title of "President" to one that coincides with the one you are applying. Most employers are looking to fill a position with someone who is employed in the same capacity. Since you are the owner, you can title yourself anything you want. After all you're the boss – or Operating Manager, if you are applying for such a job.

2.2.4 Too Many Employers

Eliminate inconsequential employment experiences, such as ones that are exceptionally rudimentary, short term, overlapping in time (second jobs), and part-time positions that don't add anything to your qualifications (usually these are part-time positions that are in addition to full-time positions).

2.2.5 Career Change

When changing direction in your career, your past may seem irrelevant. And it most likely is. Therefore, the first strategy is to identify any thread of relevant experiences and promote them in a highly visible way such as in a highlights or functional section.

Secondly, you should re-interpret your past to draw out any relevant or transferable skills and experiences. Most likely these will touch upon universal skills such as communications, leadership, project management, technical skills, etc.

Thirdly, you may have to weed out information that ordinarily would be considered good, but is now irrelevant and a distraction.

Fourthly, you should still reveal a pattern of success even if the accomplishments are not relevant. Half functional, half chronological resume formats are typically the best solution to highlight relevance.

2.2.6 Irrelevant Experience

When your background has no apparent relevance to the next job you are pursuing, rely on promoting universal aspects such as problem solving, communications, project management, interpersonal relationships, revenue generation, analysis, administration, and leadership.

Address your accomplishments to show a pattern of success and scope of your responsibility. Even an irrelevant pattern of success is still admired.

2.2.7 Returning to the Work Force

If your last serious job was more than a year ago, a functional resume or combination resume format will help focus on relevant matters before they are recognized as out of date.

If you have assisted in a family business or did volunteer work, you can use those experiences within your chronological history as previous jobs. This strategy may result in presenting an up-to-date experience history. The fact that you may not have been paid is irrelevant. If you worked, even in a volunteer capacity, you are performing an array of skills and have demonstrated certain accomplishments.

2.2.8 No Education

If you don't have a four-year degree, you can still list colleges, universities, and other forms of partial education on your resume. In addition, you could note certifications and continuing education classes taken. Moreover, you can list seminars, workshops, and other forms of corporate training to justify that you are educable.

Under most circumstances, the education section is placed on the bottom of the resume. Remember, your education helps employers predict that you can do the job; your experience and accomplishments are evidence that you can do the job.

Your experience is more valuable than a formal education, and many candidates command high-powered executive positions despite a lack of formal education. Part of that success rests on shaping a can-do image on your resume. After all, employers want candidates who can perform, not just pass a multiple-choice test in an academic setting. If you can make an employer higher profits, they will want you.

2.2.9 Too Much Education

If a higher degree is not required or advertised, listing it on your resume could undermine your efforts. Employers may consider you overqualified. At times higher degrees overwhelm an employer to

13

the point that they dismiss you believing you will not remain with them long or that you will be too hard to manage, or that you will cost them too much in salary. If you haven't had luck securing a position, see if removing your Ph.D. and Master's degrees make any difference. You can always say no to an unacceptable salary offer, but you should have the chance to negotiate a win/win conclusion after securing the interview. Also, you will always have the opportunity to convey your degrees. Your primary goal is to get the interview.

2.2.10 No Experience

Make the best case with what you have. Most people have worked somewhere in their past. You may have to consider using internships, part-time work, volunteer experiences, consulting experiences, possibly informal experiences with a hobby that happens to be relevant to your career direction.

At times you may have to use educational experiences to address relevant areas of knowledge. A bullet point might be weak but it's something. Example of an academic project: Designed architectural plans for a 3,000 square foot residential property using computer-aided design software.

The design may have been merely a class assignment and the home never built, but the academic experience is still noteworthy. You have options to describe entire class curricula or delve into actual assignments.

2.3 Basics

The writing style of a resume still rests with implied first person, active voice, and action verbs such as "developed, implemented, and directed."

2.3.1 Imply 1st Person not 3rd Person

When you see verbs that end in "s" after the root form, you are applying 3rd person. For example, the verb "plan" is the root verb. Add an "s" to it, and it becomes "plans" in third person. Test it out.

First person uses "I"–

I plan board meetings.

Third person uses "He, She, or It" –
         He plan**s** board meetings.

In resume writing, you write in implied first person as if you are speaking directly to the employer. After all, you don't speak about yourself in third person when writing a letter to someone. However, when writing in implied first person, you drop the "I" and start off with an action verb.

- *(I) Plan board meetings.*
  NOT
- *(He) Plans board meetings.*

Confusion arises when job seekers read job vacancy announcements and job descriptions, which are commonly written in implied third person. Their action verbs will have the "s" because they are <u>not</u> referring to themselves; they are referring to someone else– he or she, or the candidate. If you were describing someone else, you would describe them as so: "He (the desired candidate) plan**s** board meetings. She manage**s** large numbers of employees." But the resume is you, your voice, referring to yourself.

2.3.2   *Active Voice*

Don't bury your verbs and disassociate yourself from your actions.

Example of Passive Voice:
- Thermodynamic engines were **modified** for reduction in energy consumption and heat transference.

Active Voice "I modified…":
- **Modified** thermodynamic engine designs to reduce energy consumption and heat transference.

2.3.3   *Action Verbs*

Weak beginnings flag your resume for disposal. Examples of weak introductory verbs are "was, have, did, and is."

Instead of:
- Was the top sales associate in the company.

Start with an action verb:
- **Emerged** as the top sales associate in the company.

Instead of:
- Have knowledge of thermodynamics, hydrodynamics, and kinetics.

Start with an action verb:
- **Applied** knowledge of thermodynamics, hydrodynamics, and kinetics.

2.3.4 *Weak Beginnings*

Other candidates use crutches such as "duties include" or "responsible for" to start a bullet point. These crutches also cause wordy bullet structures such as

- Responsible for the **supervision** of seven associates.

The above structure buries the strong action verb. Once you find it, place it at the beginning:

- **Supervise** seven associates.

By using supervise instead of supervision, you also get rid of "the" and the "of."

3   What Makes a Resume Effective?

If the only differences among equally qualified
applicants are their resumes, then what about the
resume makes an employer select one candidate
over the others? This chapter reveals how you can
enhance the credibility, potency, and effectiveness
of your resume so you can stand out. You can
produce this stellar resume by showing significant
and relevant accomplishments that represent a
pattern of success.

3.1 *Strategy: Transferable Skills, Significance, and Pattern of Success*

The primary objective is to persuade prospective
employers that you will be their solution. Employers
think "How will this candidate solve our
problems?" They will draw the conclusion that you
are their answer if they believe your background
applies to their needs – that your skills are
transferable, and that you have been successful.
Employers often think, "If he's been successful in
the past, he will be successful in the future."
Therefore, you want to show the right skill set that
matches the employer's and show a pattern of
success. You do that by writing about your
significant accomplishments.

Accomplishments noted throughout your
employment history suggest that the reason for your
success is based on the qualities you possess and
your effort, which you take with you wherever you
go. In the event you cite accomplishments only at
one past employer, you risk the inference that your
success at the one place was not attributable to you
alone but rather to the economy, the success of the
company, or someone else at the company. Your
case will be less credible. On the other hand,
showing a string of successes at several past
employers suggests the opposite, that you are the
reason for successful results. When employers
believe that you possess the qualities that lead to
success, you will stand out from other candidates
vying for the same position.

Since in many cases, the position you seek may differ from what you have done in the past, you have to do more than just blindly list your past responsibilities. You will most likely have to interpret your background and carefully select points of interest that pertain to the requirements of your next position. In short, the primary theme of effective resume writing is to "interpret and selectively perceive your background to write significant resume content that addresses the needs of prospective employers."

To guide your focus in identifying accomplishments, consider the following four elements: **Relevance, Significance, Credibility, and Pattern of Success.** These essential elements bridge your background to the needs of prospective employers.

3.1.1 *Relevance*

You establish relevance by **identifying and interpreting** transferable skills/experiences/knowledge that address key requirements of the desired position. You show how well you understand and master the industry practices and knowledge areas. For example, for a Human Resource position, you would want to show that you have experience with interviewing, healthcare and retirement benefits, and laws/regulations such as the American Disabilities Act and the Family Leave Act.

Suppose you have had one job as a General Manager of a retail store. You want to apply for a Human Resources Specialist job. Instead of listing all of your General Manager duties, selectively choose responsibilities and accomplishments that relate to Human Resources, such as, "Hired and trained a Human Resources Representative to establish a Human Resources Department." Or, "Collaborated with the Human Resources Representative to arbitrate labor disputes."

Even though you may not have headed the arbitration effort or even known a lot about arbitration, you can cite any involvement you did have, which would be significant and relevant to the needs of the new Human Resources job that you are applying for.

18

If you are applying for an Accounting job, you would want to select some responsibilities that pertain to accounting. For example, "Tabulated days end and weekly revenues from eight registers. Calculated profit and loss percentages and prepared weekly sales reports."

For this accounting opportunity, you would exclude the bullet point about "arbitrating labor disputes." When applying for the Human Resources Representative job opportunity, you would exclude the "tabulated revenues" responsibility. These are examples of selectively perceiving your background so that it matches the needs of the prospective employer.

This approach is not an issue if your background is the same as your future employment direction.

You also want to show the scope/level of experiences, as explained next.

3.1.2   *Significance*

Of equal importance is to reveal not only your transferable skills but how well you have performed them. You do that by **measuring and characterizing your performance** through quantifiable and qualitative comparisons.

A great deal of this book is dedicated to explaining the various ways in which you can express significance and your performance. See "Accomplishments" in Section 3.2.

3.1.3   *Credibility*

Significant and relevant accomplishments should also be conveyed credibly with enough concrete examples, precise quantifications, and avoidance of hyperbole. See Section 3.2: Accomplishments for examples.

3.1.4   *A Pattern of Success*

You want to reveal your accomplishments from all of your previous listed employers to show a pattern of success. If you can't interpret relevancy, you want the bullet points to be at least impressive in their own right.

3.2 Accomplishments

3.2.1 Getting Beyond Responsibilities

Your responsibilities are an integral part of the resume; however, only citing responsibilities tells the employer a lot about your jobs, but little about you – how well you did the job and to what extent?

When candidates settle for responsibilities without measuring their performance, they risk presenting a bland, uninspiring resume. Such a resume does little to differentiate you from other candidates vying for the same job. After all, if you just list a few responsibilities, then how are you answering the question, "how am I better than the other equally qualified candidate who performs the same responsibilities?" The answer lies in telling employers how well you have performed those responsibilities, which is often demonstrated through quantifying how you have positively impacted your previous employers. The remainder of this section covers detailed techniques for identifying and writing your winning accomplishments.

3.2.2 But What is an Accomplishment?

Basically, it is **how you made a difference**, how you positively impacted an organization, how well you have performed the job, and how much of an improvement you made – a completion, a solution, a creation, an enhancement, or the successful implementation of an initiative. Often improvements are best expressed through measurable variables.

Some examples of measurable variables include revenue increases, account growth, volume, territorial expansion, market share domination, account development; enhanced customer satisfaction indexes, operational efficiency and productivity; technological capability, quality improvements; initiatives championed; equipment upgrades; and cost controls–(which are often represented through declining numbers: decreased labor costs, food costs, operating costs; employee attrition, etc.) At times a variable that declines is an

20

improvement such as waste, inefficiencies, complaints, penalties, error rates, employee turnover, shrinkage, and other measurable reductions.

Accomplishments may provide any of **six basic functions**:

- They may indicate your responsibilities and transferable skill set;
- To what degree you did them (scope/breadth/level);
- How well you performed them (impact/how you made a difference);
- Convey your understanding of the industry;
- Convey some quality such as innovativeness; and
- Demonstrate a pattern of success.

Even if your accomplishments are not earth shaking on an individual bullet level, your strategy is to create an impression of productivity through the collection of bullet points. One minor improvement is not necessarily impressive, but ten minor improvements establish a pattern and an impression that you make a difference.

Typically, you convey an accomplishment through a quantitative expression. After all, if you simply state that you performed a function "extremely well," who's to say what that means? Extremely well compared to what? Another example of an ill-stated accomplishment is…"Achieved a dramatic increase in revenue." What do you mean by dramatic? How much of an increase? Vague bald-faced claims lack force and credibility. They may even anger a personnel director who may be deciding whether to contact you.

Here's another shortfall, when numbers are misused. "Increased revenue 300%." Three hundred percent of what? If revenues were $100 and you raised them to $400, you've increased revenues 300%, but so what? It's an insignificant volume that fools no experienced human resource director. Plus, since the percentage is so high, it suggests an exaggeration.

4 How to Quantify

Your accomplishments are expressed with more credibility when they are measured. When you measure your performance, you are using numbers to show the extent of your success. Measuring performance means that you show how well you performed your responsibilities.

Some key concepts to guide your effort will be "Scope/Volume," "Aspect," "Points of Reference," and "Units of Measurement." The following sections describe each concept:

4.1 Quantifying Scope

The scope of responsibility is often indicated by the amount, volume, value, size, or other measurable variable. After identifying transferable skills/responsibilities, you want to show to what degree you performed those responsibilities or the level of those responsibilities.

For example, suppose two candidates both have managed facility operations. If that's all you know about the candidates, they seem equally qualified. However, if you define the scope of your management of operations, you may be able to differentiate yourself from lower level Operations Managers.

Candidate A managed a mom and pop retail store. Candidate B managed a 24,000 square foot facility with 45 employees. If you are candidate B, you would want to convey the extent of your management responsibilities to separate yourself from other candidates, such as Candidate A whose management responsibility is inferior.

Usually you can convey how much responsibility. For example:

Example 1:	
Primary responsibility	Manage numerous stores
Quantify Scope	Manage eight retail stores that generate $15 million per annum throughout a three-state territory.
Difference	By indicating the number of stores, the vastness of the territory, and the total volume of revenues, you show a big difference between this candidate and one who is managing a mom & pop store.

Example 2:	
Primary responsibility	Coordinate patients
Quantify Scope	Coordinate a caseload of 22 patients on the post-partum recovery floor.
Difference	By indicating the number of patients and the type of environment, the employer can infer that you had a great deal of responsibility. You also contrast yourself from candidates who generalize that they "coordinate patients," which could be as few as two.

Example 3:	
Primary responsibility	Promote sales
Quantify Scope	Promote sales of neurological assessment machines each valued in excess of $250,000.
Difference	Selling a $250,000 technical product takes more knowledge and professionalism than selling $20 toasters.

Example 4:	
Primary responsibility	Delivered speech
Quantify Scope	Delivered an annual kick-off speech before an audience of 5,000 key industry professionals.
Difference	Giving a speech before 5,000 industry professionals is far more significant than giving a classroom lecture to 20 attendees.

Whether any of the above bullet points are actual accomplishments could easily be debated. However, they all provide a clear understanding of the scope of responsibility in a quantifiable manner. That's crucial in convincing an employer that you can handle the responsibility at a higher level.

While the degree of your responsibility can often set you apart from others with lesser responsibility; showing improvement will distinguish you even more. You can show improvement through quantifiable comparisons with various points of reference.

4.2 Points of Reference

- Find the Story
- Compared to What? Relative (Goals, Expectations, Projections),
- Historical (time related),
- Internal (Personal Productivity, Peer to Peer),
- External (Market Share, Competition, Industry-wide)

Points of reference are used to make comparisons. You indicate how important and effective your performance is by comparing it with a point of reference. After all if your bullet read: Generated $50,000 in annual sales. How should a prospective employer interpret that? Is $50,000 a year good or lousy? Compared to what? Most corporations have goals, and most corporate goals are relatively respected universally. Therefore, comparing your performance to a corporate goal is one point of reference that conveys how well you performed.

4.2.1 Corporate Goal as Point of Reference

- **Generated $850,000 in fiscal year 2015, which exceeded the corporate goal 15%.**

Your company may have unrealistic goals or no goal system, or perhaps you simply didn't make goal. Other points of reference can be used to illustrate how well you performed. Other points of reference are obvious once you start creatively thinking about them. A few that are commonly used include peer performance, expectations, industry averages, and personal history.

For example, compare your performance with your peers' performance.

4.2.2 Peer and Geographical Comparisons

- **Generated $850,000 in fiscal year 2015, which was the highest among a staff of 10 other sales associates.**

Comparisons with peers can be extended beyond the office you work in. Explore the applicability of comparing your top performance with larger populations to see if it keeps holding up. Start with your peers in your office then to your division, across divisions, local territory, regional territory, national, and/or global level. Some geographical regions don't have distinct borders as do counties and states. For example, the Washington Metropolitan region; Mid-Atlantic; Eastern seaboard; East Coast; Tri-state territory; Metroplex; Triad, etc. Identify the largest comparison. For example:

- **Generated $850,000 in fiscal year 2015, the highest among the Arlington store consisting of 40 sales associates.**
- **Generated $850,000 in fiscal year 2015, the highest among all 35 corporate stores in the Mid-Atlantic region.**
- **Generated $850,000 in fiscal year 2015, the highest in the company consisting of 2,000 employees nationwide.**

At times, your number will fall in rank as you widen the circle of competition. That's OK, you can adjust the language a bit to accommodate the variance. For example, you can write "one of the highest" instead of just "highest." Because being 2nd, 22nd, or 122nd out of 2,000 is still phenomenal.

- Generated $850,000 in fiscal year 2015, **one of the highest** in the company among 2,000 employees nationwide.

4.2.3 Geography/Space

In addition to the number of corporate locations and the number of employees, geographical territory and or physical space are aspects that often expand.

- **Expanded the market place from Montgomery County to the Washington Metropolitan region, resulting in a tripling of the account base.**

- **Oversaw a 2,000 square foot expansion of the flagship store.**

- **Coordinated the construction of three major complexes on the university campus.**

4.2.4 Time

Apart from corporate goals, peers, and geographical points of reference is time. Time is usually expressed in annual performance, but not always as we shall explore later.

4.2.4.1   Annual Figures

The most basic point of reference is the calendar year. If your annual figures are solid, use them rather than partial year figures such as monthly or daily figures, even if you are accustomed to tracking your progress on a short-term basis. Again annual figures are impressive typically because they show a more realistic picture of long term performance as well as provide a larger number. Annual figures also play into universal protocols because most organizations think along the lines of annual performance.

4.2.4.2   Calculating Annual Figures

Dale sells about 30 shoes a day each retailing for about $100. Although he thinks about his productivity on a day to day basis, annual figures are most universal. Multiply the 30 sales with the $100 price to get a monetary daily revenues of $3,000. (100 x 30 = 3,000). Multiply the number of days worked in a week with the daily revenues (5 x $3,000 = $15,000). Multiply the number of weeks Dale works in a year with the weekly revenues (50 x $15,000 =$750,000). Dale sells not "30 shoes a day" but a whopping $750,000 per year in gross annual revenues, which should be compared to some reference point to make a powerful bullet. Other cases may require more complicated tabulations, especially if variables in your transactions change over time such as price, volume, and/or profit margin.

For now, see if your annual volumes show any growth. Has your performance from this year out performed last year? Has any particular year outperformed any previous year since you started with the company? Has your current year's performance improved since your first year? The key method here is to list your annual performances from year to year since you started with the company and find the story, which is any period of growth. Growth is the increase from one point to another point. It doesn't necessarily have to be just this year. It can be from when you started to the current day, which could be a span of many years. Or, it could be a part of your history with the company. These varying points of reference are further explained through graphs to better visualize these concepts.

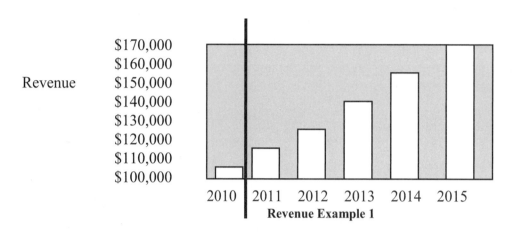

Revenue Example 1

In the above graph, suppose the employee's performance is indicated each year starting with year 2011, whereas 2010 is the performance of the company the year before the employee started. According to the graph, the company generated about $100,000 in 2010. After the employee started working, he/she improved the revenue each year. Here's the data listed for better visual understanding:

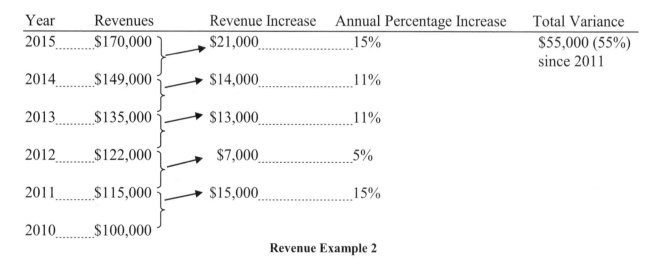

Year	Revenues	Revenue Increase	Annual Percentage Increase	Total Variance
2015	$170,000	$21,000	15%	$55,000 (55%) since 2011
2014	$149,000	$14,000	11%	
2013	$135,000	$13,000	11%	
2012	$122,000	$7,000	5%	
2011	$115,000	$15,000	15%	
2010	$100,000			

Revenue Example 2

With this gradual incline in performance from year to year, you have several options to depict how to express your performance. Three of the most common ways are "performance rate; partial variance, and aggregate variance."

26

4.2.5 Performance Rate

For the performance rate, you take the percentage of growth from year to year. For example, suppose your performance since 2011 is as follows:

Year	Growth
2015	18.4%
2014	.8%
2013	3.1%
2012	4.2%
2011	3.0%

Revenue Example 3

If your most recent year is your best year, cite it:
- Increased annual revenues more than 18% in FY 2015.

The same data since 2011 can be represented:
- Increased annual revenues for 5 consecutive years.

If each year is above a significant number then you can express your performance clearly and simply as such,

- **Exceeded** a 12% annual growth rate in revenue since 2011. See Revenue Example 4:

Revenue Example 4

If all the yearly increases were actually about the same, you can use a specific claim such as

- **Achieved** a 12% growth rate in annual revenue for 5 consecutive years.

Year	Growth
2015	12.4%
2014	12.8%
2013	12.1%
2012	12.2%
2011	12.0%

Revenue Example 5

27

If the yearly performance wasn't rigidly at 12% or all above 12%, explore averages. For example,

- **Averaged** 12% growth in annual revenue since 2011.

Rather than "Exceeded 8% a year."

Year	Growth
2015	8.0%
2014	14.0%
2013	12.0%
2012	12.0%
2011	10.0%

Revenue Example 6

4.2.6 *Partial Variance*

You can also just reference the peak at exclusion of other years, especially if the other years were poor.

Year	Growth
2015	0.0%
2014	-1.0%
2013	-3.0%
2012	16.0%
2011	-5.0%
2010	-2.0%
2009	-1.0%

Revenue Example 7

- Exceeded goals **as much as** 16% for sales of ABC products since 2009.

The operative words "as much as" provide great latitude for the applicant.

Another selective perception is to isolate the greatest swing from negative to positive revenue levels. In Revenue Example 7 above, goals were exceeded as much as 16%; however the actual increase in revenues jumped from negative 5 to positive 16, which is a 21 percentage point swing. You can also use a point of reference such as a goal to help bridge a negative to a positive figure in a bullet as such:

- **Reversed a 3-year negative trend in sales from 5% below corporate goals to 16% above goal in 2012.**

Percentage points are a different reference than a percentage growth, which would be relative to the raw volume of sales. The actual percentage increase would be 22%. For example, if 2011 production is 100, then a minus 5 percent production would equal 95; whereas a 116% of 100 would be 116. When you divide 116 by 95, you get 122%. Therefore, if you achieved 16% beyond goal, you actually achieved 22% above the previous year's production.

- **Increased annual productivity 22% in 2012.**

4.2.7 Aggregate Variance or Growth

If the annual growth rate is not consistently progressive, you may want to explore the total growth variance from when you started to your current performance. According to the Revenue Examples 1 and 2 on the previous pages, your first year was $115,000; your last year was $170,000. Whether you precisely indicate how long it took you, you in essence increased revenues from the low point to the highest point. The bullets below reflect the amount of growth from one point to another. The growth may have mostly occurred at the beginning, middle, or end. Any skewed pace is not the issue, just the ultimate amount of growth. It's a simplistic "selective perception" that makes a positive impression on your resume.

- **Increased gross annual revenues from $115,000 to $170,000.**

Or

- **Raised gross annual revenues 48% within first 5 years from $115,000 to $170,000.**

Suppose you worked 10 years, but your sales growth occurred within the first 5 years and plateaued or dropped after that. By omitting from the bullet a reference to the total amount of time, you have maximized the impact of the increase.

4.2.8 Dicing/Aggregate Methods

If parts of your past years shine more than others, you may want to use the dicing method to split time, products, people, or geographical territory; or the aggregate method to show accumulated productivity.

Dicing is isolating a part of your history as a period separate into itself at the omission of the rest of your history, especially at any one company. You may want to reference a particularly good stretch of productivity when your performance peaked.

For some people, your peak may have been within a single year. Find the longest peak, which may be a quarter (three months) or a particular month. Usually weekly or daily accomplishments don't translate credibly as bullets. A rare exception; however, would be when referencing results of a special event. "Raised $240,000 at the summerfest charitable weekend for kids with cancer." Otherwise, you can indicate, for example "Sales Associate of the Month or Quarter" which is particularly effective if you have been employed with a company for less than a year.

4.2.9 Dicing Time

If your performance plateaued or fell, or took a long time to mature, then you will have to isolate any period of your past where there was a rise in performance. Find the variance between your lowest point and your highest point, using your lowest point as your baseline.

Ultimately, you can identify any rise and compare it to a baseline, which may be last year, a period in the middle, the beginning of your employment, or even time prior your employment. You can compare your performance with your predecessor or simply what the company was performing upon your entry.

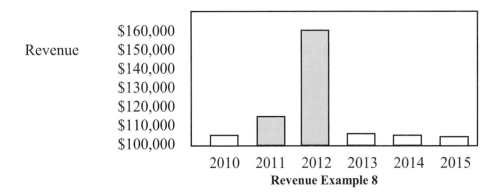

Revenue Example 8

In the graph above, only years 2011 and 2012 show increases in revenue from previous years. If you began working for the company in 2010, you could isolate the period of growth by writing a bullet as such,

- **Increased gross annual revenues from $105,000 to $155,000 within first 2 years.**

The rest of the story, being a rapid decent in revenue, would be omitted from your resume.

You can dice up time in various ways to find the best figures to represent your achievements. You may have performed an outstanding quarter, despite a mediocre year. If so, forget the year's total, and bullet the outstanding quarter. For example:

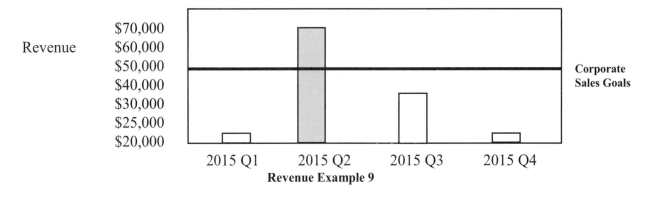

Revenue Example 9

The corporate sales goals are $50,000 per quarter. Therefore, the above graph shows that the yearly total falls short of the $200,000 annual sales goal as well as 3 failed quarters. But you can still capitalize on touting the one successful quarter, as such:

- **Exceeded corporate sales goals 20% in the second quarter of 2015.**
- **Achieved the highest sales figures in the second quarter of fiscal year 2015 among a 50-member sales force.**

Although, dicing up time is a technique to circumvent lackluster years, you would ideally want to use yearly intervals to represent solid achievements. In other words, if your yearly figures are good, use them.

4.2.10 Dicing People

Suppose your annual sales performance was not the highest and nowhere near the top or anywhere near the corporate goal. By all accounts your performance was lackluster, or is there a way to make it shine anyway?

Examine your situation, maybe you haven't been with the company too long and are competing with peers who have been there many years. They have the advantage in several ways. First, since they have lasted, they are probably pretty good at their craft. Second, they may have had time to build a clientele and contacts. How then are you going to compete with others who have 10 years more experience and many more contacts and clients?

Perhaps your performance compares better with other employees who have equal or less time at the company as you. In other words, if you're a rookie, dice up the staff in terms of rookies and non-rookies. For example, in a staff of 14 sales associates, you may be 1 of 4 rookies. If your performance was the highest or second highest among the four, you can write a bullet point, substantiating the fact that your performance is compared with the performances of the rookies.

- **Generated one of the highest sales volumes among the rookie staff.**

4.2.11 Dicing Products

Your annual performance may comprise the total of sales from numerous products and services. For example, if you sell computers, you may also sell printers, software, and carry cases, as well as intangibles such as warranties. Your sales for the year may be mediocre or poor, but the sales figures for a particular product or service may be great. Find the growth or improvement, even if it means ignoring your total annual figures and highlighting annual sales figures for a specific product or service. Your figures for warranties may be up 10%. If so, reference that in a bullet point at the exclusion of total sales of all products/services that were flat for the year.

Many pharmaceutical sales associates promote dozens of different drugs. Some sell very well, others don't. The performance of one product may be worth bragging about at the omission of the sales figures across the board. After all, poor sales of some products may be due to factors outside of your control. For example, your company's price for some products may be non-competitive, or perhaps legislation or negative media coverage has encumbered sales of a particular drug. Examine which product lines or services have advanced and choose them to represent your progress.

4.2.12 Dicing Monetary Values

4.2.12.1 Revenue

Analyze all aspects of the dollar. Although revenues are often used as a performance measure, there are other aspects of measurable dollars. For example, annual profitability is not the same as gross annual revenue.

4.2.12.2 Profitability

Despite a downward flux in yearly revenue, other variables may show better on paper, such as profitability. In this ironic situation, revenues may be down, but profitability may be up. Profitability is simply the cost of operations versus the sales. If you decreased expenses such as labor, waste, damages, theft, or rent, your operation may be more profitable despite lower annual revenues.

For a different story, explore whether you have established a larger profit margin. This is somewhat of a phantom accomplishment because you could write a bullet that you "Increased the profit margin on magazines 14%," without having actually sold a single magazine. You may have increased the margin by negotiating lower costs with the vendor or increasing the retail price. A profit margin is simply the difference between the cost to sell a product and its sales price.

For your performance measures, ask yourself, "What improved?"

4.2.12.3 Aggregate Figures

Another exception to using annual figures is the use of your total sum of production over many years, which can be more impressive than a single year. This especially works if you have been in one field for a long time but have had many different employers. A summation can provide a powerful picture that overshadows annual production. For example suppose you have been a real estate agent for the past 15 years, but never generated more than $3 million in sales in any given year. While the annual performance isn't anything to be ashamed about, you could sum up your total career with an aggregate value referenced in a highlights section of your resume.

- **Generated more than $30 million in total sales of residential and commercial real estate.**

The above bullet totals the annual production of sales over the real estate agents' 15 year career.

4.2.13 Extending Time

Sometimes reality doesn't show your real performance. So you may have to delve into the abstract world to reflect your impact on a company. Suppose you launched a start-up campaign that put into place significant systems and strategies, but then you moved on to a different employer. The results of your campaign haven't had time to mature in profitability. You may want to hinge the project, not to current revenues or production, but rather "projected" revenues and production, or potential or expected results. Although expected future returns are relatively unsubstantiable, they will resonate with greater credibility than bullet points without quantifiable references.

- **Devised and launched marketing strategies that reversed a $750,000 loss to profitability with expected revenues to exceed $100,000 by fiscal year 2018 and $500,000 by fiscal year 2019.** (When 2016 is the current year).

4.2.14 Superimpose Time

In some instances you may want to take advantage of overlapping times to express the same accomplishment in different ways. You first may want to show a solid annual volume, which may not be the best among the staff, but may still show a strong personal effort. You can then exploit the fact that during a particular period within the same year you out performed everyone else. This particular period may be just a quarter, but still resonates well as a second point of interest. That way you squeeze out two bullet points or one bullet point that addresses both aspects. For example:

One Bullet that Addresses Both Aspects:
- **Generated $5 million in gross annual sales and led a 50-member sales crew as the #1 producer for the third quarter of fiscal year 2015.**

Two Bullets that Address Both Aspects:
- **Generated $5 million in gross annual sales in fiscal year 2015.**
- **Led 50 sales associates as the #1 producer for the third quarter of fiscal year 2015.**

4.3 Units of Measure

So how do you persuade someone, regardless of the industry, that you are a productive employee? You have to continue building your case with universally applicable expressions.

To quantify your performance, you can use various units of measures such as raw numbers, percentages, dollar figures, rankings, or indexes. Other ways of demonstrating improvement such as changes in designations will be discussed in later parts of this chapter.

At times, one unit of measure will be more appropriate or advantageous to use than others. For example, suppose you're in the hospitality field and one of your many responsibilities as a hotel manager is to manage your crews to clean the rooms. If when you started your managerial position, 11 rooms were cleaned per hour on average, and then through your leadership skills, you improved operational efficiency so that 13 rooms were cleaned per hour on average, you could write a bullet point that shows improvement:

- **Increased the average number of rooms cleaned per hour from 11 to 13.**

The problem with that bullet is that by using the raw numbers, only someone in the industry would be able to understand the significance of how hard it is to improve the maintenance efficiency. However, if you used percentages as the unit of measure, you could cite that the difference between 11 and 13 is actually a double-digit figure. The difference between 11 and 13 is 2, which is actually 18% of 11. 18% is more universally understood and impressive. You would then write:

- **Improved efficiency of the maintenance crew 18%.**

An 18% improvement is universally understood as a significant improvement, whereas 2 rooms is not.

At other times, a combination of two units of measure work in unison. For example:

- **Increased revenues $3 million, representing 65% of corporate growth.**

4.3.1 Monetary Values

For other times, a small percentage such as 3% may not seem impressive; however, if the increase is of an immense figure, the representation on paper would probably seem more daunting in a raw monetary form, such as "increased division revenues $27 million in FY 2015."

Perceive the accomplishment: Greatest Figures
Suppose your percentage was a low 1% improvement. That may not sound so impressive; however, if it is based on a huge volume such as $500 million in trade, then 1% constitutes $5 million. You have choices. You could indicate that you "**generated $5 million in new business**" or exploit the larger number as well as a visually larger percentage by writing:

- **Achieved 101% of business development goal based on $500 million in trade volume.**

If you exceeded goals by 1% you achieved the initial 100% too.

4.3.2 Exploiting Losses

Suppose you assumed authority over a problem product that was losing 25% a year. Your sales effort, while admirable, still resulted in losses of 12.5% a year. While the product was unprofitable, your losses of 12.5% were less than your predecessor's losses of 25%.

Despite your revenue figures in negative territory, they are still an improvement.

- **Cut losses 50% by increasing sales of the ABC product through a new marketing initiative.**

You can also simply calculate the increase in sales. You would have to factor the percentage rise in revenue from the greatest loss to the least level of losses.

If 0 is your break-even point, and the company lost $25 then you stepped in and lost only $21, you could indicate that you improved revenues 16%. Divide 21 by 25, you get 84 less 100, you get 16%.

Some improvements can be expressed through either increases or decreases. Take for example some performance measures from Human Resources.

- **Increased employee longevity from 90 days to 4 years.**

Or

- **Reduced employee turnover 30% among a 168 member staff.**

4.3.3 Other Improvement Variables

Monetary figures and percentages are not the only units of measures to express improvement. You may find opportunity to use raw volume, designations, rankings, grades, assessment scores, indexes, square feet, and/or time to show your impact. The following bullets are examples of these types of variables.

- Improved store's ranking from #15 to #7 within a 26-store territory.
- Raised the hotel's rating from a 2-star to a 5-star status.
- Addressed sanitation complaints resulting in a lifting of a disapproval assessment status and raised the inspection grade from F to C.
- Reduced costs from above budget to below budget.
- Increased rentals of 182 commercial properties with 7 million square feet of aggregate leasing space.
- Increased employee longevity from 90 days to 4 years.
- Installed 17 miles of plumbing pipe 6 weeks ahead of schedule for the Superplex construction project.
- Expanded the customer base from 400 to 645 within the first year.
- Raised inspection scores of mystery shopper evaluations from 75 to 98/100.
- Developed and implemented individualized education plans for students diagnosed with autism resulting in a dramatic elevation of their skills by two grade levels.
- Improved the customer satisfaction index 30 points within the first year of implementing new Customer Friendly policies.
- Elevated the football team's status from a Division C to a Division A by recruiting new talent for the front line, which resulted in a three consecutive winning seasons.

4.3.4 Quantification via Association

When what you have done is routine, but the company you work for does something significant, associate yourself with the success of the company.

- **Wrote technical documents for an award-winning, Top 100 IT company in the Washington Metropolitan area.**

The fact that a successful company hired you in the first place is something to brag about.

4.3.5 Non-quantifiable Bullets

Usually, quantifiable performances take precedence in the ordinal positioning of your bullets because they not only show the scope of your responsibility and transferable skills, but also your effectiveness. However, bullets that are not quantifiable measures can still help round out your experience by addressing universal skills. Typically, it is a good idea to include if possible references to leadership qualities, communications, good judgment, problem resolution, and writing abilities, even if they aren't central themes of your history.

- **Conceived and deployed a new training initiative that improved employee's written and verbal communication skills.**

This bullet (even though does not have any quantifications) emphasizes your ability to think of ideas and bring them to fruition. That takes initiative, creativity, and leadership, which are all qualities that are marketable just about anywhere.

5 ARC Structure

Bullets can emphasize the main action, result, or characterization and its many forms, depending on how the bullet is structured. This section is dedicated to deepening an understanding of the flexible structure of a bullet. By emphasizing the most significant, relevant, or unique points of your bullets, you can maximize the potency of your accomplishments.

5.1 Basics On the Bullet Level

The essence of a bullet point is typically the Action (A) you have taken, which is composed of the verb (V) and the object (O).

$$V \qquad O$$

- Managed facility operations.

And, as we have discussed throughout this book, Results (R), especially quantifiable results, give greater impact by showing how well you have performed the action.

$$A \qquad\qquad\qquad R$$

- <u>Managed facility operations</u> resulting in a <u>15% decline in operating expenses</u>.

Action is emphasized by being first.

$$A \qquad\qquad R$$

- **Launched a new product line** that <u>increased GAR 20%</u>.

Result is emphasized by being first.

$$R \qquad\qquad A$$

- **Increased GAR 20%** by <u>launching a new product line</u>.

Results by Results

- <u>Enhanced customer satisfaction</u> by <u>improving service times and cutting errors 45%</u>.

Multiple Actions: Emphasizes various skills on one aspect, such as a marketing campaign.

- <u>Planned</u>, <u>launched</u>, and <u>managed</u> a marketing campaign promoting sales of ABC product.

Multiple Actions: Various aspects and skills as a subset of a major action to explain how you did something like "Initiated."

- Initiated the company's first national marketing campaign by <u>launching</u> a website, <u>cultivating</u> key industry contacts, and <u>developing</u> marketing literature.

5.1.1 Breadth

After selecting a strong introductory action verb, decide whether you want to elaborate on breadth, depth, or scope. A judgment at this point must be made where to take the bullet point. Using a writer for example, you can show breadth by listing a variety of types of writing:

- Perform a broad array of writing assignments, including articles, reports, summations, marketing collateral, and proposals.

Additional Examples that reveal breadth through details for other occupations:

- Counsel pediatric through geriatric patients diagnosed with <u>severe cognitive and neurological conditions such as Alzheimer's disease, schizophrenia, bipolar disorder, and dementia.</u>

- Train opticians in <u>dispensing methods, pupil measurement procedures, and frame fitting practices.</u>

- Lead weekly meetings on <u>retail procedures, sales strategies, service standards, and promotional campaigns.</u>

5.1.2 Depth

Still using the example of a writer, indicate depth by focusing on one aspect. In this example, elaborate on the intricacies, such as what the article pertained to and what it took to write the feature article.

- Wrote a feature article on the decline of Communism which featured interviews with Mikhail Gorbachev and Vladimir Putin.

5.1.3 Purpose

By introducing the purpose of your action, you reveal the scope of your responsibilities. It can also be used as a phantom bullet, when the results were dismal. The purpose states what was intended to happen, not what actually happened. Suppose you designed an HVAC system for a massive project that stalled during a recession. You could still write what was intended.

A   Purpose
- Designed HVAC systems <u>for renovations</u> of high-rises and related commercial properties.

5.1.4 Scope

A little context or perspective can also reveal the scope of your responsibility. The credibility is in providing details that show to what extent you performed your duties. See the following examples of scope:

- Planned, coordinated, and monitored special events that <u>hosted up to 2,000 attendees.</u>

- Interviewed, hired, and motivated personnel <u>for all 12 divisions.</u>

- Wrote articles on political and economic issues <u>for a leading industry magazine with a 100,000 nationwide circulation.</u>

5.2 Advanced Understanding of Bullet Structure

Characterizations (C), contexts (C), and challenges (C) are other tools to build potent bullet points. The C's interplay with the Actions/Results (AR) structure and its combinations. Actions, Results and Characterizations, Context, or Challenges (ARC) is a staple structure, which will be explained next as well as ARC's many variations.

5.3 ARC Structures

The structure of a bullet usually employs one or some combination of ARC. A characterization may involve a perspective, clarification, specification, or qualifier. Whereas the Action and Result are self-explicit, the characterization often addresses a substantiation, perspective, intent, or elaboration on complexity – what was involved to perform the function or get the result. The characterization addresses how, why, or what it took to perform an action. It builds on the AR structure, by explaining why the result is significant.

In the next examples, the action is referenced, followed by the result. Then, a second level of perspective enhances the bullet point.

- Strengthened internal controls and employee training resulting in 144% increase in annual revenues, <u>the highest sales production in the company's 10-year history</u>.

In the following example, the result and characterization are one in the same.

- Wrote articles on political and economic issues, <u>which were cited by lobbyists during congressional hearings in support of legislative changes to campaign financing</u>.

The structure may be determined based on what point you want to emphasize, which typically comes first.

5.3.1 Results, Action, Context/Challenge
- Increased gross annual revenues (GAR) 20% by launching a new product line, <u>which entailed training 20 technicians.</u>

5.3.2 Action, Results, Characterization
                      A   R   C
- Launched a new product line that increased GAR 20%, <u>the highest revenue among a 400-member staff.</u>

You are in essence giving a perspective on how significant the accomplishment is. The accomplishment is two-fold, first indicating how well you performed the function by a percentage, then the characterization that explains why the result is so significant.

5.3.3   Characterization, Action, Results

Even a characterization may be what you really want to emphasize; so place it first:

```
        C                                                      A        R
```

- Achieved the highest revenue performance among a 400-member staff by launching a new product that increased GAR 20%.

5.3.4   Parallelism/Variation

Often the structure of a bullet is influenced by what you want to emphasize. Ask yourself what do you want to emphasize: the action, result, or context? The bullet's structure is also influenced by the structure of bullets that precede and follow the one you are writing. You may want to avoid repetitive sentence structure from bullet to bullet.

Regardless of how you structure your bullets, you should keep them parallel. For example if you decide to begin with a result followed by a list of three actions, those actions should all have the same grammar as illustrated in the next bullet:

- Achieved 104% of corporate sales goal by **expanding** the customer base, **strengthening** client communications, and **improving** post sale follow-up services.

5.3.5   Prepositions

which/that	entailing	for	to	of
involving	encompassing	through	in	by
impacting	resulting in		on	

Prepositions assume a pivotal role in directing what you want to write. For example: "Developed an educational pilot program." So what? If you stop here, the employer won't understand the significance of your effort. Add context, which may also provide a quantifiable reference.

- Developed an educational pilot program, **which** included the preparation of a 200-page manual.

- Developed an educational pilot program **that** was adopted by the company and instituted in all 450 facilities nationwide.

- Developed an educational pilot program **in support of** a 40-member sales force preparing **to** rollout the company's premier product line for fiscal year 2016.

6 Re-Examination

The first five sections of *Resumes That Impress!* covered issues and strategic approaches that most affect resumes. Apply the approaches of this book to bring relevance, significance, and credibility to your resume.

By indicating how well you performed your efforts, you impress upon employers how you made a difference. When you can demonstrate a pattern of success throughout your career, your resume will effectively compete against other well-qualified candidates vying for the same open positions.

Now that you have read about the many strategies to make a resume more credible and persuasive, re-examine your own resume. Are there striking omissions or ineffective content that found their way in your original effort?

For more examples of how to portray responsibilities, transferrable skills, and accomplishments, see the next section which provides more than 100 resume samples in alphabetical order from Accountants though Writers.

7 Samples

The samples presented in this section cover skilled-laborer, professional, and executive positions that represent many different occupations. The main job title of each sample is indicated in the upper right hand corner of the page, and the samples are arranged alphabetically. Therefore, in some cases related jobs such as a real estate agent and a property manager won't necessarily be placed side by side. Likewise, an attorneys' resume will not be side by side with a legal secretary, nor will journalist be next to writer, and help desk operator will not be next to software engineer.

Feel welcome to strum through the samples, even ones that don't directly relate to your field of choice, and observe the various structures, phrasing, etc. The samples vary in length and format and are rich with quantifiable references and typical responsibilities for each featured field. Since some jobs lend themselves better than other jobs to quantify productivity, not all of the samples will contain quantifiable accomplishments.

CORY SCHULMAN

1001 Accountant Drive
Rockville, Maryland 20752
240-338-0050
accountant@gmail.com

HIGHLIGHTS

Accurate, cost-effective, and efficient Staff Accountant with extensive background performing accounting functions in accordance with GAAP, especially month-end procedures, payroll, and miscellaneous receivables. Adept at auditing, budgeting, and reconciliation procedures. Recouped hundreds of thousands of dollars in past-due accounts and eliminated severe backlogs in several processing areas. Possess strong interpersonal, verbal, and writing skills. Held governmental clearance.

Computer Skills: Experienced in using PMM, PFM, PAAR (Star System), Microsoft Dynamics GP, PeopleSoft, Peachtree, Sage, and Legal Management System.

EXPERIENCE

Staff Accountant, United Hospital, Silver Spring, Maryland   2010 – Present

Accounting:
- Perform a broad range of accounting functions, including accounts receivable, accounts payable, month-end reconciliations, journal entries, general ledger, payroll taxes, audits, and analyses of cash balancing, credit card charges, and receivables.
- Maintain the general ledger consisting of 700+ accounts that represent approximately $120 million in operating income per annum. Contribute to the preparation of financial statements.
- Facilitate internal and external annual audits by providing documentation pertaining to receivables, PAAR, and journal entries.
- Calculate Maryland State and Federal payroll taxes for more than 3,000 employees.
- Reconcile, record, and enter payroll taxes into the general ledger.
- Contribute to fiscal budgetary development by allocating funds to reclassified accounts.
- Input EIPD and EIPA statistics into 100-line journals for 200+ departments.
- Appointed by the Director of Accounting Services to upgrade PeopleSoft at the Indiana headquarters.

Cash Management:
- Reduced a backlog in processing receivables, resulting in the collection of approximately $250,000.
- Eliminated a 9-month backlog in entering and depreciating more than $100 million in assets.
- Entered 100 invoices per day to eliminate accounts as much as 90-days past due.

Communications:
- Wrote and implemented department-wide policies and procedures for collections, cash balancing, and PAAR balancing of non-efficient funds in the Accounting Services Department.
- Collaborated with the Accounting Manager and the Director on a daily basis.
- Mentored and trained new hires in asset management and related accounting functions.

Accounting Technician, International Endowment for the Arts, Washington, DC   2001 – 2010
- Reconciled and balanced accounts; prepared accounts receivable and payable records; generated cash-flow reports; made journal entries using state-of-the-art software; processed obligations and payment documents; implemented a fully integrated financial management information system; prepared special reports in a timely and accurate manner to meet established deadlines; and researched financial system database in response to outside CPA audits that required verification of account balances.

EDUCATION

Bachelor of Science in Accounting, May 2000, Bowie State University

CORY SCHULMAN

1002 Accountant Drive • Olney, MD 20832 • 240-338-0050 • cs@gmail.com

SUMMARY

Staff Accountant with 10 years of experience ensuring accurate, expedient, and highly organized accounting services to small through mid-size companies. Expertise in cost, managerial, and tax accounting with experience in auditing and business law. Performed general accounting functions for corporations, S corporations, and partnerships. Supervised a team of accountants.

Education: Bachelor of Arts, Business Administration/Economics, Wesleyan College Completed all courses in preparation for the CPA examination, Montgomery College

Computer Skills: Sage, Windows Excel, Ceridian, ADP payroll software packages, Real World general ledger software.

EXPERIENCE

CAL HOWARD & ASSOCIATES – KENNEDY INTERNATIONAL, Temporary Agency
Staff Accountant, 2011 – Present, Rockville, Maryland
- Enhanced reconciliation of daily revenues that exceeded $2 million per month by establishing and implementing a cash entry system for USA Waste. Reduced errors in accounts receivable by incorporating new data tracking methods. Reconciled general ledger accounts having deficits as large as $25,000. Eliminated a two-month backlog in accounts reconciliation. Processed general ledger.
- Verified accuracy of computer records with hard copy records for a 3-year history of client billings at Chestnut Lodge.
- Processed and maintained $500,000 in accounts payable records.

MANYARD & SONS, INC., Wholesaler
Staff Accountant, 2007 – 2011, Baltimore, Maryland
- Replaced manual accounts receivable operations with a computerized system to process $15 million per month. Automated accounts payable procedures.
- Prepared industry related tax reports for five states and health insurance reports for the union.
- Prepared commission reports for the Sales Department and personnel.
- Conducted internal audits of payroll processing.
- Processed and maintained payroll for more than 200 employees.

MARYLAND SAVINGS ASSOCIATION, Mortgagor
Staff Accountant, 2004 – 2007, Frederick, Maryland
- Ensured proper transfers of escrow accounts by developing a system to identify misapplied loan payoffs.
- Reconciled six bank statements and general ledger accounts which eliminated a 6-month backlog.

CORY S. SCHULMAN, CPA

1003 CPA Drive   240-338-0050

Rockville, Maryland 20852   E-mail: cpa@gmail.com

HIGHLIGHTS

- CFO, Financial Consultant, and former business owner with diverse capabilities in creative financing, including cash management, accounts payable, payroll, fringe benefits administration, strategic planning, budgeting, reporting, pensions, financial statements, and tax returns.
- Provided expert tax advice as a guest on a one-hour talk radio infomercial, which entailed taking questions from the public on the air.
- Developed and conducted seminars on Quickbooks for small business clients.
- Software: Peachtree, One Write Plus, Excel, Microsoft Word, Sage, Quickbooks.
- Passed the CPA Exam, November 2002.

EXPERIENCE

UNITED MORTGAGE BANKERS, LLC, Silver Spring, Maryland   2009 – Present

Controller/CFO

- Direct all financial activities of 3 branches for a mortgage loan company, which processes $37 million in loans per year.
- Initiated annual audit in collaboration with the independent auditor, which resulted in securing HUD licensure and new revenue opportunities from the FHA loan market.
- Instituted quality control mechanisms, which reduced liability.
- Allocate costs and income to each branch in accordance with banking regulations.
- Managed escrow account for the company's five branches.
- Participated in consolidating a major office, which decreased rental expenses 50%.
- Incorporated the net branch commission concept.

COLUMBIAN INTERNATIONAL, Columbia, Maryland   2006 – 2009

Independent Financial Consultant

- Provided tax and bookkeeping consultation to individuals, partnerships, and corporations. Prepared tax forms, including 1040s, 1120s, 1120Ss, and 1065s.
- Expanded the client base of corporate accounts 50% and individual accounts 166% within 4 years of inception.

ELEGANT EUROPEAN FURNITURE, Washington, DC   2002 – 2006

Accountant

- Created one of the first point-of-sale systems using dBASE III to track approximately $800,000 in annual sales and an average of $1 million in cash checking transactions.
- Prepared payroll for 9 employees and devised a budget of $160,000 for the physical inventory. Developed short- and long-term forecasts based on market trends, sales history, and profit margins.

EDUCATION

B.A., Economics, Minor in Math, 2001, University of Maryland, College Park, Maryland
Graduate Studies in Economics, University of Maryland, College Park, Maryland

CORY S. SCHULMAN, CPA
1004 CPA Avenue
Baltimore, MD 21215

Home: 240-338-0050
Work: 555-220-0800
E-mail: cpa@hotmail.com

OBJECTIVE

To ensure the most profitable, accurate, and compliant accounting practices in an executive level Controller/CFO position or a related career opportunity.

EXPERIENCE

SCHULMAN ASSOCIATES, INC., Rockville, Maryland   2003 – Present
Controller, Secretary of Treasury, Consulting Engineering Firm

Accounting Operations Management:
- Oversee accounting and reporting of contracts ranging from $30,000 to $5 million with corporate and government client guarantors such as USAID, The World Bank, Asian Development Bank, and domestic/foreign governments.
- Restructured the entire accounting department and downsized staff 40% without compromising quality or efficiency.
- Revamped and updated the cost accounting system, which enabled determinations of profit and loss of company profit centers throughout the world.
- Devise strategic plans to reinvest resources and/or dissolve unproductive branches.
- Replaced under-skilled employees with experienced staff accountants, resulting in a dramatic upgrade in proficiency, industry knowledge, and professionalism.

Budgeting and Auditing:
- Formulated and allocated the company's first corporate overhead budget of $9.5 million, which included 7 separate divisional budgets.
- Ensure compliance and passage of DCAA, IRS, and CPA external audits. Prepare DCAA indirect cost submissions and audit representations.

Financial and Asset Management:
- Modified banking relationships and successfully negotiated lower interest rates and credit fees, saving the company $75,000+ per annum.
- Negotiated a rise in the company's line of credit from $2.5 million to $3 million and increased the threshold of asset based financing.
- Recouped approximately $200,000 within 6 months by initiating collections efforts.
- Challenged and successfully reduced disallowances from $225,000 to less than $50,000.
- Eliminated a 9-month backlog in accounting and project accounting.
- Prepare financial statements and perform cash management.

EDUCATION

Accreditation:
Earned Certificate as Certified Public Accountant in New York, 2002

Education:
Bachelor of Arts in Mathematics, 2001, University of New York City, New York

CORY S. SCHULMAN

2001 Attorney Drive
Gaithersburg, Maryland 20878

240-338-0050
attorney@gmail.com

EXPERIENCE

Associate Attorney, Ellison & Associates, P.C., Silver Spring, Maryland   2009 – Present
- Review and prepare for trial approximately 50 cases per day pertaining to collections, contract law, landlord/tenant law, and bankruptcies.
- Provide legal representation for cases ranging up to $500,000 in support of such clients as Mercedes Benz Credit Corporation, Chrysler Financial Company, L.L.C., Key Bank and Trust, and Household Automotive Finance Corporation.
- Exceeded the firm's annual billable hour projections 33% by generating approximately $300,000 per annum.
- Achieved an outstanding win/loss record for 3 consecutive years for clients in the automotive, financial, and property management industries.
- Draft informational memoranda that address legislative changes in real property law in Maryland. Update clients on Article 9 of UCC and the revamped bankruptcy rules.
- Prevent unnecessary litigation by conducting successful mediations between clients and consumers. Negotiate complex settlements involving financial analyses, contract interpretation, cost/benefit analyses, and financial loss tabulations.
- Write leases, business organization contracts, and employment contracts as well as complaints, briefs, motions, appeal memoranda, and settlement agreements.
- Conduct trials, argue motions, and handle appeals in state and Federal district courts of Maryland for criminal cases through $5 million civil suits with multi-counts of action.

Associate Attorney, Stein, Myer, & Gold, Rockville, Maryland   2007 – 2009
- Provided legal representation to clients in a general practice law firm, including family, contract, traffic, criminal, landlord/tenant, and business law.

Legal/Legislative Intern, International Publishing Association, Harrisonburg, Pennsylvania   2006
- Summarized legislation for Association publications, answered member inquiries on legal publishing issues, and assisted with lobbying for or against various legislation.

Law Clerk, Morgan and Klein, Washington, Pennsylvania   2003 – 2005

EDUCATION

Juris Doctor, 2002, Widener University School of Law, Harrisburg, Pennsylvania
Bachelor of Arts, 1997, Political Science, Jefferson College, Washington, Pennsylvania

SUPPLEMENT

Honors: Admitted to United States District Court, February 2002
                Admitted to Maryland Bar, December 2002

Affiliations: Member, Jay Admission Council, Jefferson College, 2000 – Present
                Member, Maryland State Bar Association
                Member, Bar Association of Montgomery County
                Member, American Trial Lawyers of America

Technical Skills: Westlaw and Lexis

CORY S. SCHULMAN

2002 Attorney Drive
Potomac, Maryland 20854
240-338-0050
lawyer@gmail.com

OBJECTIVE

To apply expertise in civil litigation, legislative representation, and legal counsel in a position that is commensurate with extensive background as an Attorney at Law.

EXPERIENCE

UNIVERSAL INSURANCE COMPANY, Fairfax, Virginia   2005 – Present
Resident Attorney
- Achieved a 96% winning percentage rate for civil lawsuits regarding malpractice, personal injury, product liability, property damage, and wrongful death.
- Represented UIC insureds for approximately $600 million in aggregate claims since 2005.
- Increased billable hours from 1,800 to 2,400 hours per year.
- Defended claims against UIC insureds often nullifying multi-million dollar litigation.
- The following are sample cases:
  - Defended a national chain department store in a $300 million assault/defamation case resulting in a $500 verdict.
  - Eliminated a $4 million personal injury claim against a national trucking company.
- Exhibited strong courtroom presence with in-depth knowledge of law and procedure to effectively analyze evidence, cross examine witnesses, and persuade jurors to secure desired verdicts.
- Prevented unnecessary litigation by conducting successful depositions. Negotiated complex settlements involving financial analyses, contract interpretation, cost/benefit analyses, and financial loss tabulations.
- Directed staff comprising two attorneys, paralegal, and four legal secretaries.

LAW OFFICE OF MAXWELL T. SCHMELLING, Fairfax, Virginia   1998 – 2005
Attorney
- Grew this general practice approximately 10% per annum over tenure and represented both individual and corporate clients in civil litigation matters.
- Represented an NFL franchise in proposing legislation pertaining to tax credits and counseled a team owner in legislative affairs.
- Traveled to Madrid, Spain to represent an international airline to secure landing rights and ensure compliance with IATA requirements.
- Litigated general practice cases involving commercial, criminal, family, environmental, employment, and traffic law.
- Conducted revealing witness interviews and depositions; wrote subpoenas, complaints, briefs, affidavits, motions, appeal memoranda, and settlement agreements. Argued motions and handled appeals in all state and Federal district courts of Virginia and Washington, DC.

EDUCATION

Juris Doctor, 1997, Georgetown Law Center, Washington, DC
Bachelor of Arts, 1993, English, University of Notre Dame, Notre Dame, Indiana
Notre Dame Man-of-the-Year and Who's Who in American Law

AFFILIATIONS

- Court Memberships: U.S. Supreme Court, U.S. District Court for 4th Circuit, and all courts in Washington, DC and the State of Virginia
- Virginia and Washington, DC Bar Association
- Member, Board of Governors, Congressional Country Club, Bethesda, Maryland, 2005 – 2011

CORY S. SCHULMAN, ESQUIRE

2003 Attorney Road
Silver Spring, Maryland 20905
240-338-0050
esquire@gmail.com

OBJECTIVE

To maximize settlement/judgment awards, billable hours, and new client generation as an astute and highly influential Attorney at Law.

HIGHLIGHTS

- Emerged as the highest revenue generating non-partner attorney for Klein & Goldman, P.C. by successfully litigating broad ranging cases involving personal injury, wrongful death, medical malpractice, employment discrimination, domestic relations, and criminal law.

- Interfaced with Johnny Cochran in high-profile personal injury cases, including a wrongful death from the Dulles tunnel collapse and a police brutality case with a potential multi-million dollar award.

- Persuasive and articulate attorney with commanding court presence and proven ability in plea bargaining, settlement negotiations, plaintiff/defendant interviewing, depositions, networking, and media relations. Skilled in arguing complex matters with insurance companies.

EXPERIENCE

KLEIN & GOLDMAN, P.C., College Park, Maryland   2008 – Present

Attorney, Licensed in the State of Maryland
- Negotiated, settled, and closed hundreds of legal cases, involving personal injury matters. Represented clients as a defense trial lawyer in criminal law cases.
- Secured favorable settlement awards, prevented client incarcerations, and reduced fines and sentences through persuasive plea bargaining and client negotiations.
- Drafted contracts, articles of incorporation, settlement/stipulation agreements, motions, pleadings, and related legal documents. Drafted and answered interrogatories, and performed depositions and related discovery matters.
- Researched case law using various resources such as LEXIS and Westlaw.

RICHARD RENQUIST, ESQUIRE/RENQUIST & PELE, Washington, DC   2002 – 2008

Legal Assistant
- Served as legal assistant to an attorney who represented clients in cases of personal injury, bankruptcy (Chapter 7, 11, & 13), immigration issues, criminal law, corporate law, contract review and negotiation, and real estate title search.
- Drafted offer of settlement and demand packages on behalf of personal injury clients.

SUPPLEMENT

Juris Doctor, 2002, Antioch School of Law, Washington, DC
Clinicals: Landlord/Tenant, Bankruptcy, and Civil Litigation

Bachelor of Arts Degree, Business, 1998, Rutgers University, New Brunswick, New Jersey

Affiliation: Member of Montgomery County Bar Association

CORY SCHULMAN
3001 Bank Manager Way
Germantown, Maryland 20876
240-338-0050
bankmanager@gmail.com

HIGHLIGHTS

- District Vice President experienced in managing 16 branches consisting of $1.6 billion in assets and 150 employees.

- Achieved double-digit growth in bank assets by providing profit-driven leadership, especially in operational efficiency, employee productivity, and quality service.

- Possess expertise in team building, staff development, and portfolio management.

- Adept at financial analysis, pricing strategies, budget management, and marketing.

- Acquired Life and Casualty licenses in the State of Maryland.

EXPERIENCE

SUNCOAST BANK, Bethesda, Maryland   1996 – Present
Vice President of the Montgomery County District, 2006 – Present

Operations Management:
- Manage a $145 million branch while overseeing 15 other branches employing 150 banking personnel.

- Improved ranking of the Bethesda branch from #32 to #3 within first 2 months and reached #2 among all 185 branches nationwide.

- Increased the deposit base from $73 million to $125 million within 2 years by effectively implementing relationship acquisition strategies throughout the business sector.

- Exceeded corporate goals 30% for sales of financial investment services, netting approximately $5 million in 2 quarters.

- Led efforts to revamp troubled branches, which resulted in improving the Montgomery Mall branch from #105 ranking to #8 within 9 months.

- Grew assets of the Montgomery Mall branch from $15 million to $88 million as a result of strategic coaching.

- Initiated retraining of loan underwriters and platform staff.

- Closed 45 home equity loans, which tripled the volume in the Wheaton branch.

Marketing:

❑ Achieved 25% new account growth primarily by networking extensively and conducting financial management seminars as a member of the Montgomery County, Bethesda, and Hispanic Chamber of Commerce associations.

❑ Developed and launched a marketing program for three demographically divergent areas.

❑ Established a new revenue channel based on sales of financial products/services, which generated approximately $500,000 in FY 2011.

System Implementation:

❑ Implemented a tracking system that monitored staff's product knowledge, especially consumer loans, mortgages, financial services, and alternative delivery channels.

❑ Oversaw conversion of the transaction processing system from Retail Delivery Service to Hogan Financial Systems throughout the 18 branches in Washington, DC.

❑ Coordinated the implementation of the emergency Y2K back-up system for all 18 branches.

Human Resources:

❑ Eliminated labor shortages as large as 40% in 3 branches within 5 months.

❑ Conducted informational and behavioral interviews and personality assessments.

❑ Instituted exit interviews to mend employee – management relations.

❑ Curtailed high turnover rate from 45% to 10%.

❑ Lengthened average employee longevity from 3 months to 1 year.

❑ Proposed the use of the Myers Briggs personality test, an action plan that was adopted by the President and implemented throughout the company.

❑ Revamped employee training in sales and customer service by conducting intensive workshops.

❑ Enhanced employees' effectiveness in giving presentations, converting objections into agreements, closing transactions, diffusing conflicts, and building relationships.

EDUCATION

B.A. in Business Administration, 1990, University of Maryland, Adelphi, MD

Life and Health Insurance, 1998, NASD Series 6/63, Baltimore, MD

CORY SCHULMAN

3002 Banking Place
Gaithersburg, Maryland 20879

Home: 240-338-0050
banking@gmail.com

OBJECTIVE

To enhance branch-level profitability by attracting new customers, increasing the asset base, and enhancing quality services as a Manager in the banking industry.

EXPERIENCE

IMPERIAL BANK OF AMERICA, Bethesda, Maryland   2000 – Present

Branch Manager, 2005 – Present

Operations Management:
- Increased the asset base from $23 million to $28 million by strengthening internal controls, financial sales productivity, processing accuracy, and customer relations.
- Improved the branch ranking from last among 189 branches to #37 within 4 months.
- Led the entire bank in achieving the highest sales ratio among 760 employees.
- Generated new business by launching effective marketing campaigns, which entailed social media promotions, prospecting, in-person presentations, and benefit banking.
- Produced triple-digit increases in sales of financial products, which included 200% improvement in sales of CDs and business loans and 150% rise in sales of home equity loans and cash management services.
- Curtailed operating expenses approximately 25% by eliminating procurement of unnecessary equipment and revising policies for document transfers.

Human Resources:
- Hired, coached, and supervised an eight-member staff, resulting in improved transaction processing accuracy and team cooperation.
- Conducted workshops to implement customer relations and product knowledge programs.

Awards/Recognition:
- Earned outstanding performance awards throughout tenure, including Manager-of-the-Year in FY 2010 for the Washington Metropolitan region.
- Achieved flawless customer relations record since inception of employment.

Assistant Manager, 2003 – 2005
- Oversaw operations of the Potomac branch and facilitated a rise in ranking from #140 to #25 as well as a rise in the deposit base from $68 million to $85 million.
- Generated $10 million out of the $17 million increase in the deposit base.

Sales and Service Associate, 2002 – 2003
- Emerged as the leader in sales ratio per customer throughout the corporate network.

Lead Customer Service Representative, 2001 – 2002; **Teller**, 2000 – 2001

SUPPLEMENT

Education: **B.S. Physics**, Minor: **Business Management**, 1999, University of Michigan

CORY SCHULMAN

3003 Banking Drive
Rockville, Maryland 20855

240-338-0050
banking@comast.com

SUMMARY

Generated robust profits and growth of financial operations consisting of more than $100 million in assets. Facilitated corporate mergers, revitalized troubled units, and strengthened internal controls, resulting in greater sales production, marketing effectiveness, employee productivity, and corporate profitability. Maintained operations far below budget while enhancing overall operational integrity. Knowledgeable in Accounting, Economics, and Marketing. Exceeded corporate goals and earned numerous awards throughout tenure.

EXPERIENCE

FAIRQUEST BANK   1995 – Present

Assistant Vice President, Branch Manager, Germantown Branch, Maryland, 2007 – Present
- Served in numerous capacities and earned many promotions and awards for exemplary performance.

Business Development/Management:
- Oversaw branch operations consisting of a $57 million deposit base and an 8-member staff.
- Increased the deposit base more than $15 million within first 14 months.
- Achieved 127% of annual goal for new deposits valued roughly $2.8 million in FY 2015.
- Spearheaded a 180% rise in loan originations and 140% increase in business development, FY 2015.
- Increased the Flower Hill branch's deposit base from $11 million to $29 million as a result of across-the-board enhancements and effective marketing initiatives. Exceeded goals three-fold for fee income.
- Improved the ranking of the Flower Hill branch from near the bottom to within the top 25 among 190.
- Grew the deposit base of the Air Park branch from $10 million to $20 million in 4 years as a result of strengthening service standards and employee coaching.

Financial Management:
- Managed approximately $100 million in consumer commercial loans.
- Curtailed compensation budgets $70,000 below annual budget.
- Performed unannounced audits in 14 branches to ensure compliance with corporate policies and federal regulations.

Customer Service/Personnel Management:
- Received numerous customer-written commendations and positive corporate mystery shopper evaluations for outstanding service and customer satisfaction.
- Reversed high employee turnover rate and eliminated severe understaffing.
- Expanded the staff from two to nine members to maintain full staffing capacity.
- Sustained employee longevity as a result of effective communication and training.

Honors/Recognition:
- Earned one of two Presidential Awards given in 2010 for exemplary branch management.
- Received recognition by Regional Manager who used the Air Park location as a model branch and training center.
- Invited by Regional Manager to speak on successful operational management and service techniques to a group of 30 managers.

EDUCATION

Bachelor of Arts in Business Administration, 1994, University of the District of Columbia

CORY SCHULMAN

3004 Banking Drive
Rockville, MD 20853

240-338-0050
bankteller@gmail.com

EXPERIENCE

BANK OF CITIZENS TRUST, Bethesda, Maryland   2006 – Present

Customer Service Specialist (Managerial Level), 2012 – Present

- Direct customer service operations for the branch, which entails lobby management, personnel coaching, customer relations, and problem resolution.
- Oversee and coach the staff in transaction procedures, sales techniques, and public relations.
- Increased the bank's service rating as the primary point-of-contact for customers.
- Improved processing time and accuracy while increasing the volume of transactions per day.
- Exceeded corporate performance goals for all quarters in FY 2015 since appointed as a Customer Service Specialist.
- Cross sold various financial products and services, including home and personal loans, credit cards, certificates of deposits, and new accounts.
- Achieved approximately 105% of the banking center's branch sales goal for FY 2014.
- Applied bilingual skills as a liaison between customer service and Spanish-speaking patrons.

Personal Banker, 2006 – 2012

- Generated more than $2 million in new business through sales of financial products and services, which entailed canvassing existing customers and establishing new accounts.
- Opened 250 individual and corporate accounts for checking, savings, CDs, money markets, and related banking products and services valued in excess of $10 million.
- Processed applications for personal, unsecured, and home equity loans as much as $100,000.
- Applied fluency in Spanish to bridge communications with non-English speaking customers.

SUNCOAST BANK, Bethesda, Maryland   2002 – 2006

Teller

- Opened new accounts, notarized documents, and processed various transactions such as deposits, withdrawals, and transfers.
- Achieved corporate goals for sales of financial products and services for 4 years.
- Audited travelers' checks on a monthly basis.
- Reconciled the bank vault containing more than $50,000 and prepared two ATMs daily.
- Earned high marks for customer service based on periodic mystery assessments.
- Addressed customer inquiries on financial products such as certificates of deposits and consumer/home equity loans.
- Trained new tellers in opening/closing accounts, processing transactions, financial sales, customer service, and reconciling end-of-the-day figures.

EDUCATION • COMPUTER SKILLS • LANGUAGES

Education: University of Maryland University College, College Park, Maryland
         B.S. Degree in Communications, 2001, Minor: Business Management
Computer Skills: Windows, Microsoft Word, Excel, PowerPoint, Access, Photoshop
Language: Fluent in Spanish

CORY SCHULMAN
27001 Biological Science Laboratory Road
Germantown, MD 20876
240-338-0050
science@gmail.com

RESEARCH SKILLS

- Senior Biological Science Laboratory Technician and former Project Manager, Research Scientist, and Virologist with extensive knowledge of immunology, microbiology, virology bacteriology, blood banking, immunochemistry, and chemistry. Knowledgeable of immobilized enzymes and proteins.

- Possess in-depth experience in performing various laboratory procedures, including antigen and/or antibody detection using enzyme-immuno assays, radio-immuno assays, hemagglutination assays, fluorescent staining techniques and other serological and/or immunological techniques.

- Adept at using techniques for virus isolation and identification, tissue culture technology, hybridoma cloning and maintenance and serologic procedures utilizing monoclonal and polyclonal antibodies.

- Conduct statistical, numerical, and/or graphic analyses to record experiments and data.

- Co-authored approximately 40 scientific papers and presentations.

EXPERIENCE

U.S. NAVY	2005 – Present

Viral and Rickettsial Diseases Program, Infectious Diseases Division (IDD), The Research Institute, Bethesda, Maryland
Senior Biological Science Laboratory Technician

- Develop and improve methods to prevent, diagnose, and treat infectious diseases that may threaten U.S. Navy personnel. Prepare viral antigens that have been used to develop rapid diagnostic procedures for research scientists from two divisions.

- Train junior personnel in viral lab procedures, including preparation of living cultures to study viral agents; preparation of various types of complex mediums needed for living cells for propagation of viral agents. Supervise junior technical staff in maintenance of various cell lines for the propagation of virus antigens.

- Develop rapid diagnostic assays for arbovirus diseases. Ensure highest quality control of reagents, assays, and standards used in protocols.

- Purify and quantify viruses by performing various biochemical procedures involving protein assay, plaque assay and immunoassays such as enzyme-linked immunosorbent assay (ELISA) and immunofluorescence assay for characterization of antigens and antibodies.

- Optimize serological assays for antibody to viral antigens and conduct antibody titrations and/or viral isolation on large number of human serum specimens from endemic areas.

- Relocated the Naval Research Center for Infectious Disease Laboratories from Bethesda to Forest Glenn in an expeditious time frame that minimized down time. Moved equipment, reagents, and tissue cultures within 3 weeks which facilitated the propagation of the dengue vaccine program.

54

NRC, (NAVAL RESEARCH CENTER), Lima, Peru   2004 – 2005

Research Scientist

- Functioned as Head, Department of Virology of Naval Research Center, Lima, Peru.

- Established the virus division of NAMRID and served as Head of the Virology Division to conduct medical research, assess the distribution and prevalence of infectious disease threats of South America, and assess laboratory diagnostic and clinical therapeutics.

- Worked closely with military and civilian scientists in Peru to investigate outbreaks of disease where viral etiology was suspected. Identified hepatitis and initiated vaccinations.

- Established monitoring system for the first documented outbreak of the dengue fever in Peru.

- Trained a vast number of physicians and technicians in viral laboratory procedures in Peruvian public health blood banks, resulting in the prevention and reduction of contaminated transfused blood products.

- Ensured laboratory safety was in compliance with Federal, State, NAVOSH, and NAVMEDRSCHINSTITUTE guidelines.

- Executed the entire virology and serology research program by designing, implementing, evaluating, and modifying research techniques to achieve research goals.

NAVAL HEALTH INSTITUTE, San Diego, California   1998 – 2004

Project Manager

- Directed primary research efforts of the Virology section, Biological Sciences Department toward the development and evaluation of methods for the rapid detection and identification of infectious disease agents.

- Tested various materials, configurations, and modifications for their ability to facilitate detection of viral and bacterial antigens from body secretions.

- Supervised the production of high affinity monoclonal antibodies, both viral and bacterial, by using current hybridoma technology.

WASHINGTON RESEARCH INSTITUTE, Washington, DC   1997 – 1998

Virologist

- Supervised a section of the virology laboratories, as well as fiscal and personnel matters.

- Wrote research proposals, designed laboratory protocols, allocated assignments, and trained laboratory personnel.

- Conducted studies to identify specific strains of dengue virus associated with outbreaks of the disease in the Caribbean and Central American regions, and investigation of the immune response of individuals infected with this agent.

- Isolated and propagated chlamydial agents in tissue culture systems.

- Developed more efficient methods to monitor sentinal animals for exposure to viral agents with emphasis on group A and B arbovirus.

- Investigated selected human sera which yielded aberrant patterns when tested in standard procedures for the presence of rubella antibody.

- Used various techniques and procedures: animal and insect tissue culture, direct and indirect immunofluorescence, radioimmunoassay, serum fractionation, immundodiffiusion, 1-dimensional and 2-dimensional gel immunoelectrophoresis, extraction and purification of antigens, production of mono-specific antisera, enzyme linked immunosorbent assay systems, lyophilization, dialysis, and other tests.

CORY SCHULMAN

1008 Full Charge Bookkeeper Lane
Germantown, Maryland 20874
240-338-0050
bookkeeper@gmail.com

OBJECTIVE

To apply generally accepted accounting procedures as an experienced Full Charge Bookkeeper or in a related career opportunity.

SUMMARY

Bookkeeping Skills: Payroll, Payroll Taxes, Accounts Payable, Accounts Receivable, Sales Taxes, General Ledger, Financial Statements, and Employee Benefits

Computer Skills: Sage, Quick Books, Peachtree, Great Plains, and Excel

EXPERIENCE

INFORMATION DATA CENTER, Gaithersburg, Maryland   2004 – Present
Full Charge Bookkeeper

- Prepare monthly financial statements and payroll for a multi-million dollar computer hardware wholesaler consisting of 18 employees.
- Manage a $2.5 million asset baseline of credit and all bank reports.
- Provided accurate, well organized records approved by outside auditors on a quarterly basis for 11 consecutive years. Ensured end-of-the-year certification of financial statements.
- Administrated employee benefits, especially insurance and profit sharing.
- Researched and rectified financial discrepancies among thousands of account records and general ledgers.
- Identified and corrected overages on accounts payables from 30+ national vendors.
- Verified that the fiscal inventory matched the general ledger.
- Ensured accuracy of state withholdings and sales tax for the District of Columbia and numerous states, including New York, New Jersey, Pennsylvania, West Virginia, Virginia, and Maryland. Processed W-2s and 1099s.
- Transitioned manual bookkeeping to computerized systems using Great Plains.
- Set up computerized accounts payables and receivables.

ADDITIONAL EXPERIENCE

- Performed bookkeeping functions prior 2004 for Books International, Medical Consultants, the Lifestyle Group, and the Maryland Real Estate Commission.
- Processed medical insurance claims, reconciled bank statements, developed monthly profit and loss statements, prepared taxes with accountants, and prepared monthly reports for Board of Director meetings.
- Coordinated office staff and supervised the Quality Assurance Department.
- Prepared individual and corporate State and Federal tax forms.

CORY SCHULMAN

1007 Budget Lane
Germantown, Maryland 20874
240-338-0050
budget@gmail.com

OBJECTIVE

To program budgetary preparation and strategically defend budgetary proposals as a Budget Manager knowledgeable in contemporary Public Financial Administration.

HIGHLIGHTS

Master of Science in Accounting, GPA: 3.8, Southeastern University, Washington, DC
Bachelor of Commerce, University of Maryland, College Park, Maryland

Budget Administration: Senior Budget Analyst experienced in preparing and administrating $200+ million proposed budget for the Maryland-National Capital Park and Planning Commission consisting of 2,000+ employees.

Fiscal Planning: Verify budget sufficiency for $3 million in capital outlay purchasing. Apply knowledge of fiscal planning and procurement when performing analyses of trends, projections, quarterly reviews, available funds, and expenditures. Attended various training classes and seminars on performance measures conducted by the Commission and Government Finance Officers Association. Performed contingency planning, tax filing, Medicaid billing, and budgetary/financial management.

Communications: Interview, hire, train, and evaluated staff. Interface with various levels of management and department staff to obtain information for research, analysis, and preparation of proposed and adopted budgets. Led staff meetings to discuss cost-reduction methods regarding manpower, equipment, and operations.

Technical Skills: Possess strong computer skills, especially in using Sage and Microsoft Excel spreadsheets. Use the Performance Budget System and Computerized Accounting System to balance and control budgets.

EXPERIENCE

Architectural Planning Committee of Maryland, Silver Spring, Maryland   2007 – Present
Senior Budget Analyst, Department of Human Resources and Management, Budget Office

Budget Management:
- Provide significant leadership in the preparation, management, and evaluation of the proposed and adopted annual operating budget of approximately $251 million for the Maryland-National Capital Park and Planning Commission.
- Manage personnel budget projections for 2,210 career employees. Analyze personnel parameters such as salaries and benefits projections.
- Improved quality and accuracy of analytical studies on trends of the Commission's expenditures and revenues in nine departments and offices for the Department Head, Planning Board, and County Council staff.

Budgetary Functions:
- Analyze all aspects of the bi-county budget, including the operating budget impact of capital projects, employee fringe benefits, salary lapses, and leave accrual. Prepare program budgets, which includes spreadsheets, fund and department summaries, position/employee parameters, and analytical graphs.
- Balance all funds with tax rate and revenue calculations.
- Review and analyze performance measures, especially regarding outcome and efficiency data submitted by departments. Prepare performance measures for the Budget Office.
- Coordinate line item budget processing in the Performance Budget system.
- Verify availability of purchasing funds for nine departments and offices with an aggregate of $3 million for capital outlay.
- Perform quarterly reviews that compare budgeted versus actual expenditures to determine available fund balances.
- Budget funds for contracting external professional services for the Commission.
- Prepare impact analyses of various state legislation affecting the Commission.
- Prepare Commission's budget resolution.

Communications:
- Provide technical budgetary support to the Commission's offices and departments.
- Represent the Budget Office in the absence of the Budget Manager by giving presentations before the Montgomery County and Prince George's County's Planning Board and Commission meetings.

Writing Skills:
- Draft the Commission's budget manual, which facilitates improvements in budget uniformity, compliancy, and accuracy.
- Co-develop written policies and procedures for departmental budget projections.
- Prepare budget transfer reports and secure approval from the Planning Board for significant budget transfers.
- Prepare budget narratives for various funds.

Data Systems Corporation, Rockville, Maryland   1998 – 2007

Financial Analyst
- Performed budgetary analyses, including explanation of variances and financial and operational trends.
- Developed budget and financial statements, financial forecasts, and cost proposals.
- Determined impact of critical program variances.
- Analyzed operating and financial reports; maintained graphic charts for management.
- Performed various accounting functions, including billing, accounts reconciliation, accounts receivables/payables, and journal entries.

SUPPLEMENT

Member of the Government Finance Officers Association (GFOA), United States and Canada
Member of GFOA Budget Review Committee
President of VMC Group Home, Inc., Assisted Living Program, 1998 – 2007

CORY SCHULMAN
4001 Buyer Road
Damascus, MD 20872
240-338-0050
buyer@gmail.com

OBJECTIVE

To procure high-quality materials by negotiating advantageous contracts as an experienced Buyer.

EXPERIENCE

INDUSTRY TECHNOLOGIES SYSTEMS, Gaithersburg, Maryland   2003 – Present
Buyer
- Procure materials and equipment worth hundreds of thousands of dollars in support of government and private sector contracts. Negotiate single contracts as large as $160,000.
- Conduct competitive bid analyses with the primary focus on securing the highest quality and Just-In-Time (JIT) delivery at the lowest cost.
- Ensure compliance with the Material Requirement Plan (MRP), contractual terms and conditions, company policies, and public law.
- Apply knowledge of commodity, inventory, and supplier terms to determine quantities for requisitions.
- Resolve discrepancies pertaining to receiving and invoices. Minimize rejected materials by maintaining clear communications with engineering, manufacturing, and quality assurance departments. Document purchasing negotiations and provide feedback on supplier performance.
- Administer purchase orders, which entails pre-expediting and follow-up on revised delivery dates.
- Identify and establish new procurement sources by researching, surveying, and negotiating with vendors.
- Manage inventory of metal, machine tools, printed circuit boards, labels/decals, and related materials, components, and equipment. Reduced excess inventory items.
- Apply extensive MRP and database knowledge of purchase order entry and view screens, cross reference information, price history information, receiving transactions, gross requirements information, access supply/demand, requisition view screens, access and requisition pool, and purchasing and manufacturing shortage reports.
- Train co-buyers in administrative support procedures.
- Promoted to Buyer from Senior Process Specialist, which involved image printing, photo plotting, Optek photo tool inspections, reading drawings, and inspecting photo art-work to master prints.

EDUCATION, SKILLS, & AWARDS

Business Management, 2002, University College, Germantown, Maryland
Awards: Two Employee-of-the-Month Certificates for Outstanding Performance

CORY SCHULMAN

4002 Buyer Terrace
Frederick, Maryland 21701
240-338-0050
buyer@hotmail.com

OBJECTIVE

To ensure the highest cost-effectiveness and quality assurance as a high-level Purchaser or a related position.

SUMMARY

Purchasing Agent/Senior Buyer: Source, qualify, and negotiate purchase agreements with domestic and international suppliers/distributors in the electronics industry. Manage multi-million dollar procurement budgets; prepare short and long-range materials forecasts; develop price quotes, bids, and proposals. Expedite and trace purchase orders and shipments, negotiate freight costs, and coordinate deliveries.

EXPERIENCE

SUPER COMPUTER INDUSTRIES, INC., Frederick, Maryland   2001 – Present
Senior Buyer

- Secured $20 million in aggregate purchasing and leasing engagements in support of SCI as a contractor for the National Cancer Institute of the National Institutes of Health.
- Closed lease agreements for multi-million dollar supercomputers. Purchased capital equipment ranging in value from $50,000 to $4.1 million.
- Applied extensive knowledge of GSA schedules, FAR, and related government regulations to procure medical, scientific, and IT equipment and a vehicular fleet.
- Authorized $8.1 million in leased supercomputer technology for the largest advanced biomedical computing center in the country.
- Purchased flow cytometers, centrifuges, bioreactors, SEMs, blood culturing systems, etc; and supercomputers (IBM, SGI, and SUN), mainframes, network equipment (servers, routers, hubs, muxes, PCs, peripherals), software, licensing agreements; and environmentally friendly and energy efficient fleet of 35 alternate fuel and electric delivery trucks and vans.
- Conduct Internet research to evaluate hundreds of vendors and prepare cost/product analyses, RFQs/RFPs, and solicitation contract agreements.
- Saved the Federal Government approximately $75,000 for purchases of Dell computers by capitalizing on a corporate purchasing agreement.
- Identified dozens of small, minority-owned and HUB-zoned businesses to meet government spending requirements.
- Interfaced with numerous division-level directors and architectural, maintenance, and facility engineers regarding contract negotiations, risk assessments, and quality assurance.

- Appointed by the Director of Acquisition and Logistical Services to coordinate special projects such as procurement of multi-million dollar leases.
- Identified and resolved export issues for capital and medical equipment purchases for the Health and Human Services AIDS Initiative and Research Lab in Mali, Africa.

SECURITY ELECTRONICS, LTD., Houston, Texas   1997 – 2000

Buyer – Security Systems Division

- Planned and managed procurement of electronic security systems, parts, and components for a wholesale distributor of Panasonic, Mitsubishi, Sony, Pelco, Silent Witness, Telex, and Toshiba electronic security systems.
- Sourced and qualified vendors and suppliers, and negotiated purchase of sensors, cameras, monitors, multiplexers, cables, wiring, speakers, intercom systems, transceivers, carbon monoxide detectors, and fire and smoke alarms.
- Maintained an approved vendors list comprising Signal Cable, Spectrum Wire, Atlas Cable, Wheelock, Marshall Electronics, Video Mount Products, Sentrol, System Sensor, Peterson Products, M&S Systems, Napco, Telex, Phillips, Transaction Verifications Systems, and Network Video Technologies.
- Monitored stock inventory levels valued in excess of $12 million, utilizing ROBINET in-house database system and PeopleSoft in electronic processing of purchase orders.
- Negotiated more than $26 million in purchases of electronics equipment, parts, and supplies for 8 warehouse operations located throughout Texas, Florida, Georgia, California, and Connecticut.
- Provided accounting support in the investigation and resolution of freight charges, return authorizations, approval and payment of invoices, and establishment of credit lines.

SUPPLEMENT

Education – Professional Development:
Computer Science, University of Maryland, College Park, Maryland
Interior Design and Fashion Merchandising, Hood College, Frederick, Maryland
Negotiations, Government Regulations, Contractors, Legal Issues, and Vendor Sourcing

Affiliations:
NCMA (National Contract Management Association), Member 2001 – Present
Vice President of Programs for Frederick Chapter, 2001 – 2003
Secured guest speakers on purchasing and contracting issues.

CORY SCHULMAN

4003 Procurement Lane
Olney, Maryland 20832

240-338-0050
procurement@gmail.com

EXPERIENCE

Procurement Agent, High-Tech Solutions Corporation, Vienna, Virginia   2012 – Present

- Procured approximately $1.5 million per annum in computer hardware, software, furniture, supplies, and maintenance contracts.
- Improved order fulfillment approximately 20% for 150 internal employees and 75+ accounts, which included colleges/universities, small businesses, and international corporations.
- Reviewed spreadsheets consisting of as many as 50 line items that detailed system specifications. Interfaced with the systems manager to verify the necessity of line items.
- Established and managed the Shipping/Receiving Department.
- Collaborated with the Controller to hire shipping and receiving personnel by conducting candidate interviews and making recommendations. Provided training in SBT, an internal purchasing inventory control system.

Procurement Agent, Electronic System Technologies, Inc., Reston, Virginia   2006 – 2012

- Facilitated the relocation of Electronic System Technologies upon the company's acquisition by High-Tech Solutions Corp.
- Headed full-scale pre/post move inventory audits; led the transfer of the Shipping and Receiving Department without loss of equipment; set-up a new stock room at the Vienna location.
- Identified and rectified discrepancies when conducting semi-annual inventory audits.
- Negotiated terms and conditions of blanket and bulk order agreements as large as $400,000 with local and national vendors. Reduced expenses as much as 25% per item and periodically eliminated shipping/receiving costs.
- Curtailed expenditures by enforcing purchase justifications from all employees submitting purchase requisitions.
- Authorized approval/denial of purchasing requisitions valued up to $5,000 for internal orders.
- Eliminated a backlog of 30 unfulfilled purchase orders within the first month.
- Strengthened security of the stock room, which contained goods valued in excess of $200,000.
- Customized computer software by meeting with technical consultants and defining specifications for shipping, receiving, and purchasing modules.
- Created inventory tracking procedures for equipment transferred throughout six departments.

Purchasing Agent, ATP Systems, Inc., Reston, Virginia   2004 – 2006

- Earned two promotions culminating to Purchasing Agent responsible for procuring audio-video systems and parts valued approximately $1.2 million per annum.
- Filled orders from large corporate customers such as FedEx, PNC park stadiums, malls, and restaurants; non-profit organizations and government agencies.
- Interfaced with manufacturers' representatives to ensure timelines of order fulfillment and to verify the accuracy of costs, quantities, quality, brands, and related specifications of orders.
- Evaluated vendors for adequate stock levels, delivery capabilities, and shipping/receiving terms and conditions.
- Curtailed shipping rates approximately 10% through negotiations with freight companies.
- Improved on-time completion of purchases approximately 40% by enforcing receivable requirements and by effectively coordinating warehouse processes.

SUPPLEMENT

Education: Fundamentals of Purchasing, National Association of Purchasing Management
University of Maryland, College Park, Maryland, 2003

Knowledge: Postal rates/regulations, mail classes, mail sorting, and data entry

Cory Schulman

7001 Carpenter Drive
Gaithersburg, MD 20878
Work: 240-338-0050
carpenter@gmail.com

EXPERIENCE

Planner, Estimator, Carpenter, 1995 – Present
United States Navy, Public Works and Maintenance Division

- Supervise renovations, installations, repairs, and new construction involving office spaces, industrial testing laboratories, technical research areas, and computer facilities. Work primarily in an assigned zone of 22 buildings containing 748,000 square feet of floor space and over 1,000,000 square feet of roofing.

- Apply knowledge of architectural, civil, structural, mechanical, fire protection, and electrical engineering disciplines.

- Perform a broad range of carpentry and facility maintenance functions, which include welding, sheetmetal, roads and grounds, security fencing, locks and security devices, painting, rigging, roofing, masonry, foundation, water/sewer, heating, ventilating, air conditioning, steam supply, fire protection, communications/security systems, and related electrical, plumbing, and structural projects.

- Evaluate projects and prepare cost estimates, specifications, drawings, and other technical documents. Use database, spreadsheet, and estimating software.

- Select and procure materials, plan job sequences, and oversee completion of large-scale projects on time and within budget. Maintain awareness of the latest industry standards and State and Federal laws/regulations.

Project Planning and Coordinating:

- Develop project execution plans and estimate costs of construction projects for the Naval Surface Warfare Center (NSWC), which hosts 60+ buildings on a 185 acre campus.

- Inspect sites and prepare detailed technical specifications, instructions, sequences, material orders, and sketches, especially for work involving buildings, structures, roads, walks, parking lots, paved areas, fences, walls, land drainage, soil erosion, equipment, and any other civil aspect of the NSWC. Plan and estimate major moving, rigging, and personnel moves.

- Manage schedules in accordance with milestones and the necessity to resolve conflicts in scheduling, material incompatibility, customer time tables, occupancy schedules, hazardous material removals, and other circumstances.

- Plan and estimate projects valued in excess of $500,000. Oversee large-scale interior remodeling projects as large as 6,000 square feet.

Light Engineering:

- Design and oversee construction of free standing buildings, roofing systems, concrete foundations, repairs, and other structural projects on time and within budget. Calculate ceiling/floor loads, size location/type of footings; create renderings; select steel and roofing materials; reconfigure mechanical systems.

Technical Knowledge:
- Use Ilsmus, AutoCAD, Pulsar, CCB applications and several other off-the-shelf software programs to prepare detailed estimates and plans for projects valued up to $400,000.

- Interpret technical documents, including blue prints, schematics, specifications, renderings, and job sequences. Use transits, builders' levels, engineering scales, and related measuring devices.

- Provide detailed computer aided design (CAD) sketches, working drawings, and full-sized engineered drawings.

- Use estimating standards such as Means Construction Price Standards, NAVFAC Engineering Performance Standards, Unit Price Standards, ANSI Standards, NAVFAC Guide Specifications, ASTM Standards, ASME Standards, and historical data.

- Apply knowledge of construction materials such as load bearing steel and wood joists, rafters and trusses, wall types and coverings, masonry and concrete strengths and applications, construction fasteners and hardware, roofing materials, high strength adhesives, various ceiling types, floor coverings, trim, fire rated metal doors and related hardware. Assess and remove lead, asbestos, PCB contaminants, and other hazardous materials.

- Conduct detailed annual and bi-annual physical inspections of more than 748,000 square feet of interior areas and 1,000,000 square feet of roofing.

Administration:
- Document issues pertaining to customer impact and regulatory compliance with health, safety, and environmental standards. Apply knowledge of Occupational Safety and Health Administration (OSHA), Environmental Protection Agency (EPA), Federal Acquisition Register (FAR), Naval Facilities Engineering Command and Naval Supply Systems contracting requirements, the Federal Handicap Accessibility Standards, and the Environmental and Natural Resources program.

- Maintain accurate digitized records. Write inspection reports, which contain written statements, sketches, cost estimates, and repair recommendations. Prepare material take-offs, cost estimates, justifications, and job plans.

- Saved the government thousands of dollars by effectively negotiating line item costs, base realignment and closing costs, and contract terms.

Financial Matters/Procurement:
- Prepare bid proposals and estimates for all facets of construction for material acquisition and contractor procurement services. Track costs of 15 - 20 jobs per month on the Work Control Management System. Balance monthly financial statements for submission to supply departments.

- Determine, cost, procure, and track diverse materials and contracting services: lumber, piping, sheet metal, welding, carpentry, roofing, lock smithing, masonry, wall board, ceiling tiles, electrical, HVAC, plumbing, and many others.

- Attend pre-construction finance conferences with contractors; identify and rectify discrepancies in contracts and cost estimates.

Communications:

- Maintain productive communications with customers, laborers, professionals, and division heads. Discuss highly technical issues with architects, engineers, administrative, safety, environmental offices, supply system personnel. Served as a liaison between contractors and the government.

- Negotiate project requirements with Command management, customer representatives, administrative offices, Federal Support Contracts (FSC) personnel, Public Works Division management, Occupation Safety and Health representatives, the Environmental Program Office, Industrial Hygiene personnel, and Fire Safety managers.

OTHER QUALIFICATIONS

Award:
Environmental Employee-of-the-Year, 2015

Additional Employment:
Framing Carpenter, 1992 – 1995, Holland Company, Gaithersburg, Maryland
Assistant Superintendent, 1990 – 1992, Superior Construction, Washington, DC

State Licenses:

- EPA AHERA Project Designer Recertification, 1999, Aerosol Monitoring & Analysis, Inc.
- EPA AHERA Inspector Recertification 1999, Aerosol Monitoring & Analysis, Inc.
- AHERA Building Inspector Certificate, 1998, Man Tech
- Asbestos Building Inspector Refresher Certificate, 1997, ATC Associates, Inc.
- AHERA Project Designer Course, 1994, BCM Engineers, Inc.
- Building Inspectors for Asbestos Hazards, Abatement and Protection, 1993, Biospherics, Inc.

Education & Professional Development:

- Initiated continuing professional development through seminars and additional training.
- Confined Space Refresher Training Certificate, 2010, Department of Navy
- Maintenance Supervisors Class, 2003, NAVFAC
- Maryland Lead Based Paint Abatement, 2003, Aerosol Monitoring and Analysis
- CADD Microsystems, Inc., AutoCad Release 12
- Maintenance Supervisors Class, 2003, NAVFAC
- Blanket Purchase Agreements, 2002, NRCC
- Basic Electricity, 2001, Montgomery County Community College
- Principals of Construction Specification Writing, 2000, NAVFAC
- Construction Contracts and Specifications, 1998, Montgomery County Community College
- Corrosion Control, 1997, NAVFAC
- Federal Acquisition Processes, 1997, GSA
- Construction Plans Reading, 1996, Montgomery County Community College
- Facilities Support Contracting, 1996, NAVFAC
- Contract Inspection, 1996, NAVFAC
- Control Inspectors Training, 1996, NAVFAC
- Architectural Blueprint Reading, 1995, Montgomery County Community College
- Structural Mathematics Algebra, 1995, NSWC

Cory Schulman

5001 Chef Farm Court
Silver Spring, Maryland 20889
H: 240-338-0050
chef@gmail.com

Visionary Chef de Cuisine

Trend-setting Executive Chef of award-winning restaurants: Le Elegante, Provence, Americano, Radisson Hotel, and Pavillon. Earned celebrated reviews by industry leading food critics Phyllis Richman and Mimi Sheraton.

International Acclaim:

- Received rave reviews throughout tenure by national and international press: *Gourmet Magazine, New York Times, Washingtonian Magazine, The Washington Post, Bon Appetit Magazine, Connoisseur, Playboy, LA Times, Chicago Tribune, Harpers*, and the *Japanese, Hong Kong, German*, and *English Magazines*.
- Won Chef-of-the-Year in 2015, (Le Elegante) *Washingtonian Magazine.*
- Elected Best New American Restaurant (Americano) & Best New Restaurant (Radisson Hotel) in 2004, *Esquire Magazine.*
- Nominated for the James Beard Award for Best Mid-Atlantic Chef (Provence Restaurant in 2008 and Radisson Hotel in 2003).

Culinary Innovation and Global Influences:

- Introduced fusion cuisine 15 years prior its national trend and emerged as a force behind contemporary French movements in the United States. Developed more than 2,200 creative recipes based on acquired insights into native cuisines and spices through worldwide travels to India, Middle East, Thailand, Japan, and Latin America. Born, raised, and apprenticed in France with initial training from numerous renowned chefs, including Pierre le Donje.

Executive Management:

- Generated 200% rise in gross annual revenues for Le Elegante during an economic downturn in the Washington, DC market; cut food and labor costs as much as 21 percentage points. Achieved 89% revenue increase in multi-million dollar 4-star restaurant spanning 11,000 square feet (Radisson Hotel); and managed up to 38 employees with improved productivity and staff stability. Commanded the highest average price per plate in the country at $257 in the mid-1990s while maintaining food costs below 21% for Pavillon.

Change Management:

- Revamped menus, pricing structures, large staffs, and interior decor. Designed creative and technically prudent kitchen layouts that have been replicated by culinary experts throughout the country. Selected new sites, negotiated construction contracts, and planned expansions with seamless implementation.

Public Relations:

- Interfaced with world famous celebrities, VIPs, political dignitaries, military officials, business executives, investors, royal family members, and other affluent patrons.

OBJECTIVE

To generate robust financial success and the finest reputation for quality and service as a visionary restaurateur and renowned Executive Chef.

EXPERIENCE

LE ELEGANTE RESTAURANT, Great Falls, Virginia   2008 – Present
Chef de Cuisine
- Achieved the highest sales in Le Elegante's 7-year history despite an industry-wide depression in business throughout the Washington, DC market.
- Doubled gross annual revenues from $750,000 to $1.5 million and brought national acclaim as one of the most celebrated and expensive French restaurants in the Washington Metropolitan region.
- Revitalized bar operations which enhanced daily sales from $100 to $1,000; and re-established private parties averaging $200 per person.
- Received 3 stars by *Washingtonian Magazine* in first year after re-engineering the original bistro into a fine-dining establishment specializing in south contemporary French cuisine.
- Revamped all aspects of operations: replaced staff with high caliber sous chefs; cut food costs from 40% to 27%; and increased average cost per plate from $54 to $95, the most expensive in the area.

CONSULTANCY, Boston, Massachusetts   2007 – 2008
Consultant
- Provided consultation to Le Monea in Boston, Massachusetts, a $7+ million a year restaurant with 150+ seat capacity and a South of France theme. Overhauled menu items, broadened cuisines, and mentored 22-member kitchen staff to sustain this establishment as one of the most reputable in Boston.
- Advised 15 Beacon Hotels in Boston, Massachusetts to change executive chefs, resulting in enhanced coordination of its multi-level kitchen and service sections.

PROVENCE RESTAURANT; AMERICANO RESTAURANT, Washington, DC 2004 – 2007
Co-Founder

Provence Restaurant:
- Established a regional rustic French cuisine that earned 3 stars by *Washingtonian Magazine*; ratings of 27 out of 30 by *Zagat Guide*, and acclamations from the *National Press*, *Bon Appetit Magazine*, *Esquire*, *Veranda*, and *The Washington Post*.
- Won Chef and Restaurant-of-the-Year in 2006 by *Washingtonian Magazine*.
- Nominated for James Beard Award for Best Mid-Atlantic Chef in 2006.
- Averaged double-digit increases in gross annual revenues and brought annual sales from $2.4 million to $3.8 million. Increased average guest checks from $60 to $100.

- Designed an award-winning layout of kitchen and dining room, which captured the simple elegance of the Auberge decor featuring decorative ironwork, ocher tiles, and cobblestone mosaics. Collaborated with architects and designers to create this original design, which has been copied throughout the culinary industry.
- Reduced employee turnover 70% within first year and maintained loyal and stable staff for 4 years.
- Raised the value and reputation of a below-market sector by converting a neglected location into a robust restaurant attracting affluent clientele.

Americano:
- Co-founded, co-designed, and opened this 320-seat "talk of the town" bar/restaurant featuring contemporary Mexican tapas and Brazilian churrascaria cuisines.
- Elected Best New American Restaurant by *Esquire Magazine*, 2005.
- Elected Best Restaurant by *Washingtonian Magazine*, 2005.
- Rejuvenated gross annual revenues from $1.8 million to $3.8 million after returning from a multi-year hiatus managing Provence Restaurant.
- Secured seed capital from investors as a result of a nationally acclaimed reputation.
- Designed specifications for a nightclub expansion and introduced catering services that increased the bottom-line approximately 21%.

RADISSON HOTEL, Alexandria, Virginia   2002 – 2004
Chef de Cuisine
- Achieved 89% rise in revenue since opening this fine-dining signature restaurant recognized as Best New Restaurant by *Esquire Magazine*, 2004.
- Nominated for the James Beard Award for Best Mid-Atlantic Chef, 2003.
- Earned the Conde Nest Award and received inspiring reviews from food critic Mimi Sheraton.
- Trained and directed staff of 38 employees throughout the establishment, which spanned 11,000 square feet and consisted of 160 seats.

PERSONAL CHEF FOR FRANK PEARL, Washington, DC   2001 – 2002
Chef de Cuisine
- Satisfied the sophisticated pallets of billionaire Frank Pearl and his international guests, including investors, political dignitaries, military officials, and other renowned high-profile invitees.

PAVILLON, Washington, DC   1992 – 2001
Chef de Cuisine
- Reversed annual losses of $250,000 to annual profits of $180,000 within first 18 months after assuming ownership.

- Brought the nearly bankrupt original operation to become one of the best restaurants in the country for 7 consecutive years and generated up to $2.6 million per annum.
- Sold the business in 1997 and opened a new location in 1998, which was awarded 4 stars by *Washingtonian Magazine* in 1998 and 1999.
- Increased gross annual revenues 30% from $2 million to $2.6 million and maintained food costs as low as 21%.
- Secured the highest priced restaurant in the country with guest checks averaging as high as $257 with evening sales as much as $14,000.
- Developed the "Best Burgundy Wine Cellar in America" as recognized by Robert Parker, Wine Advocate and won the Grand Award of Excellence from *Wine Spectator* for the wine cellar selection.
- Received laudable coverage from national and international press.
- Hired, trained, and directed a 23-member staff to serve a 70-seat capacity.

LE COUP DE FUSIL, New York, New York   1991 – 1992
Chef de Cuisine and Partner
- Co-founded the first contemporary French cuisine restaurant in the United States with Countess Marina de Brantes, sister-in-law to French President Giscard D' Estaing.
- Received stand-out reviews by *The New York Times*, *New Yorker*, and *French Press*.
- Served political officials, business executives, and celebrities averaging $100 a plate, which led the market as much as 40%.

FOUR SEASONS RESTAURANT, New York, New York   1990 – 1991
Chef de Partie, Saucier
- Organized French seminar Gastronomique with Chefs of 3 star *Michelin Guide* rating.
- Chefs: Paul Bocuse, Pierre Troisgrois, Jean Troisgros, Michel Guerard, Gaston le Notre, Alain Chapel, and Roger Verge.

LASSERRE, Paris, France   1989 – 1990
Chef de Partie Fish Station and Saucier
- Restaurant 3 star *Michelin Guide* rating.

ROYALE HOTEL, Deauville, France   1987 – 1989
Chef de Partie, Garde Manager and Fish Station
- Five star hotel rating.

MOULIN DE ROSMADEC, Pont Aven, France   1986 – 1987
Premier Commis
- Restaurant 2 star *Michelin Guide* rating.

CAP DE CUISINIER, Pont Aven, France   1984 – 1986
Apprentice
- Ty Chupen Gwuen for Monsieur Le Donge.

CORY SCHULMAN
5002 Sous Chef Road
Poolesville, Maryland 20837
240-338-0050
souschef@gmail.com

OBJECTIVE

To maximize guest satisfaction as a Sous Chef while ensuring efficient and cost-effective kitchen operations.

HIGHLIGHTS

- Highly disciplined Sous Chef experienced in preparing and presenting modern American cuisines with precise timing, balance, and distinct flavors. Co-developed menus with fresh combinations, including use of regional ingredients to create popular and profitable dishes.

- Prepped and prepared stocks, soups, sauces; butchered meat and poultry; cleaned and portioned fish for a four-star, four-diamond "preferred" hotel.

- Coordinated banquet operations, controlled inventory, contained costs, and enforced sanitation/safety controls. Achieved consistent guest satisfaction as evidenced by numerous letters of appreciation throughout tenure.

- Food Service Certification, Montgomery County.

EXPERIENCE

ROLLING MOUNTAINS COUNTRY CLUB, Darnestown, Maryland   January 2012 – Present
Sous Chef
- Collaborated with the Executive Chef to develop menu items and launch the grand opening of American cuisine dining operations. Set up the hot line and facilitated the maintenance of food costs 10% below industry averages by enforcing strict portion controls.
- Coordinated timely food preparation for both on and off-premise social events.
- Supervised a staff of five in the absence of the Executive Chef.
- Kept abreast of 200%+ growth in the member base by assisting the Executive Chef in instituting a dinner shift and an outside grill operation.

THE VINO COMMISSION, Charleston, South Carolina   April 2006 – January 2012
Banquet Chef for Hotel Restaurant
- Supervised five cooks/stewards to execute banquet kitchen operations and off-premise functions, which attracted up to 350 attendees. Created refreshing, cost-effective, and popular menu items. Assisted in preparing for the grand opening of the banquet kitchen.
- Maintained food costs approximately 20% below management projections.
- Participated in the Chaine de Rotisseurs' Dinners, the James Beard Foundation Dinners, and the Cellarmaster's Wine Tastings. Saucier for the Hampton's Restaurant.

LE PUIANCE RESTAURANT, Baltimore, Maryland   January 2005 – April 2006
P.M. Line Cook
- Promoted from Garde Manger to prepare soups and sauces; operated the sauté/grill stations.
- Provided support in planning menus, private functions, and wine tastings.
- Portioned game and poultry, operated grill/sauté stations, and performed other Garde Manger functions as a member of an internship program with the Baltimore Culinary College.

SHOPPERS FOOD WAREHOUSE, Germantown, Maryland   February 2004 – January 2005
Butcher Department Assistant

EDUCATION

Baltimore International Culinary College, Graduate, January 2004

Cory Schulman

5003 Executive Chef Drive
Gaithersburg, MD 20879
240-338-0050
executivechef@gmail.com

Executive Chef

- Executive Chef of renowned establishment highlighted in national magazines as one of the "very best restaurants" in the Washington Metropolitan region.

- Developed a sterling reputation among culinary sophisticates and affluent patrons, including international dignitaries and celebrities for exquisite preparation and presentation of world regional cuisine.

- Increased gross annual revenues from $92,000 to $600,000 within 3 years.

- Hired, trained, and directed as many as 60 employees. Maintained longevity of original kitchen crew members over 9 years.

- Managed multiple sites concurrently, and possess experience in financial management, inventory control, kitchen design, interior decor, marketing, and human resources.

PROFESSIONAL AWARDS & REVIEWS

- Highlighted on the *Washingtonian Magazine's* cover for its annual edition featuring the 100 very best restaurants as one of the top 14 Chefs to watch in New York, 2012
- Feature Story, *First Sunday Magazine, Hamptons News*, May 6, 2010
- Favorable Review Article, *Hamptons Spree*, March/April, 2009
- Phyllis Richman's 50 Best Award, *Washington Post Newspaper*
- *The Washingtonian Magazine* People's Choice Award, 2008
- *The Washingtonian Magazine* 100 Best Restaurant Award, 2002

EXPERIENCE

THE RESTAURANT AT THE HAMPTONS, Hamptons, New York
Executive Chef   2002 – Present

- Achieved a 4-star status, the highest possible and only one of three in Hamptons, New York as highlighted in the *Hampton News Gusto* review.

- Managed all food services for an upscale, modern American restaurant and jazz club, a Spanish-Caribbean nightclub, and a banquet facility with a total of 315 seats. Provided oversight of 60 employees.

- Maintained food/labor costs approximately 20% below industry averages.

- Revamped menu items for all facilities, which enhanced patronage and revenues while cutting expenses.

- Coordinated banquets for corporate and private events, including weddings, retirement parties, business meetings, and other formal celebrations.

- Won a televised chef competition judged by a panel on ABC affiliate WKBW.

CAFÉ CHEVY CHASE, Chevy Chase, Maryland
Co-founder, Executive Chef   1995 – 2002

Operations Management:
- Co-established a 50-seat, fine-dining restaurant and grew annual sales from $92,000 to $750,000.

- Opened a second upscale location consisting of 75 seats, which also flourished in patronage, reputation, and robust corporate profits.

- Curtailed operating expenses by successfully negotiating cost reductions with local/national vendors for food, beverages, and liquor. Handled purchasing, ordering, finance, and accounting.

- Enforced strict adherence to portion controls and maintained food costs below the industry average.

- Designed and remodeled the interior layout and determined the decor to create an upscale atmosphere.

- Hired, trained, and led staffs as large as 35. Maximized employee productivity through training, motivational leadership, and selective hiring of quality conscious and seasoned support staff.

THE ATLANTIC RESTAURANT, Washington, DC
Entremetier   1993 – 1995

- Worked on all line positions in two kitchens; advanced from the grill to the formal, upscale saloon; provided staff meals for 75 people daily.

BETHESDA COUNTRY CLUB, Bethesda, Maryland
Preparation Cook   1992

- Served up to 1,200 club members as an assistant to the Chef. Planned menus, controlled the inventory, and prepared meals.

EDUCATION

L'ACADEMIE De CUISINE, Gaithersburg, Maryland   1989 – 1992
Culinary Career Training Program

- In-depth study of food purchasing, preparation, and presentation with emphasis on both theory and technique, kitchen management, and restaurant operations.

PERSONAL ATTRIBUTES

Highly disciplined and creative Executive Chef with artistic flair for presentation of modern American and French cuisines.

Exude passion for preparing classic dishes with precise timing, balance, and distinct flavors. Exhibit profound understanding of such ingredients as balsamic vinegar, ancho chilies, ginger, and cilantro without overwhelming the natural tastes of the main course. Superb use of Mediterranean flavors such as peppers, lemon, garlic, and parsley.

Developed menus with fresh combinations, including use of regional ingredients to create popular and profitable dishes with low cholesterol, sodium, and fat.

CORY S. SCHULMAN, Ph.D.
27004 Chemist Avenue
Walkersville, MD 21793-0037
240-338-0050
chemist@gmail.com

OBJECTIVE

To apply extensive FDA experience to expedite drug approval in a Regulatory Affairs position within a pharmaceutical company.

SUMMARY

Review Chemist with 20 years FDA experience managing and/or performing application reviews of anti-inflammatory, antineoplastic, radio-opaque, anesthetic, antihistamine, pulmonary, gastrointestinal, coagulation, radiopharmaceutical, metabolic, endocrine, reproductive, and urological drug products.

EXPERIENCE

FOOD AND DRUG ADMINISTRATION, Washington, DC, 1996 – Present
Office of Pharmaceutical Science, Office of New Drug Chemistry
Director of the Division of New Drug Chemistry II, 2006 – Present

- Manage review of Investigational and New Drug Applications (INDs and NDAs) on human subjects within a $3 million annual budget.
- Direct efforts of review teams, consisting of 46 Ph.D. chemists and other support personnel in 6 clinical areas: critical care/drugs of abuse, radio-pharmaceutical drug products, gastrointestinal and coagulation drugs, metabolic and endocrine drugs, pulmonary drugs, and reproductive and urological drugs.
- Complete reviews within stringent time constraints established by the Prescription Drug User Fee Act (PDUFA). Ensure drug safety and efficacy post-manufacturing.
- Streamlined chemistry reviews resulting in a 10% – 15% reduction in review time without sacrifice to safety and efficacy.
- Keep abreast of a rapid rise in the number of reviews performed annually.
- Develop, implement, and monitor Division plans and policies as well as evaluate budget, fiscal, and administrative controls.
- Develop guidelines to assist FDA reviewer and drug applicants by streamlining as well as clarifying requirements of new drug applications.
- Serve as the FDA's topic leader for residual solvents in the International Conference for Harmonization discussions.
- Perform the tertiary chemistry reviews of NDAs for new molecular entities.
- Interface with industry representatives, public interest groups, and professional/trade organizations.

EXPERIENCE, Continued

Supervisory Chemist, 1999 – 2005
- Created and trained a chemistry review staff as the first supervisory chemist of the newly established Division of Gastrointestinal and Coagulation Drug Products (DGCDP).
- Led the DGCDP chemistry review team to achieve a sterling reputation for conducting timely reviews for INDs, NDAs, or Abbreviated New Drug Applications (ANDAs).
- Recruited seasoned and new reviewers and provided effective training that enabled the team to work independently.
- Maintained a nearly perfect retention of review team members.

Chemist, 1998 – 1999
- Served on a multidisciplinary scientific/medical team to review, evaluate, and determine approvability of scientific submissions and applications requiring FDA regulatory permission/approval for clinical research, human testing, and marketing of human drugs.
- Reviewed and evaluated NDAs, INDs, supplemental applications, amendments, and reports pertaining to chemistry, manufacturing and processing, controls, stability, labeling, and environmental impact.

EDUCATION, AWARDS, & FELLOWSHIPS

Ph.D. Chemistry, Clemson University, Clemson, South Carolina

B.S. Chemistry, College of William and Mary, Willamsburg, Virginia

National Merit Scholarship

NASA Predoctoral Fellowship

AFFILIATIONS

- FDA Representative to the International Committee on Harmonization of pharmaceutical requirements for residual solvents in drugs and drug products.

- Co-Chair of Post Approval Change-Sterile Aqueous Solution (PAC-SAS) Guidance.

- Member, Drug Substance and Drug Product Stability Committee

CORY SCHULMAN

6001 Claims Square Court
Decatur, Georgia 30030
240-338-0050
claimsanalyst@gmail.com

EXPERIENCE

SECURE STATE INSURANCE, Rockville, Maryland   2005 – Present
Claim Specialist

Customer Service and Interpersonal Communications:

- Provide prompt, accurate, and courteous customer service, which entails reviewing and explaining policies and coverages to insureds and claimants; address both complaints/complex coverage questions.
- Interface with underwriters and agents to ensure proper claims processing from initial reporting through settlement.
- Provide first contact at disaster sites as Fire Claim Assist Team Specialist to coordinate claim files, inspect damages, and conclude prompt settlements for natural disasters.
- Coordinate car rentals, lodging, and related emergency logistical arrangements.
- Apply background in social work and psychology to facilitate communications with distraught individuals during crises.
- Provide leadership and training to new claim representatives in claim processing procedures and customer service.

Investigations:

- Investigate accident scenes, including traffic-light sequences, street configurations, vehicle damage, skid marks, and related material evidence.
- Interview all parties, including insureds, claimants, police officers, and witnesses.
- Secure recorded statements and prepare comprehensive reports to determine liability.
- Identify and investigate red flags pertaining to potential fraudulent claims.
- Ensure proper subrogation recovery. File and defend arbitration.
- Provide testimony in court and surcharge hearings regarding property damage and bodily injury investigations.

Claims Processing:

- Maximize processing efficiency of property and liability damage claims in collaboration with a team of claim specialists.
- Inspect and review property damage estimates to issue payments according to applicable coverages for insureds and claimants.
- Conduct first contact BI settlements.
- Perform market surveys to determine ACV of total loss vehicles; negotiate settlements.
- Perform garage surveys to determine prevailing competitive prices.
- Prepare files to investigate and determine Secure State's subrogatable rights.

EDUCATION

Claims School, Certificate of Completion, 2005, Bloomington, Illinois and Austin, Texas
M.A. in International Business, 2004, University of Maryland and Bowie State University
B.A. in Business, 2002, Salisbury State University, Salisbury, Maryland

Cory Schulman

6002 Coach Drive
Beavercreek, Ohio 45431
240-338-0050
coach@ohio.edu

OBJECTIVE

To obtain a position as a Women's Basketball Head Coach at an institution committed to the development and overall experience of the student-athlete.

EXPERIENCE

WRIGHT STATE UNIVERSITY, Dayton, Ohio, 2012 – Present
Assistant Women's Basketball Coach, Division I, Horizon League

UNIVERSITY OF MARYLAND, Baltimore County (UMBC), 2008 – 2012
Assistant Basketball Coach, **Recruiting Coordinator**, Division I, Northeast Conference

AMERICAN UNIVERSITY, Washington, DC, 2005 – 2008
Graduate Assistant Basketball Coach, Division I, Colonial Athletic Association

TOWSON STATE UNIVERSITY, Towson, Maryland, 2004 – 2005
Part-time Assistant Coach, Division I, America East (Formerly in Big South)

HIGHLIGHTS

Recruitment
- Signed two Smith and Street honorable mentions, (20105) including a player who became the 1st Team All Horizon League and the 5th leading scorer in the country.
- Organized nationwide recruiting efforts resulting in two signed players: one emerged as Rookie-of-the-Year (2014) 2nd Team All Conference; the other earned a spot on the 2nd Team All Conference for 2 years (2014 and 2015).
- Signed two overseas players, one who made the All-Rookie Team.
- Recruited all of the current starters and returning players who posted victories against VCU, a team 18 conferences higher than UMBC.
- Recruited and signed one of the highest ranking high school senior point guards in the Mid-Atlantic Region (2011).
- Conducted nationwide scouting efforts at regional tournaments and recruiting camps, including the AAU National Tournament, Junior Nationals, Blue Star Tournaments, and Blue Chip Shootouts.
- Organized on-campus and nationwide recruiting efforts.
- Coordinated all official visits by prospective student athletes.

Coaching
- Facilitated WSU's highest league placement in the past 6 seasons, earning 4th place despite a last place conference projection. Provided intensive development of guard positions, which led to three more wins over the previous 2014 season. Supported development of an unranked player, which resulted in her averaging 24.1 ppg and becoming the #5 leading scorer in the country (2015).

- Emerged as the only team in the Horizon League to beat #16 nationally ranked University of Wisconsin-Greenbay (2012).
- Led victories over the #1 team in the NEC Conference as the Acting Head Coach (2013).
- Assisted in coaching defense, resulting in the UMBC's #1 ranking in the NEC Conference for scoring defense at 59 ppg (2009); and #2 ranking (2010).
- Spearheaded an intensive skill development program for 1 – 5 positions.
- Led coaching initiatives to develop a post player's scoring average, which improved from 1.3 to 9 ppg.
- Achieved a new precedent with the starting center who ranked 1st in rebounding among Division I players in the nation and Northeast Conference (2007).
- Coordinated and directed pre/post season conditioning programs.
- Introduced new skill development techniques, which dramatically improved players' agility, shooting, defensive footwork, ball handling, and offensive proficiency.
- Scouted basketball opposition to develop and execute game strategies.

Productivity
- Facilitated an improvement of the American University women's team from a losing season to a winning season to rank 4th in the Division I Colonial Conference.
- Analyzed offensive effectiveness and made half-time adjustments that helped lead the team to its first televised victory in UMBC history.

Logistics
- Coordinated the film exchange program, which doubled amount of film footage on opponents.
- Scheduled all non-conference games and coordinated travel arrangements.
- Organized and supervised a community service project for AU student-athletes.

Additional Experience
- Editor-in-Chief of monthly newsletter for alumni, parents, and associates.
- Organized and directed a community service project that involved American University student-athletes to tutor underprivileged children.
- Directed the Excel Academic Support program, entailing supervision of the freshmen and academically at-risk student-athletes to maintain high academic performance.
- Improved team GPA from 2.5 to 3.0 in 2004 – 2005.
- Microsoft Word for Windows, Photoshop, Access, InDesign.

SUPPLEMENT

Education: **American University**, Washington, DC, Major: Special Education, 2003
Towson State University, B.A., Physical Education, 2002, Honors: Dean's List

Affiliations: WBCA Member, 2004 – Present
NCAA Convention, 2004 – Present

Honors: Full Scholarship at the Division I Level
Most Valuable Player, 2000 – 2001

Cory Schulman
6003 Coach Road
Syracuse, New York 13215
240-338-0050
coach@gmail.com

COACHING EXPERIENCE

UNIVERSITY OF MARYLAND, Baltimore, Maryland   2008 – Present

Head Women's Basketball Coach, 2005 – Present
- Achieved the first winning conference season since 1994.
- Team led Northeast Conference in scoring defense, 2014; finished second in scoring defense, 2013 and 2012.
- Converted team from 9th place pre-season selection to the 3rd place regular season finish, the most significant turnaround in the Northeast Conference, 2008 – 2009.
- Only Head Coach appointed to the University President's Exploratory Committee for enhancement and advancement of UMBC athletics in preparation for potential change of conference participation.
- Oversaw operating budget for the women's basketball program.

Significant individual player awards and statistical accomplishments:
- Placed one player on Northeast All-Conference 2nd Team.
- Coached NCAA Division One leading rebounder.
- Recruited and coached the Northeast Conference Newcomer-of-the-Year.
- Recruited and placed three players on the Northeast Conference All-Rookie Team.
- Recruited and signed Honorable Mention High School All-American, November 2009 with the eighth ranked recruiting budget in a 12-team conference.
- 2010 – 2011 squad achieved highest grade point in the school's Division One history for spring semester (3.144) and for overall academic year (2.974).

THE UNIVERSITY OF IOWA, Iowa City, Iowa   2005 – 2008

Assistant Women's Basketball Coach
- Developed and maintained a $500,000 annual budget for the women's basketball program.
- Contributed in attracting All-American, international, and WNBA caliber players. Won four Big Ten Championships and participated in NCAA tournament play 4 consecutive years.
- Coordinated all travel logistics. Scouted basketball opposition and scheduled professional scouting services.

ROCKVILLE HIGH SCHOOL, Rockville, Maryland   2002 – 2005

Head Women's Basketball Coach
- Finished regional state tournament semi-finalist. Improved the conference record to 8 – 4. Took 2004 3A State Champions into overtime.
- Signed the number one recruit in Michigan who set the all-time scoring record among men and women.

EDUCATION

Bachelor of Science, 2001, The Pennsylvania State University, Pennsylvania

CORY SCHULMAN

24002 Community Relations Drive
Gaithersburg, MD 20879
240-338-0050
community@gmail.com

OBJECTIVE

To apply advanced planning, organizational, and interpersonal skills as a Community Relations Specialist or a related Outreach Coordinator position.

HIGHLIGHTS

Fifteen years' experience with Montage International, Inc. includes public relations, outreach development, business management, and sales/marketing for Lodging and Senior Living Service Divisions. Dynamic public speaker driven to provide professional representation, conduct individual and group presentations, and build team leadership. Demonstrated highest attention to detail and organization while coordinating multiple projects concurrently.

EXPERIENCE

MONTAGE INTERNATIONAL, INC., Gaithersburg, Maryland   2000 – Present

Director of Community Relations, Montage Senior Living Services, 2006 – Present
- Lead programmatic development and management involving community outreach, sales support, and public relation initiatives while sustaining high standards for independent living, assisted living, and healthcare.
- Earned the Silver Circle Award, Montage Senior Living Services, 2006 and 2007.
- Earned the Teamwork Advocacy Manager Award, Bedford Court by Montage, 2006.

Community Outreach:
- Promote public awareness of Montage Senior Living Communities by conducting presentations to as many as 500 attendees at hospitals, churches, schools, Fortune 500 businesses, senior educational fairs, and county senior centers.
- Develop a public lecture series, which entails coordination of guest speakers, advertising, and follow-up evaluations.
- Expanded the referral resource network by securing partnerships with hospitals, hospice organizations, and other senior providers.
- Develop diverse programs involving seniors in social, recreational, educational, and service functions, which include senior mentoring, Adopt-A-Highway, and seasonal events.
- Conceive and coordinate intergenerational programs throughout the public school system, which paired seniors with primary/secondary school students.
- Established a computer center and a resource outreach center, resulting in an increase in referral business.
- Revised and distributed welcome manuals for all three levels of care.
- Opened Brighten Gardens of Tuckerman Lane in 2007, a senior living community that provides assisted living and skilled nursing services.

Marketing:
- Represent all 10 Senior Living Communities as a booth manager at tradeshows to promote senior living services and establish alliances with prospective referring entities.

- Collaborate with the Sales and Marketing team to devise quarterly marketing plans in addition to advertising and promotional collateral.
- Use partnerships, cable TV, newsletters, and social media to launch effective promotional campaigns in the community.
- Conduct internal marketing by hosting events for resident family members, staff, and prospective residents.
- Prepare market analyses and competition updates to support corporate pricing initiatives.
- Manage the marketing budget while meeting/exceeding census objectives for independent living, assisted living, and healthcare communities.

Executive Meeting Manager, Montage Suites Bethesda, Bethesda, Maryland, 2003 – 2006
- Solicited business through polished in-person sales presentations and effective telemarketing blitzes. Performed preliminary qualifications to identify viable leads and negotiate rates for various social/corporate business and catering events.
- Received "Bill Tiefel Awards" for outstanding customer service.
- Emerged as Manager of the Second Quarter, 2005.
- Earned corporate recognition for achieving the Most Referred Booked Revenue in the Mid-Atlantic Region 4th/1st Quarter, 2003, 2004.

Sales Coordinator, Montage Suites Bethesda, Bethesda, Maryland, 2000 – 2003
- Made dynamic presentations to groups throughout the business sector. Qualified prospective candidates, closed sales agreements, and coordinated final stages of booked functions from rooming list, BEO completion, and communication of special requests.
- Associate of the Month, August 2001.

Senior Sales Coordinator, Courtyard by Montage, Rockville, Maryland, 1999 – 2000
- Worked closely as a team player with the Regional Director of Sales and Property Management. Coordinated administrative functions in support of marketing and sales efforts in the regional office. Handled customer inquiries and bookings for groups and meetings. Trained, supervised, and evaluated performance of support sales personnel. Participated on sales calls, market reviews, sales blitzes, and open houses.
- Associate of the Quarter, November 1999.

SUPPLEMENT

Additional Experience:	Coordinated and monitored athletic programs for youths as a Recreator at gymnasiums throughout Montgomery County. Supervised as many as 63 youths as a Director of Camp Blue Devil, Gaithersburg High School, Montgomery County Recreation Department.
Education:	Shepherd College, Shepherdstown, West Virginia **Bachelor of Science in Business Administration**, May 1999 Minor: Speech Communication Certified Level I Hospitality Maryland Style

CORY SCHULMAN

7002 Construction Street • Rockville, MD 20853 • Home: 240-338-0050 • construction@gmail.com

OBJECTIVE

To complete technically challenging construction projects on time and within budget as a Construction Manager or a related position.

HIGHLIGHTS

Construction Management:
- Quality and cost-conscious Construction Superintendent with 25-years' experience managing more than 300 tenant build outs, renovations, and other intricate design/build projects, including historic restorations and state-of-the-art facilities for Fortune 500 clients.
- Directed as many as 100+ subcontractors of diverse trades for various office and retail commercial renovations, additions, and new construction.
- Coordinated all phases of construction from design and excavation through punch out.
- Prepared RFBs, RFPs, and RFIs; obtained all permits and licenses; ordered custom materials.

Honors:
- Earned the National Construction Excellence Eagle Award for the Parklawn Office Building renovation in 2015.
- National Excellence Merit Award for the Inn at Little Washington project.
- Artery Service and Quality Award (For speed of completion and quality of the Arlington Courthouse Plaza office complex project).
- Exceptional Craftsmanship Award, Washington Builders Congress; nominated in 1993.

Security Clearance:
- Held security clearances, which have since expired, to oversee construction projects for NSA, Westinghouse, and Architect of the Capitol.

EXPERIENCE

THE CAPITOL CONSTRUCTION COMPANY, Rockville, Maryland   1998 – Present
Senior Construction Superintendent
- Managed all phases of a $5 million expansion for the Inn at Little Washington, which retained its 5-star status throughout the 22 month construction period.
  - Completed the project on time and within budget without disruption to the Inn's 7-day a week operations.
  - Installed a state-of-the-art kitchen with customized appliances such as the Vulcan-Hart range.
  - Oversaw 25 subcontractors from all trades, including electrical, plumbing, masonry, trim carpentry, cabinet makers, stucco, kitchen appliances, artists/painters, ceramic tile, excavation, concrete/brick, and landscaping.
  - Collaborated and coordinated five designers; modified blueprints to rectify design flaws while ensuring feasibility. Kitchen features included 8-foot-tall window, 12-foot vaulted ceiling, hand-painted ceramic tile, and intricate wood finishes.
- Directed 100+ trade subcontractors to restore the True Reformer Building, a historic property from 1903 that spans 40,000 square feet and encompasses a high-tech, 200-seat auditorium and sound stage, MEP and life safety systems, vintage-era portico, and custom beech millwork paneling.
  - Identified and cleaned contaminated soils, refurbished parapet walls, and relocated permanent power.
  - Ensured compliance with National BOCA, DC, and ADA codes.
  - Completed the project within the $7 million budget and a stringent 11-month schedule.
- Led an intensive 6-week renovation of the Parklawn corporate office building, which consisted of 55,000 square feet, exterior improvements, curved walls, open ceiling plan, dramatic skylight, and slate flooring in complementary geometric patterns.

- Coordinated 100+ subcontractors to completely gut and upgrade obsolete systems.
- Installed elevator, water line, and fire/life safety systems.
- Designed a modern environment, which earned the prestigious Eagle Award.

- Designed and revamped MEP and life safety systems of the main MCI facility in a dust free environment without disruption to operations.
  - Prevented downtime valued at $1 million per minute.

- Modernized 1600 K Street, a 1950s office building north of the White House with 90,000 square feet.
  - Retrofitted and upgraded all life safety, MEP, sprinkler, and water/gas systems.
  - Upgraded elevators and refurbished lobbies, storefront, entrances, rest rooms, and common areas.
  - Incorporated custom cherry millwork panels, finished metals, marble flooring, granite vanities, and custom carpets.

HOFFER & BENSON, Linthicum, Maryland   1995 – 1998
Construction Superintendent/Construction Manager
- Coordinated tenant build-outs for such projects as the Westinghouse facilities while maintaining 100% operability.
- Won a Construction Excellence Award for work on high-end office buildings.

TELEPORT CIRCLE, Linthicum, Maryland   1993 – 1995
Senior Superintendent
- Directed all tenant build outs for 21 office buildings.
- Managed various design/build construction projects for major clients such as NSA, Lockheed, Northrop Grumman (Westinghouse), and U.S. Army Corps of Engineers.
- Coordinated aggressive schedules and high-level security demands for such projects as a 17-story high-rise office building with steel-frames, brick clads, screen rooms, and sciff systems.

WATERFALL ORGANIZATION, INC., Bethesda, Maryland   1991 – 1993
Senior Construction Superintendent
- Oversaw the completion of two major office complexes for the Fairfax County, Virginia government.
- Supervised two Assistant Construction Managers and a full labor force.
- Obtained all final permits. Worked closely with Fairfax government A&E staffs to build a state-of-the-art day care center and playground, special satellite installations, and a cafeteria.
- Directed all tenant build outs for the Arlington, Virginia Courthouse Plaza complex.
- Accommodated all construction warranties, change orders, and repairs to the full satisfaction of all tenants.
- Turned over 34 tenants and 6 retail businesses in 12 months, involving over 210,000 square feet of commercial office space.
- Completed punch-outs in less than 2 weeks without compromising quality or tenant service.
- Directed all scheduling, ordering, and tracking of materials.
- Monitored safety and work completion inspections.

EDUCATION

Architectural Technology/Construction Management, Dean's List, Montgomery College
Awarded a Certificate of Completion, The Waterfall Organization, Inc., Management School

PROFESSIONAL CERTIFICATION

Certified Journeyman Carpenter, United Brotherhood of Carpenters and Journeyman, Local #132
Certified Welder, ¾" plate, all positions

CORY SCHULMAN

7003 Construction Court
North Potomac, Maryland 20878

240-338-0050
construction@hotmail.com

OBJECTIVE

To enhance corporate profits, cost-containment, and project integrity by applying expertise in construction and/or telecommunications as an Operations Manager.

SUMMARY

- Operations Manager and Certified Fiber Designer with turn-key expertise completing $30+ million telecommunications and construction projects on-time and under budget.

- Possess expertise in voice/data, fiber/copper backbone, fusion and terminations, mapping and design, CATV aerial, fiber restoration, and underground installations.

- Converted corporate losses into profits by turning around troubled commercial projects, such as piling, caisson, bridges, concrete, paving, road work, and duct work.

EXPERIENCE

KINGSTON CONSTRUCTION COMPANY, Baltimore, Maryland   2005 – Present

Electrical Superintendent/Consultant

- Co-direct $277 million in construction projects ranging from design through installation of Level III fiber-optic communication systems throughout the North East and Mid-Atlantic regions.
- Manage installation of network systems consisting of 1,600+ miles of long haul fiber optics for major clients such as Level (3) Communications, BWI/Dulles airports, and the U.S. Government.
- Coordinate 70+ subcontractors and up to 12 projects concurrently throughout 7 states.
- Hire and supervise diverse contractors/subcontractors and union carpenters for structural construction, paving, sewer work, road work, concrete/masonry, and electrical installations.
- Provide oversight of road, concrete, and building construction for government dams and military bases requiring runways, sewer systems, and related infrastructure.
- Use ProCAD, AutoCAD, and Atviso to produce and revise architectural plans.
- Ensure compliance with new building codes and local, State, and Federal regulations for all new construction, renovations, and upgrades.
- Conduct inspections and provide troubleshooting support to turn around troubled projects, prevent corporate losses, and ensure completion of projects.

Sample Projects and Accomplishments:

- Manage a $38 million expansion of roads and terminals as part of a $2 billion project for BWI. Plan and coordinate the installation of multi-mode/single-mode fiber optic backbone to upgrade and expand the power/telecommunications system.

- Led initiatives for new duct banks and manholes, new traffic signals and loops, and upgraded lighting and communication services. Accomplished 60% of first year's work load within the first 2 months.

- Completed installation of 16,000 miles of fiber optic network, valued $44 million of a $3 billion project, 5 months ahead of schedule. Saved the company $19 million by finishing the project 40% under budget.

- Turned around severe losses of a $7+ million fiber optic network installation in New Jersey to a robust profit. Brought the project from 1 year behind schedule to completion 8 months ahead of schedule, while reducing construction costs per square foot from $160 to $26.

- Increased open trench work from 200 feet to 1,000 feet per night for a restoration project on Rt. 128 in Boston, Massachusetts. Completed 5 miles in first 3 months.

- Finished a $50 million fiber/trenching relocation for a DOT/SEPTA railroad; secured the sign off on the project and a $20 million performance bond.

MANCOR COMMUNICATIONS, INC., Bridgeport, Connecticut   1997 – 2005

President
- Increased gross annual revenues from $100,000 to $5 million as a result of developing and implementing a team of 29 engineers, technicians, and laborers certified and highly trained in cutting-edge technologies.
- Managed the installation of telecommunication systems, including fiber optics, copper, and coaxial networks.
- Established major clients from the North East to the Mid-West, which included Cablevision System, DOT, Brandeis University, and Kennedy Airport.
- Provided diverse services such as design, installation, splicing/terminations, training, and maintenance.

EDUCATION

Bachelor of Science in Electronic Engineering, 1994, Ferdowsi University

LICENSE

Electrical Limited License, State of Connecticut, 1998 – Present

CORY SCHULMAN

8001 Contract Drive
Clarksburg, Maryland 20871
240-338-0050
contract@comcast.net

OBJECTIVE

To apply industry expertise in major commodity areas, negotiations, and supplier relationship management as a cost-saving and quality-conscious Contract Manager.

EXPERIENCE

DALIANCE, LLC, Rockville, Maryland   2007 – Present

Founded by Marriott International and four other hotel and resort corporations.

Contracting Manager

- Negotiate $150+ million in annual legal contracts with domestic and international distributors and manufacturers for five founders and 3,000 corporate accounts in the hospitality industry.
- Close 40 contracts per year ranging from $500,000 to $100 million per contract within stringent timeframes, the highest volume among a five-member team.
- Secure contracts with minority suppliers in accordance with MBO and founders' requirements.
- Kept pace of contract negotiations during exponential growth of the account base, which grew from 0 to 3,000 in 3 years with the number of contracts increasing from 100 to 900. Exceeded corporate expectations roughly 50%.
- Prepare RFPs based on specifications of service components.
- Address final prices, allowances, and business/legal concerns with the General Council.

HARRISON INTERNATIONAL, Washington, DC   1998 – 2007

Contract Manager

- Negotiated and established Furniture, Fixtures, and Equipment (FF&E) contracts ranging from $1 million to $15 million per agreement.
- Closed more than $30 million per annum during corporate re-organization.
- Adapted to change management needs stemming from the abolishment of Harrison national contracting system.
- Saved the company more than $1.5 million through effective cost analyses and negotiations with 12 manufacturers.
- Collaborated with Interior Design Department to define manufacturers' specifications for FF&E in regard to aesthetic appeal, quality, and cost effectiveness.

EDUCATION

Accounting, Montgomery College, Rockville, Maryland
Professional Development: Management, Negotiations, Team Building, and many others.

CORY SCHULMAN

8002 Contract Lane, Chevy Chase, MD 20815   manager@gmail.com 240-338-0050

Senior Management

EXPERIENCE

UNISCRIBE PROFESSIONAL SERVICES, INC., Gaithersburg, Maryland, 2008 – Present
Facility Director

Direct a national facility that provides high-volume imaging and coding services to law firms and corporations across the country.   Oversaw as many as 140 technical, managerial, and support professionals.

Business Start-up and Expansion: Established a national document scanning and coding facility and grew revenues from zero to $6 million within the first year. Co-developed the business plan, secured 25,000 square feet of commercial space, hired and trained 140 staff members, procured cutting-edge equipment, and devised operational protocols. Transitioned off-the-shelf applications to more cost-effective, leading-edge proprietary applications, which enhanced ease of use, reduced training time, and minimized required technical support. Beta tested as SQL server-based coding application, which was rolled-out throughout the company. Provided dynamic demonstrations and presentations of technology, software, and operations to prospective clients.

HOWREY & SIMON, Washington, DC, 2006 – 2007
Manager, Technical Support and Operations

Directed the firm's automated litigation support division encompassing document imaging, discovery, and trial support to more than 500 attorneys and paralegal staff.

Business Restructuring and Expansion: Re-engineered the firm's organizational and management structure resulting in a dramatic increase in annual revenues from less than $1 million to more than $1.7 million in 2007. Marketed, negotiated, and closed an $800,000 contract for automated legal services, the largest transaction in the firm's history. Prepared and presented cost benefit analyses, estimates, and schedules to clients. Expanded the staff approximately 58%.

CACI, INC., Arlington, Virginia, 2004 – 2006
Senior Project Manager, 11/2004 – 4/2005; *Account Executive*, 5/2005 – 7/2006

Managed a $100 million litigation for the Department of Navy/Department of Justice, supporting 60 attorneys and 70 staff members. Increased monthly billable revenues 30% from $500,000 to $650,000.

Marketing and Business Development: Marketed litigation support, document management, and imaging services to federal civilian agencies. Developed leads, team partners, and proposal strategies for a $250 million litigation support contract. Targeted government agencies and private law firms by leading presentations, lectures, and demonstrations to as many as 25 technical and non-technical staff members.

ASPEN SYSTEMS CORPORATION, Washington, DC, 2001 – 2004
Associate Deputy Contract Manager, 2/2002 – 10/2004

Managed multi-million dollar civil and criminal litigation cases for the government and private law firms. Solicited and responded to proposals ranging from $250,000 to $2 million per case. Hired and trained up to 75 clerks, paralegals, and managerial staff. Directed logistics for a landmark environmental trial in New Orleans, supporting 20 attorneys and 15 paralegals.

Productivity: Spearheaded $12 million in sales since 2001; expanded supervisory and managerial staff from approximately 15 to 35; increased caseloads, billable hours, and database coding capacity; generated new cases by winning bids and earning additional business from existing accounts.

EDUCATION

B.A., Economics, The American University, Washington, DC, May 2000, Cum Laude

CORY SCHULMAN

1010 Counselor Way
Gaithersburg, Maryland 20886
240-338-0050
counselor@gmail.com

HIGHLIGHTS

Experienced Counselor adept at active listening, counseling, academic development, and behavioral management of youths. Provided support in domestic affairs, daily living skills, and emotional/cognitive matters. Planned and coordinated youth-oriented events in academic and social settings. Supervised individuals and large groups comprising toddlers, children, and teenagers including underprivileged and troubled youths. Possess strong leadership skills in financial management, program development, and oversight of commercial operations, academic classes, and events. Directed as many as 80 youths concurrently. Trained and supervised staff.

EXPERIENCE

CAMP SPRINGS SUMMER CAMP, Kunkletown, Pennsylvania   2011 – Present

Counselor
- Directed 8 programs per day for up to 80 co-ed teenagers for an overnight summer camp.
- Planned and coordinated daily programs involving athletic, social, and educational activities.
- Provided individual counseling on broad-based issues such as family, relationships, social integration, self-esteem, eating disorders, anger management, and cognitive disorders.
- Led group discussions on drug and alcohol abuse as well as other societal matters.
- Interfaced with team of counselors to address deviant behavior and determine appropriate disciplinary actions.
- Planned and chaperoned monthly trips to New York and Boston.
- Conferred with parents by providing updates on their child's adaptation to the camp.

THE WELLNESS PLACE, Allentown, Pennsylvania   2007 – 2010

Event Coordinator Volunteer
- Oversaw as many as 15 students in support of an after-school program for troubled middle and high school students.
- Drafted proposals outlining event plans and systemic improvements for program development.

THE STARTERS PROGRAM, Allentown, Pennsylvania   2005 – 2007

Assistant Teacher
- Assisted in instructing a class of 25 financially and nutritionally underprivileged children.
- Applied various one-on-one teaching techniques, resulting in responsive and engaged students who advanced in academic, social, and emotional development.
- Provided instruction in daily living skills, social etiquette, self-discipline, reading, writing, and other skills.

EDUCATION

B.A. Psychology, 2004, Muhlenberg College, Allentown, Pennsylvania

CORY SCHULMAN

23004 Probation Road
Rockville, Maryland 20853

240-338-0050
probation@gmail.com

OBJECTIVE

To apply extensive experience in case management, resource coordination, and counseling as a Social Worker, Patient Advocate, or related position within the social services field.

EXPERIENCE

JUVENILE COURT OF MONTGOMERY COUNTY, Rockville, Maryland   2003 – Present

Probation Counselor II, Children's Bureau, 2008 – Present

Case Management:
- Managed 75+ cases involving oversight of juveniles ages 8 – 18 arrested on possession, assault, robbery/burglary, grand larceny, carrying weapons, and first degree murder.
- Drafted petitions, prepared paperwork, and coordinated attorneys.
- Set bond for misdemeanor offenses and arranged court dates for felonies; contacted parents/guardians; authorized community service, and referred qualifying cases to drug treatment sections.
- Aided the Court in making appropriate dispositions by assessing children before/after adjudication.

Resource Coordination and Communications:
- Coordinated educational, employment, psychological, and legal resources.
- Collaborated with social workers, case managers, probation officers, attorneys/district attorneys, and court advocates.
- Interfaced with various agencies such as the Department of Human Services and the Department of Children's Services, as well as non-profit private organizations such as Mediation and Restitution Services, Rape Crises, CASA (Court Appointed Special Advocates), and the YWCA (Young Women's Christian Association).
- Trained new counselors in scheduling appointments, managing cases, leading conferences, setting bonds, and coordinating resources.

Child Support Mediator, 2004 – 2007
- Mediated child support resolutions between custodial and non-custodial parents.
- Secured court ordered resolutions for delinquencies as much as $100,000.
- Determined legitimacy of children's biological-relationship with defendants. Verified legitimacy of legal papers such as birth certificates, passports, and green cards. Determined appropriate legal action and corresponding petitions.
- Advised clients on legislation, legal procedures, and government and private resources.

Probation Counselor II, 2003
- Facilitated placement of children in the Department of Children Services in support of investigation of cases involving the possible termination of parents' rights.
- Counseled clients and assessed their cognitive, emotional, and behavioral status.
- Documented clients' family, medication, mental health, and educational history.
- Ensured clients' participation in court ordered mental health services and drug treatments.

YWCA, Potomac, Maryland   1999 – 2002

On-call Advocate
- Answered crisis calls and led group counseling sessions in this shelter for abused women dealing with domestic violence, co-dependency, abusive cycles, unresolved childhood issues, and substance abuse.

EDUCATION

Bachelor of Social Work, 1999, University of Maryland, College Park, Maryland

CORY SCHULMAN

24001 Customer Relations Drive
Gaithersburg, Maryland 20877

240-338-0050
customerrelations@gmail.com

OBJECTIVE

To enhance corporate profitability in a Customer Relations position or a related career opportunity requiring experience in writing, research, investigations, and/or public relations.

EXPERIENCE

MARC RAILROAD PASSENGER CORPORATION   2000 – Present
Customer Relations Advisor (CRA), Washington, DC

Writing/Public Relations Experience:

- Draft executive correspondence at the National Headquarters' Office of Customer Relations for the company President and executive staff of the only nation-wide provider of passenger rail services to 22 million passengers a year throughout 500 cities.
- Represent the corporation's final and highest level of arbitration as one of 10 CRAs that resolves and/or addresses customer complaints/inquiries pertaining to service and delivery, reservations, scheduling, stations, policies, fares, Internet, and related issues.
- Investigate and respond to incidences, natural disasters, and catastrophic accidents, which entails in-depth knowledge of corporate policies, interviews with relevant persons, and research of routes, schedules, and status of trains throughout the system. Provide verbal and written responses to inquiries regarding a wide variety of corporate affairs. Achieved 153% of production quotas on a weekly basis.

Policy Development/Committee Experience:

- Served on committees to propose, develop, and/or recommend new policies and procedures as well as to represent the customer perspective and matters related to enhanced security.
- Recommended a "Best in Industry" refund and exchange fee policy that was adopted in part by the company and was projected to generate significant revenue increases while improving both fairness and customer satisfaction.
- Participated in the Contract of Carriage Committee that rewrote intricate legal language into plain English for user-friendly access on the Internet.
- Appointed to the 2012 President's Achievement Awards Committee to research nominees for the President's Award.

BLUE SKIES AIRLINES   1995 – 2000
Senior Executive Communications Representative, Dallas, Texas, 1996 – 2000
Customer Relations Writing Representative, Dallas, Texas, 1995

- Represented the CEO and executive management as a member of their premier communications unit that produced highly-polished written correspondence. Averaged 117% of monthly production goals.
- Interfaced with all departments, including legal, finance/accounting, management, station operations, dispatch, maintenance, and many others.

SUPPLEMENT

Press Secretary, United States Congress, 1992 – 1995

- Prepared and launched press releases for United States Representative. Worked with all district print and electronic media. Wrote editorials for district newspapers and introduction statements in the *Congressional Record*. Served as a liaison between administrative and legislative aides.

Education:
University of North Texas, Denton, Texas
Bachelor of Arts, 1991, Journalism/Advertising, Minor: Business Administration

CORY SCHULMAN

27002 Cytometric Drive
Gaithersburg, Maryland 20878

240-338-0050
technician@gmail.com

OBJECTIVE

To lead corporate growth as a Director of Operations or a related career position within the pharmaceutical or biotech industries.

HIGHLIGHTS

Executive Leadership:

- Corporate Vice President of Research Systems, Inc., one of three contract research organizations in the United States that sorts and purifies human chromosomes.
- Oversee preclinical, clinical, and research laboratory services and 35 employees.
- Implemented quality assessment programs for the DoD and the National Institutes of Allergy and Infectious Diseases.
- Provided assistance in experimental designs and interpretation of results for the NCI, NHLBI, NIDDK, NIAID, LIG, the Human Genome Project, and many other government and private sector organizations.

Scientific Background:

- Possess expertise in flow cytometry, product development, laboratory setups, new lab techniques, project management, human resources, research, data analysis, pricing, and proposal development.
- Oversee flow cytometry laboratory services, hematology assays, Elisa assays, phenotyping, immune function evaluations, and cell culture.
- Skilled in immenophynotyping, cytotoxic assays, detection of cytokines, natural killer activity, flow cytometry analysis/sorting/cloning of bacteria, phytoplanctum, cell lines, cells, particles, and chromosomes.
- Experienced in specimen preparation. Operate Becton Dickinson and Coulter flow cytometers.

EXPERIENCE

RESEARCH SYSTEMS, INC., Gaithersburg, Maryland   2006 – Present
Corporate Vice President & Director of Laboratories

- Direct up to 35 laboratory technologists/technicians and the operations of a 9,500 square foot facility that provides laboratory and quality assessment services for government and private industry, especially pharmaceutical and biotechnology companies.
- Facilitated a dramatic 5-fold growth from $1 million in 2006 to $5 million in gross annual revenues by 2010.
- Instrumental in writing RFP for a 10-year, $30 million contract involving quality assurance for 80 laboratories throughout the United States.
- Provided cloning services and new techniques that enabled a client to increase their production $75 million. Shortened the time to bring a product to market as much as 2 years.
- Re-engineered the company and cut unnecessary labor 25% by upgrading flow cytometers, programming robotic arms, devising new reagents, and transitioning the laboratory to a paperless operation. Curtailed processing time, errors, and expenses by eliminating manual entries, implementing bar-coding capabilities, and instituting a 100 megabytes per second networking environment.

- Adapted instruments to specific client needs.
- Developed and implemented computer data entry, analysis, and specimen tracking programs for laboratory specimens, including patient data, specimen receipt, frozen vial inventory, and enhanced data processing. Created a website, cytometrylabs.com, using MS Frontpage.

Scientific Expertise:
- Oversee a broad range of licensed clinical and GLP preclinical laboratory services: hematology assays, Elisa assays, phenotyping, immune function evaluations, and cell culture.
- Developed a natural killer activity assay that reduced the clinical trial budget for FDA approval from 3 years to 1 year, which saved the host company approximately $7 million.
- Facilitated the development of flow cytometric analysis, cloning, and sorting techniques. Improved cell preparation methods.
- Prevented the deterioration of blood and pre-stained controls by resolving logistical challenges to prepare, aliquot, and ship whole blood samples, pre stained and fixed samples, and controls to 80 laboratories throughout the United States.
- Developed and perfected methods to produce and preserve bulk quantities of pre-stained biological control materials, which would remain stable up to 2 weeks.
- Designed and produced a prototype of a small lightweight temperature recorder, which monitored the temperature of blood in transit.
- Interface with client investigators, which involves polished presentations on flow cytometry and related research projects. Review proposed projects with clients; recommend appropriate antibody panels, controls, preparation methods, and analyses; review data; explain the meaning of data and its relationship to the clients' anticipated experimental outcome.
- Co-developed QuickStain, a one-stop procedure for performing DNA analysis with highly reproducible results.

DoD CLINICAL CYTOMETRY TRAINING COURSE, Rockville, Maryland   2002 – 2006

Instructor
- Provided training to military lab personnel in flow cytometry for 1 week per year.

NATIONAL INSTITUTES OF HEALTH, Bethesda, Maryland   2000 – 2002

Chemist
- Participated on a three member team that established a state-of-the-art flow cytometry facility.
- Oversaw and participated in more than 80 concurrent clinical and research projects.

EDUCATION

AVERETT COLLEGE, Northern Virginia Campus, Virginia
Master of Business Administration, 2007

MOUNT SAINT MARY'S COLLEGE, Emmitsburg, Maryland
Bachelor of Science, Chemistry, 2000

CORY SCHULMAN (ASCP)
27003 Cytology Road
Gaithersburg, Maryland 20878
240-338-0050
Cytology@yahoo.com

EXPERIENCE

CYTOLOGY SERVICES, INC., Rockville, Maryland   8/2002 – Present
Supervisor of Cytology, Immunology, and Processing

Cytology:
- Examine, diagnose, and document gynecologic and non-gynecologic specimens for infectious, pre-malignant, and malignant conditions.
- Facilitate in overseeing the accurate processing of approximately 100,000 conventional and ThinPrep cytology slides per year.
- Document examinations and reviews of slide interpretation results of each gynecologic (gyn) and non-gynecologic (non-gyn) cytology case. Maintain section logs, ensuring all test specimens are recorded and accessioned.
- Provide QC oversight of daily production for five cytotechnologists, and coordinate both daily schedules and workflow for the Cytology Department.

Immunology:
- Supervise the Immunology Department, which conducts tests for such STDs as Human Papillomavirus (HPV), *Chlamydia trachomatis* (CT), and *Neisseria gonorrhoeae* (GC).
- Direct and supervise three laboratory prep technicians for accurate results and proper use of quality control procedures set forth in standard operating procedures manual for cytology and immunology.
- Process all incoming specimens for HPV, CT, and GC according to standard operating procedures for virology and immunology.
- Perform and examine monoclonal antibody assay tests for precise identification of viral and bacterial microorganisms such as HPV, GC, and CT using DNA probe techniques (Digene Hybrid Capture 2 technology, which is nucleic acid hybridization microplate assay with signal amplification).
- Instituted new testing procedures that expanded testing volume 10-fold from 20 to 200+ per week. Implemented HPV testing for all patients showing signs of abnormalities, resulting in greater diagnostic accuracy as well as improving laboratory revenue roughly $520,000 per annum.
- Advise the Marketing Department in strategies for improving test volume, which includes establishing alliances with medical facilities such as hospitals, clinics, and private practices.
- Prepare the laboratory to convert assay procedures from Gen-Probe PACE 2 CT/GC to Digene Hybrid Capture 2 CT/GC DNA tests.
- Participate in various Digene research projects involving (HPV, CT, and GC).

Processing:
- Prepare gyn and non-gyn slides for review by cytotechnologists and pathologists.
- Process, stain, and coverslip all fluid base ThinPrep specimens, conventional cytologic preparations, both gyn and non-gyn cytologic specimens.
- Train staff in processing gyn and non-gyn cytologic specimens on the Cytyc ThinPrep® 2000 Processor and Cytyc Image System.

Ancillary Responsibilities:
- Perform general maintenance on all laboratory equipment in assigned section.
- Ensure compliance with OSHA, CAP, and related federal regulations and prepare the lab and the department for periodic inspections.

93

Educational Coordinator
- Trained students from Old Dominion University in quality control and cytologic procedures such as preparing and screening slides; diagnosing abnormal cells; and conducting tests of gyn/non-gyn conditions.
- Prepared students for the Board of Registry examination by the American Society of Clinical Pathologists.

Cytology Lab Inspector
- Performed QC audit under the auspices of The College of American Pathologists in support of a CAP inspection of a Maryland cytology lab, January 2002.

EDUCATION • REGISTRATIONS • CERTIFICATES

B.S. in Cytotechnology, August 1999, Old Dominion University, Norfolk, Virginia
A.D. in Medical Laboratory Technology, September 1997, Shiraz Medical School, Shiraz, Iran

Registrations:
Registered Cytotechnologist, March 2000
Board of Registry and Membership, American Society of Clinical Pathologists
Medical Laboratory Technician, November 1999
Certified by International Education Resource Foundation

Certificates of Training:
Hybrid Capture 2 CT/GC Test, Digene Corporation, Beltsville, Maryland, September, 2004
Certificate, Cytyc Imaging System and Review Scope, Cytyc Corporation, May, 2004
Hybrid Capture 2 HPV Test, Digene Corporation, Beltsville, Maryland, June 2003
Certificate, CORTEX Medical Management Systems, Inc., 2002
Certificate, Cytotechnologist in the Evaluation of the ThinPrep Pap Test, Cytyc Corporation, 2001

OTHER QUALIFICATIONS

Research/Publication:
- Collected specimens, conducted tests, and gathered data used in publication, "Detection of *Neisseria gonorrhoeae* in Swab Specimens by the Hybrid Capture," *STD* 2015, P. 150, Volume 4, #8, Cory S. Schulman, Ph.D.

Laboratory Software and Equipment:
- Gen-Leader; ThinPrep 2000 Processor; Centrifuge; Microcentrifuge; Microscope; Automated Coverslipper; Isotemp Waterbath; Automated Plate Washer; Microplate Heater; Shaker; Automated Diversified Stainer; Cytyc Imager; and Review Scope

Recognition:
- Earned annual Certificates of Appreciation, The Cytotechnology Program, Old Dominion University, School of Medical Laboratory Sciences and Environmental Health, 2000 – 2003

Additional Knowledge:
Areas of knowledge and clinical laboratory experience, includes cytopreparatory techniques, microscopic analysis and evaluation of the body sites; Physics; Mathematics; Organic/Clinical Chemistry; Histology; Parasitology; Hematology; Bacteriology; Urinalysis; Physiology; Serology; Blood Banking

CORY S. SCHULMAN

9001 Physician's Court
Derwood, MD 20855-2566
240-338-0050
doctor@gmail.com

SUMMARY

Successful Medical Doctor with extensive experience in general practice and surgery. Served in hospitals, clinics, and medical facilities. Adept in cardiology, gyneco-obstetrics, pediatrics, psychiatry, and neurology. Recognized by hospital medical boards for outstanding medical performances throughout tenure.

Research Skills / Medical Knowledge:

- Facilitated research and assay development under the auspices of Cell Physiologist and Geneticist for nucleus and DNA material analyses and Mandalian genetics studies.

- Conducted differential diagnoses, planned treatments, observed procedures, and assisted physicians during rotations in Urgent Care, Internal Medicine, Surgery, OB/GYN, Pediatrics, Radiology, and Psychiatry wards.

- Keep abreast of ongoing research and emerging practices in the medical community by reading journal articles from *JAMA*, *The Lancet*, *New England Journal of Medicine*, *Reuters Health*, and other credible literary sources.

- Reviewed cutting-edge information on diseases, technological advances, treatment modalities, and guideline changes by using various on-line sites and database resources, such as Medline, National Medical Library, Medscape, WebMD, and others.

- Wrote an undergraduate honors thesis on xenophobia and racism.

- Drafted more than 150 editorials on legislative issues and foreign policy matters.

EXPERIENCE

SANTA ARAINA HOSPITAL, Cochabamba, Bolivia, 1995 – Present
Physician
- Obtained medical histories and performed initial physical examinations; recorded pertinent data in patient charts. Reviewed reports of patients' general medical conditions, reactions to medications, and medical history. Prepared patient summaries.

- Ordered laboratory tests and x-rays to facilitate diagnoses of patient conditions; performed venipuncture, intradermal tests, and EEG's and EKG's. Analyzed reports and findings of tests and examinations to develop accurate diagnoses. Developed patient care and therapy plans.

- Treated emergency room patients. Conducted triage and initiated appropriate emergency management for crisis situations such as cardiac arrest, respiratory distress, injuries, burns, hemorrhages, dehydrations, etc.

- Performed operations using a variety of surgical instruments. Removed superficial foreign bodies; conducted neurological examinations and auditory screenings. Treated and sutured lacerations; casted and splinted broken bones. Controlled hemorrhages and applied dressings and bandages; and administered medications, intravenous fluids, and blood transfusions.

- Assisted other doctors in neurosurgery and cardiosurgery.

- Managed and treated psychiatric patients suffering from schizophrenia, alcoholism, bipolar disorder, paranoia, and drug addiction. Treated epilepsy with specific drugs and techniques.

- Administered and prescribed medications, injections, IVs, and blood transfusions to treat injuries.

- Provided prenatal/postnatal care to mothers and infants.

EDUCATION

Medical Doctorate, 1991, San Simon University, Faculty of Medicine, Cochabamba, Bolivia

Jack Schilling, M.D.

9002 Doctor's Lane
Silver Spring, Maryland 20905
howardrein@yahoo.com

H: 240-338-0050
C: 240-338-0050

EDUCATION

Doctor of Medicine, May 2015, University of Sint Eustatius School of Medicine, Sint Eustatius, N.A.
B.A. with Honors, December 2011, University of Maryland, College Park, Maryland

HIGHLIGHTS

Rotations: Medical Center, ABR Hospital, VA Hospital, DC Examiner's Office, and Private Practices

- *Family Practice* – Documented histories, conducted physicals, and provided differential diagnoses of patients suffering from chronic diseases and conditions, including obstructive pulmonary disease, diabetes, and sciatica. Observed conventional and alternative treatments, including lower spine manipulation. Examined lab results from blood and urine tests.
- Examined patients in an outpatient center and diagnosed chronic diseases and rare congenital conditions, such as situs inversus. Identified a palpable mass during a physical exam, resulting in the successful identification of a uterine tumor in an early stage.
- *Internal Medicine* – Participated in post diagnostic sessions with patients to convey terminal prognoses. Contacted patients to communicate lab test results regarding cholesterol, thyroid, glucose, and other chemistry values. Examined pathology reports and conferred with the pathologist. Performed EKGs, inoculations, and venipuncture. Negotiated exceptions to formularies and healthcare entitlements with insurance companies.
- *Medicine* – Participated in a team comprising the attending physician, residents, and medical students to examine, diagnose, and treat patients suffering from acute conditions, such as congestive heart failure, liver cirrhosis, nonketotic hyperosmolar state, and scleroderma.
- *Surgery* – Assisted surgeons in femoral popliteal bypasses, lobectomies, appendectomies, laproscopic surgeries, and Nissen fundoplications. Assisted residents by closing surgeries involving hiatal hernias, gerd, and gall bladders.
- *OB/GYN* – Conducted vaginal deliveries, performed episiotomies, and dealt with perinatal complications such as preeclampsia and eclampsia. Assisted in Cesarean sections and dilation and curettage procedures (for fetus with hydrocephalous). Assisted with cryo procedures and used ultrasound equipment.
- *Radiology* – Examined and interpreted CT films, radiographs, mammograms, tomograms, and angiograms. Observed angiographs, esophagrams, CT scans, CT guided biopsies, and ultrasounds.
- *Forensics* – Assisted in autopsies of both intact and severely decomposed corpses revealing deaths by strangulation, gunshots, asphyxiation, drug overdose, and other causal factors. Participated in onsite forensic investigations.
- *Psychiatrics* – Interviewed and assisted in counseling patients diagnosed with paranoid schizophrenia, psychosis, Alzheimer's disease, depression, and suicidal tendencies. Drafted daily progress notes.

SUPPLEMENT

Experience: **Pharmacy Technician**, NVM, Silver Spring, Maryland, 2013 – Present
Radiopharmaceutical Courier, Balar Pharmaceuticals, Calverton, Maryland, 2006
Veterinary Technician, Embrey Animal Clinic, Baltimore, Maryland, 2005
Translator/Sergeant, U.S. Army, Berlin, Germany, 2002 – 2004
Certifications/Exams: USMLE (Steps 1 and 2), ECFMG, Clinical Skills Assessment Test
Foreign Languages: Fluent in German; conversant in medical French and Spanish
Security Clearance: **Held Top Secret Security Clearance**

JACK SCHILLING, M.D.

9003 Pharmaceutical Terrace
Ashburn, Virginia 20147

C: 240-338-0050
pharmaceutical@csu.edu

OBJECTIVE

To apply knowledge of pharmaceuticals, medication administration, and community resources in a health management position or a related career opportunity.

HIGHLIGHTS

Pharmaceuticals: Treated patients with various cardiovascular, respiratory, diabetic, and rheumatoid conditions, as well as pain management by administering medications under the supervision of medical physicians. Possess broad-based knowledge of betablockers, ACE inhibitors, CNSs, anti-inflamatories, glucocorticoides, insulin, sulfanaurases, glucotriens, sulfanomides, and narcotics. Completed medical school courses in Pharmacology, Neurosciences, and Biochemistry.

Diagnostic/Treatment Experience: Assess and diagnose patients with central nervous system trauma, cardiac infarctions, blunt trauma, acute vital signs, orthopedic trauma, and related maladies. Diagnosed disease through analysis of MRIs, x-rays, CT scans, and test lab results. Administered medications using oral, injection, intravenous, and related methods in short/long term care settings, such as trauma, critical care, and emergency room units.

Communications: Fostered extensive network among various medical personnel during clinical rotations at hospitals, clinics, and private practices. Interfaced with pharmaceutical representatives and evaluated proposed medicines and verified pharmaceutical information through PDR clarifications. Gave presentations to as many as 50 doctors, residents, and students on various issues pertaining to internal medicine, pediatrics, surgeries, and OB/GYN, such as AIDS, febrile seizures, appendectomies, and Bartholian cysts. Conveyed pre-op/post-op issues, including diagnoses, medical procedures, health risks, death, and post-operative care to patients, families, and care takers. Prepared reports on up to 20 patients per shift in ER covering physical examinations, histories, manifestations, tests ordered, treatments administered, and results.

EXPERIENCE

Project Manager, Ali-Baba Hospital, Addisbaba, Ethiopia, April 2014 – Present
- Procured radiology equipment (x-ray and ultrasound machinery) and established radiology units in a new 100-bed privately-funded general hospital.
- Conducted cost analyses, researched international import regulations, and negotiated price reductions to ensure compliance with $600,000 annual capital budget.

Volunteer, St. Jude Hospital, Washington, DC, May 2010 – March 2014
- Assisted in providing patient care as a volunteer in the Operating Room aiding with surgeries, deliveries, abortions, tumorectomies, fibroectomies, hysterectomies, and GI surgeries.

EDUCATION

M.D., 2007, Ross University School of Medicine, New York, New York
Clinical Rotations: Massachusetts, New Jersey, New York, and Maryland
B.A., Biology, 2003, California State University of San Bernardino, California

JACK SCHILLING, PA-C

9004 Physician Assistant Drive
Olney, Maryland 20832

240-338-0050
physicianassistant@hotmail.com

OBJECTIVE

To facilitate the highest quality of surgical interventions and pre/post operative patient care as an experienced and dedicated Surgical Physician's Assistant.

EXPERIENCE

ELI PATTERSON PA-C, HOSPITAL CENTER, Washington, DC   2013 – Present
Physician's Assistant, Neurosurgery Department
- Support physician assistants by treating patients diagnosed with subdural hemotomas, strokes, seizure disorders, electrolyte deficiencies, and related neural conditions.
- Consult with radiology specialists to diagnose conditions.
- Aid a physician assistant with histories/physicals (H&Ps), incisions, closures, drainage procedures, and simple surgeries.
- Analyze chest x-rays, CT scans, MRIs, and lab reports, especially CBCs, blood gases, PTs, PTTS, BUN, cratning and other elements to assess patient conditions, develop treatment and therapeutic plans, and write discharge summaries.

FAMILY PRACTICE, Oxen Hill, Maryland   2012 – 2013
Physician's Assistant
- Diagnosed and treated patients with acute through chronic illnesses, such as congestive heart failure, myocardial infarctions, prostate/lung cancer, renal failure, as well as untreated cases of hypertension, diabetes, and depression.
- Performed physical examinations and treated newborns through geriatric patients.
- Interpreted diagnostic laboratory tests and radiographic images. Administered pap smears and immunizations.
- Distinguished best use of ACE inhibitors, beta blockers, calcium channel blockers, and diuretics.

GENERAL CAPITOL HOSPITAL, Azmara, Eritrea   2012
First Assistant to Surgeon
- Assisted surgeon in a 100-bed hospital serving a 2.1 million population by suturing incisions and lacerations.
- Examined patients and prescribed pharmaceuticals for patients diagnosed with diabetes, malaria, and infections.
- Addressed epidemic crisis by conducting educational initiatives targeting youths and individuals at risk for sexually transmitted diseases, especially AIDS and HIV.
- Educated patients on diabetes, GERD, hypertension, congestive heart failure, and other health conditions.

SUNRISE MEDICAL GROUP, Rockville, Maryland   2009 – 2012
Physician's Assistant
- Assessed, diagnosed, and treated pediatric through geriatric patients for a broad spectrum of health problems under the guidance of the physician staff.
- Rendered primary care to chemotherapy and radiation oncology patients, including multiple myeloma, malignant melanoma, renal cell carcinoma, and other cancers.
- Documented patients' medical and family histories, including reported/observable symptoms, prescribed medications, and related information. Took vital signs, performed venipuncture, prepared IV treatments, and collected specimens, biopsies, and cultures when necessary.
- Conducted and/or ordered a variety of diagnostic tests, including pulmonary, urine, blood, and pregnancy tests. Performed phlebotomy, EKGs, etc. Reviewed and interpreted laboratory and other diagnostic data.

ROTATIONS [Emergency, General Surgery, Internal Medicine, OB/GYN]   2007 – 2009
DC General Hospital
- Supported a 7-member team performing emergency surgeries on up to 10 trauma patients per night involving gunshot wounds, stabbings, drug overdoses, rapes, motor vehicular collusions, assaults, and other severe maladies.
- Served in major trauma surgery, emergency room, medicine, and pediatric units.
- Addressed the General Surgery Department's staff including the attending with presentations on various issues: electrolyte deficiencies in the pre/post op department; coagulation disorders involving surgery; new CHF treatments; and differential treatments for inflammatory bowel diseases.

Washington Hospital Center
- Participated in scheduled and code-call surgeries, such as MVCs, hernias, appendectomies, and cholecystotomies.

Howard University Hospital
- Gained extensive knowledge of OB/GYN by preparing patients and serving on-call for delivery and labor surgeries, including Cesarean sections, D&Cs, and suctions.
- Conducted and observed alpha fetal protein tests, amniocentesis tests, sonograms, and pap smears.

EDUCATION • AFFILIATIONS

B.A. in Physician Assistance, 2006, Howard University, Washington, DC
- Honors, Johnson S. Simpson Award; Dean's List 2 year. A+ Surgery Department by attending; only award winner among class of 42 colleagues.

A.A. in Biology, 2004, Montgomery College, Rockville, Maryland
Member of American Association of Physician Assistants and Maryland Association of Physician Assistants

CORY SCHULMAN
1005 Economist Street, Apt. 100
Silver Spring, MD 20910
240-338-0050
Economist@gmail.com

OBJECTIVE

To apply economic, financial, and business principles as a Business Analyst or a related position.

EXPERIENCE

NATIONAL LABOR STATISTICS, Washington, DC, 2006 – Present
Office of Prices and Living Conditions, Division of International Prices
Economist/Industry Analyst

- Record and interpret import/export pricing for 1,200 items in the paper, fruits/vegetables, rubber/plastics, and tobacco industries in support of the International Price Program.

- Perform qualitative and quantitative analyses based on price indexes to identify market trends and accuracy of current price data.

- Analyze exchange rates, trading factors, shipping/insurance, transaction prices, production costs, supply and demand, and other micro/macroeconomic variables.

- Quantify, measure, and identify economic relationships, and use statistical methodologies in computerized data collection and processing systems.

- Review and prepare preliminary interpretative reports on product, expenditure, and price data.

- Summarize economic trends and related pricing data in tabular, chart, and narrative form.

- Research industry websites, publications, periodicals, and the Library of Congress to assess market movements.

- Interview industry analysts, company officials, and other industry leaders to gather historical, current, and projected pricing trends.

- Develop statistical graphs and spreadsheets to indicate industry pricing movements.

- Reassess accuracy of industry pricing reported from 60+ small businesses through Fortune 500 companies that participate in the International Price Program. Streamline sample refinements, coordinate item remappings, and reevaluate publishability.

- Compose market analyses and brief the Publications Department on import/export pricing trends. Use micro/macroeconomic theory during round table meetings to verbally present findings on industry pricing trends for agricultural commodities, pulp, and paper.

SOCIAL SERVICES ADMINISTRATION, Division of Policy Evaluation
Policy Analyst Intern, 2005

- Participated in a five-member team, which performed data analysis and economic modeling to provide projections of retirement income and demographic statistics for new beneficiaries.

- Collected data based on the 2000 Census Bureau and Bureau of Labor Statistics figures and tabulated a statistical report using the SAS, Windows, Microsoft Word, and Excel to update the effects of demographic population and income changes on Social Security recipients.

- Notified senior economists about project conditions during monthly section meetings.

- Conducted a PowerPoint presentation for numerous policy analysts and junior and senior economists.
- Composed a 15-page report using descriptive econometric statistics as well as theoretical and quantitative reasoning for a study published in the Social Security Bulletin.
- Updated research data pertaining to the effects of welfare reform on Social Security recipients.

INDUSTRY KNOWLEDGE/SKILLS

Public Finance: Analyzed the government's role in promoting allocation of resources and equitable distribution of income.

Financial Intermediation – International Commercial Policy: Adept in financial decisions, intermediation, and the role of financial institutions affecting economic development. Acquired knowledge of economic policy variables such as exchange rates, interest rate tariffs, and other trade controls. Studied unions, common markets, balance of trade devaluation, and economic integration in open economies.

Price Theory: Examined consumer behavior, production and cost, market structure, monopoly, and oligopoly. Used mathematical techniques, graphical analysis, and algebraic proofs, which entailed application of linear algebra and differentiation.

Statistics: Used probability distribution functions, expected values or random variables and their functions, conditional probability and independence, sampling and central limit theory, estimation, and Bayesian inferences.

Macroeconomics: Researched comparative statistic analysis of partial equilibria in product, labor, money, and bond markets. Determined output, employment, price level, interest rate and bond price. Critically examined fiscalist and monetarist policy issues.

Econometrics – Computer Skills: Performed matrix algebra, parameter estimation and significance testing, forecasting, multiple regression analysis, and matrix approaches. Use SAS to recalculate a computer model describing Welfare and Social Security recipients. Completed Lexis-Nexis course. Updated harmonized listing from the tariff schedule using VISTA software. Used Windows, FoxPro, Excel, and PowerPoint.

EDUCATION

HOWARD UNIVERSITY, Washington, DC
Master's Degree Program in Monetary and Fiscal Policy, Completed all course requirements.

Bachelor of Arts Degree, Major: Economics; Minor: Philosophy, 2004
Former Charter Member of the Abrams Harris Economic Society
Former Member of the Alaine Locke Philosophical Society

CORY SCHULMAN

7004 Electrician Terrace
Olney, MD 20832
240-338-0050
electrician@gmail.com

SUMMARY

Facilities Engineering:

- **Master Electrician** with 22 years engineering experience at the Health Institute. Plan, design, and coordinate new construction, renovations, and alterations for as many as 22 on-going projects ranging from $500,000 to $10 million.

- Managed value engineering in support of 27 institutes comprising more than 70 on-campus and off-site facilities involving intricate coast-to-coast relocations.

- Analyze, develop, write, and evaluate the architectural/engineering SOWs; RFPs; PORs; and project budgets/schedules, including design/support service construction costs and project requirements.

Regulatory/Code Compliance:

- Participated in architect and engineer (A/E) selection boards; analyzed design submissions for compliance with local and national building, electrical, and mechanical codes and regulations such as OSHA, NEC, NFPA, BOCA, FAR, NIH Design Policy and Guidelines, laboratory animal care accreditation requirements, and fire protection/disabilities accessibility standards.

- Familiar with safety practices needed for work involving chemical, radioactive, and biomedical substances, as well as high voltage electricity and sophisticated electronic equipment.

Computer Systems/Construction Specifications:

- Adept at using various software and management systems, including CADD, Visio, MEANS estimating program, AutoSketch, Microsoft Project, Enterprise Project, DOC, and spreadsheet programs.

- Skilled in using blueprints, schematics, and written instructions to plan materials, tools and methods to execute work orders. Prepared engineering drawings by hand and using architectural design software.

Communications:

- Interface with ICs and DES contractors to resolve technical, budgetary, and procedural issues.

- Well versed in NIH system of funds acquisition and budget management; federal contracting methods and requirements; engineering principles and practices; and construction techniques and management.

EXPERIENCE

THE HEALTH INSTITUTE, *Bethesda, Maryland*   July 2001 – Present

National Eye Institute, July 2012 – Present
Intramural Program Coordinator/Technical Advisor to the Director

- Manage operations for 190,000 aggregate square feet of office buildings, laboratories, clinics, and animal care/use facilities located on campus and in the Twinbrook complex.

- Cost projects ranging from $20,000 to $10 million which often require development of architectural/engineering designs/specifications, safety measures, and milestone schedules for all phases of new construction and renovations from demolition and excavation through occupancy.

- Coordinated 6 – 8 projects concurrently with varying timelines. Directed seamless relocation of a 1,800 square foot microbiology laboratory from Berkley, California to Bethesda, Maryland. Relocated up to 75 professionals without disruption to intricate clinical studies and cutting-edge research. Led numerous major relocations during critical live experiments and requiring movement of scientific equipment such as deionized water systems, computers, monitors, incubators, centrifuges, shakers, and freezers/refrigerators.

- Planned and directed a $1 million renovation of a 1,800 square foot laboratory and animal room within budget and ahead of schedule in preparation for the relocation of the Berkley laboratory.

- Participated in bi-weekly team meetings to preside over design, construction, and budgetary matters.

Design, Construction and Alterations Branch, DES, ORS, OD, November 2003 – July 2012
Technical Representative
- Provided leadership in engineering/architectural design and communications as a liaison between the Engineering Department and construction/alteration services for any of the 27 institutes.

- Contracted architectural and engineering firms; monitored design process; and conducted periodic review meetings for projects ranging typically from $500,000 to $10 million. Participated in projects valued as much as $300 million.

- Managed new construction and alterations of any of 70+ buildings located on campus and satellite areas; monitored and controlled expenditures within budgetary limits.

- Used Microsoft Project to schedule asynchronous milestones for 20+ concurrent projects.

- Designed construction projects of facilities ranging from 50,000 square feet to 600,000 square feet using Visio and CADD. Interfaced with architects, construction contractors, customers, lab chiefs, investigators, institute administrators, and directors.

- Directed a $5 million renovation of a 1929 building spanning 14,000 square feet, which required complete overhaul of the infrastructure (plumbing, electrical, and HVAC systems); restored exterior and much of the interior to its original condition, replaced interior millwork finishings, and removed hazardous materials while preserving the building's registered historic status.

- Earned numerous monetary awards for completing projects on time, within budget, and in strict adherence to federal regulations.

Design and Construction Branch Design Team, August 2002 – November 2003
Engineering Technician
- Designed electrical schematics, completed engineering drawings, wrote formal construction specifications, and estimated costs for electrical portions of laboratory, conference, and office space renovations ranging from $20,000 to $500,000.

- Determined power requirements and specifications that supported clinical operations and research studies. Reviewed entire designs to ensure completeness and timely execution within the fee for service budget. Coordinated post design services with respect to construction submittal review and site inspections.

- Developed division-wide design and construction detail/specification standards.

- Devised construction cost information for materials and items unique to NIH.

- Acted as focal point and Lead Designer briefing DCB management on project status, communicating scope changes that impacted the budget or schedule, and giving presentations to upper NIH management for project approval.

- Attended construction contract negotiations as the government's technical representative.

- Reviewed construction submittals in a timely manner.

- Collaborate with the Executive Administrative Officer of the ICD, the researcher, and ICD Director or Deputy Director to coordinate daily projects.

Construction Planning, Shops Branch, DES, OD, July 2001 – August 2002
Construction Planner, Electrical
- Prepared electrical portions of plans for facility renovation projects, which were completed on schedule and within the fee for services budgeted.

- Wrote the formal scope and statement of work for shop personnel; estimated construction costs and additional necessary work; ordered special materials; provided all electrical technical support to the planning team; briefed supervisors on project statuses, problems, and/or scope changes impacting the schedule; consulted with the planning team to coordinate between disciplines.

CORY SCHULMAN

30001 Electrocardiogram Terrace
Montgomery Village, Maryland 20886
240-338-0050
electrocardiogram@gmail.com

OBJECTIVE

To apply expertise in electrocardiogram interpretation in a clinical, research, or educational environment.

HIGHLIGHTS

- Senior Non-Invasive Electrophysiology Technician with CPR Certification and 20 plus years' experience conducting and processing various cardiac tests accurately, efficiency, and in accordance with the highest standards.

- Perform complex cardiology procedures: Holter monitoring, ambulatory cardiac event monitoring, EKGs, and pacemaker surveillance. Evaluate, recommend, and troubleshoot state-of-the-art cardiac monitoring systems.

- Recruit, train, and manage cardiac technicians and related medical staff. Delivered informational talks on technical and clinical electrophysiologic topics to as many as 100 attendees.

- Possess a high-spirited demeanor and natural ability to bond with in/out patients ranging from neonates to geriatrics. Maintain highly professional relationships and polished communications with visitors, colleagues, nurses, specialists, and physicians.

EXPERIENCE

WASHINGTON MEDICAL CENTER, Washington, DC   2006 – Present
Non-Invasive Electrophysiology Technician

Electrocardiogram Responsibilities:
- Emerged as the hospital's key resources analyzing electrocardiograms in this 500-bed teaching hospital rated within the top 13 in the country.
- Prepare and relax patients of all ages, including pediatrics, with an engaging demeanor and polished communications. Explain purposes of tests and technical procedures in a simplified and non-threatening manner.
- Process and analyze Holter recordings, summarize diagnostic results, and report findings to Neurology, Cardiology, and General Internal Medicine units.
- Detect atrial, ventricular, and other abnormalities, including early/missed beats, wide/thin beats, and other conduction disturbances.
- Promote congenial, proactive, and cooperative relations with all patients, visitors, and medical personnel, especially when working closely with Electrophysiologists and GI Physicians.

Electrocardiogram Apparatuses:

- Manage the MUSE system, a central computer that stores cardiac data from Holter, EKG, and stress test devices.
- Evaluated, operated, and maintained various apparatuses, such as EKG cart, Holter monitors, Holter scanning systems, and Event monitors.
- Upgraded the operating system of the main computer from Windows XP to Windows 2010, resulting in enhanced output efficiency, greater capacity, and more reliable functionality.
- Persuaded procurement officer to replace wet gel electrodes with solid gel electrodes, which improved recording quality and enabled faster turnaround of critical reports.

Leadership:

- Retrained hospital-wide staff in correct use of cardiac equipment, resulting in a rapid reduction in poor quality tracings and noninterpretable results from 60 EKG carts used throughout the facility.
- Directed inservices for testing procedures to Respiratory Therapists, Clinical Technicians, Nurses, Emergency Room Personnel, and Same Day Surgery Staff.
- Cut uninterpretable electrocardiogram tracings approximately 80% as the MUSE system coordinator.

HOLY CROSS HOSPITAL, Silver Spring, Maryland   2000 – 2006
Non-Invasive Electrophysiology Technician

Electrocardiogram Responsibilities:

- Prepared Holter and event monitors for neonate through adolescent patients in a tertiary care environment to identify congenital heart abnormalities and related high-risk conditions.
- Conducted approximately 120 Holter tests per month.
- Engaged in collaborative efforts with GE Medical Information Systems to conduct beta tests of a new Holter scanning computer, resulting in the implementation of this system.
- Evaluated and debugged new products over a 3 year period and provided recommendations for equipment upgrades that enhanced quality of services, efficiency, and cost effectiveness.

GERMANTOWN MEDICAL CENTER, Germantown, Maryland   1999
Holter Technician

- Processed cardiac arrhythmia recordings in support of multiple, large-scale pharmacological trials at the central processing site for nationwide studies.
- Gave presentations on Holter analysis findings to audiences as large as 100 from research study sites throughout the nation.
- Interpreted clinical recordings of inpatients and reported results to Germantown Medical Center staff.

EDUCATION

Ursinus College, Collegeville, Pennsylvania
Bachelor of Science, 1999
Major: Biology

SUPPLEMENT

MEDICAL ONE CENTER, Washington, DC   1996 – 1999

Electrician Leader

- Allocated assignments to approximately 20 electricians and apprentices on a daily basis.
- Directed project site operations, evaluated workers, and wrote weekly progress reports.
- Inspected electrical work to ensure compliance with code and job specifications.
- Ordered electrical materials in accordance with NIH ordering procedures.
- Collaborated with medical and scientific personnel in hospital and medical research facilities to coordinate renovations, repairs, and maintenance of facilities, equipment, and electrical systems.
- Installed, repaired, and maintained motor controls, A.C./D.C. motors, transformers, operating room isolation systems, emergency generators, transfer switches, fire alarm systems, fire detection devices, burglar alarms, security door holders, and load bank emergency generators.

CLINICAL CENTER, Bethesda, Maryland   1995 – 1996

Electrician

- Maintained and repaired 700 electrical and hydraulic bed hospital, nurse call systems and TV controls, emergency generators, motors, and motor control centers.
- Prepared hospital for accreditation inspections.
- Trained apprentices, helpers, and new employees.

Additional Education:
Master Electrician, May 2003, Montgomery County and Prince George's County, Maryland
Advanced Project Officer, February 2003, 24 hours, U.S. Department of Health and Human Services
Design of Electrical Power Systems, February 2003, 24 hours, Technical Training Group, Inc.
Project Officer Safety Course, September 2001, 16 hours, Harford Community College
Project Officer Course, April 2000, 32 hours, U.S. Department of Health and Human Services
Means Data for Delivery Order Contracting, March 1999, 8 hours, R.S. Means Company, Inc.
Job Order Contracting Course, December 1998, U.S. Army Engineering and Housing Support
Power Monitoring and Control Systems; Remote Power Switching Systems, October 1998, 8 hours, Square D Company
CADD Electrical Planning Software (40 hours) and **Architectural Software** (40 hours), 1997
Preparation for Master Electrician Examination, 1996– 1998, 180 hours, Montgomery College
Motor Control, Maintenance and Troubleshooting, Part II, May 1995, 32, GE Corporation
Asbestos Hazard Abatement and Protection, October 1995, 24 hours, NIH
Generator Maintenance Troubleshooting and Repair, 1995, 40 hours
Biohazard Safety, August 1990, 8 hours, NIH Safety Branch

Diploma, June 1994, High School, Lima, Peru

Languages:
Fluent in reading, speaking, and understanding Spanish and Portuguese

Awards:
The National Eye Institute's Director's Award, 2004
NIH Director's Award, 1999
Section Employee of the Year, Team 4/DCAB, 1996

CORY SCHULMAN

11001 Engineer Street
Arlington, Virginia 22205
240-338-0050
engineer@gmail.com

OBJECTIVE

To perform project or product engineering as a Mechanical Engineer for a customer oriented engineering or manufacturing company.

EXPERIENCE

DYNAMIC CONTROLS, Frederick, MD, 2006 – Present
Principal Environmental Control System (ECS) Engineer
- Perform ECS engineering which involves integrating Vapor Cycle Systems (VCS) with heating, filtration, and flow control methodology to provide cooling, ventilating, and heating for personnel and electronics.
- Provide in-depth knowledge of applied thermodynamics, fluid flow and heat transfer with special applications to refrigeration and key components: compressors, heat exchangers, pumps, fans, valves and controls.

Proposals:
- Conduct analyses of customer requirements and provide thermal architecture to meet customers' needs.
- Write technical specifications, perform trade studies and design iterations using compressor modeling as well as component sizing and layout.
- Wrote three winning proposals: Apache Longbow, Pendant and ATFLIR, and co-wrote the AAIS proposal. Seven other proposals were found to be technically very good or excellent, but were not accepted for commercial reasons.

Project Engineering:
- Project Engineer on the AAIS pod ECU with full responsibility for all aspects of design, including discussion with the customer and vendors, preparation of specification and design reviews, and all performance calculations. Project Engineer for the ATFLIR pod and Assistant Project Engineer for Apache Longbow.

Development Test Engineering:
- Design test stands to test ECS unit performance, or component performance, write procedures, supervise tests and evaluate results. Designed and used two "Hot Benches." One replicates the Apache Longbow heating loads and flow conditions, and allows Fairchild ECS to be tested at various design conditions. The other is a versatile table top system which is used for evaluation of components such as valves.

GEES CORPORATION, Division of Mark IV, Hamden, CT, 2003 – 2006
Senior Mechanical Systems Project and Development Engineer
- Performed project engineering for HVAC systems in land vehicles, aircraft and stationary equipment, which included the following general responsibilities:
  - Specifications reviews, proposal writing, thermal cycle analyses, specification of components, including compressors, blowers, pumps, heat exchangers, heaters, valves, accumulators, and control and plumbing components.
  - Flow and control schematics, preliminary packaging layouts, and work with design drafting to produce detailed fabrication and procurement drawings.
  - Additional analysis included air duct design, fluid flow analysis, static stress analysis, heat transfer, corrosion prevention, human factors, EMI, and electrical bonding consideration.
- Collaborated with manufacturing to ensure the selection of cost effective fabrication techniques such as welding, machining, sheet metal, and fasteners.

- Interfaced with customers on technical and scheduling matters, including Critical Design Review presentation.
- Maintained documentation to implement all design changes and calculate cost changes as appropriate.

KRAMER COMPANY, Wethersfield, CT, 1999 – 2003
Senior Mechanical Product and Component Design Engineer

- Designed desiccant type compressed gas driers to customer specifications; developed new line of driers from marketing requirements to finished projects, including economic analysis. Drier design included desiccant selection, regeneration cycle analysis, tower sizing, valving and control selection and structural design.
- Component development projects included a shuttle valve, a line of blowdown silencers, a PC area measurement devise.
- Provided support to the Marketing Department for a line of hygrometers.

CORPORATE NUCLEAR ENGINEERING, Windsor, CT, 1996 – 1999
Senior Nuclear Plant Apparatus Engineer

- Wrote specifications, reviewed proposals and worked with vendors to ensure technical and schedule requirements were met in support of the technical aspects of procurement of Nuclear Class 3 and ASME Section VIII pressure vessels, heat exchangers and skid mounted chillers.
- Performed pressure and static seismic stress analyses. Designed systems to define requirements for piping, valves, pressure vessels, pumps, heat exchangers, and controls as a Nuclear Auxiliary Systems Engineer. Additional projects included a boron recovery system and heat exchanger transient analysis.
- Awarded a patent for temperature control scheme.

PRATT AND WHILEY AIRCRAFT, East Hartford, CT, 1994 – 1996
Mechanical Performance Analysis Engineer

- Performed comparative analyses of TF-30 turbofan engine test performance to check effect of performance improvement design changes. Reviewed plots of data for consistency based on engine thermal cycle analyses, and wrote memos to present results.
- Analyzed JT-9D turbofan engine stall problems based on 747 operational field data and flight test results. Parameters included response to the fuel control, aircraft speed and crosswind data.

DRESSER CLARK, Olean, NY, 1992 – 1994
Mechanical Design and Analysis Engineer

- Conducted performance analyses of centrifugal compressor tests. Supported marketing through application engineering of compressors. Performance analysis and aerodynamic design of centrifugal compressors, and performed hand heat transfer analysis of the intercoolers.
- Development work included writing test programs, analyzing results, refining designs and providing reduced data to Marketing.
- Performed development on a variable geometry diffuser which was designed to reduce power requirements during off design load conditions.

EDUCATION

University of Connecticut, West Hartford, CT
Masters in Business Administration, Marketing and Strategy, 1992

Cornell University, Ithaca, NY
Bachelor of Science, Mechanical Engineering, Analysis and Fluid Mechanics, 1990, Five year program

Licensed Professional Engineer, State of Connecticut

Hartford State Technical College, completed course in AUTOCAD

CORY SCHULMAN

12001 Event Planner Avenue
Gaithersburg, Maryland 20879

240-338-0050
eventplanner@gmail.com

OBJECTIVE

To provide leadership in logistical planning, communications, and event implementation as a Promotions Director or a related career opportunity.

HIGHLIGHTS

- Quality-conscious and cost-effective Events Planner with sterling reputation for satisfying such clients as Google, Marriott Corporation, Merrill Lynch, Morgan Stanley, the French Embassy, NBA Players' Association, PBS, and many others.

- Coordinated a broad range of events, including conferences, expos, concerts, product launches, holiday celebrations, and charity sponsorships on-time and within budget.

- Directed as many as 35 support personnel and coordinated space, catering, lodging, transportation, entertainment, audio/visual equipment, and related logistics.

- Gave dynamic presentations and negotiated contracts valued as high as $1 million.

- Prepared press releases and drafted proposals to secure additional funding from sponsors.

EXPERIENCE

MIAS CHANNEL COMMUNICATION, January 2013 – Present
Promotions Assistant (P/T) WXSH-FM 100.5, Rockville, Maryland
- Represent the #1 radio station in the Washington, DC market by coordinating up to 15 promotional events per month at the MCI Center, Wolf Trap, and other high-profile settings.
- Plan and implement logistics in support of expos, concerts, philanthropic sponsorships, sales/office events, and holiday celebrations in collaboration with the Promotions Director and team of assistants.
- Conduct site inspections and plan placement of audio visual equipment, lighting, tables, seating, catering, and related specifications.
- Assess budgetary requirements for promotional items, maintain inventory, and generate new promotional concepts.

FREELANCE EVENT PLANNING, June 2011 – December 2012
Events Planner, Washington, DC
- Establish clients through effective networking, marketing, and referrals. Achieved highly-successful events and satisfied clients through timely and on-budget execution.
- Present, negotiate, and close contracts to coordinate weddings, bar mitzvahs, luncheons, conferences, and retreats.
- Curtailed client expenses approximately 10% without compromising quality by conducting cost analyses and negotiating price reductions with vendors.

NORTH EASTERN EVENTS COMPANY, September 2005 – May 2011
Director of Operations, New York, New York
- Directed operations of high-profile events such as a celebration for a New York Mets athlete and product launch events for the Lanvin Company.
- Negotiated $200,000 contract and planned corporate event hosting 350+ celebrities, which entailed scheduling security and coordination of catering, staffing, menu preparation, and related logistics.

EDUCATION

Certificate in Event Management, 2005, George Washington University, Washington, DC
Bachelor of Arts in Business, 2004, American University, Washington, DC

CORY SCHULMAN
12002 Event Planning Lane
Germantown, Maryland 20874
240-338-0050
eventplanning@gmail.com

OBJECTIVE

To optimize attendance, publicity, and logistics management of special events as a quality conscious and cost-effective Events Planner.

HIGHLIGHTS

Event Management:
- Planned and coordinated logistics for various corporate, social, and philanthropic events, including product launches, retail sales promotions, award ceremonies, business luncheons, employee morale parties, celebrations, and fashion shows.
- Ensured seamless implementation of large-scale events, which included a city-sponsored marathon that attracted as many as 120,000 spectators and participants.
- Generated as much as $100,000 per retail promotional event.
- Skilled in researching site selections, space planning, creating thematic decorum, arranging guest appearances and musicians, and generating publicity. Contacted and secured celebrity guest speakers, MCs, and sponsors.

Media:
- Incorporated various print, telecommunications, radio, and Internet media for marketing, public relations, and fundraising campaigns.
- Prepared marketing collateral, including brochures and newsletters; used social media, direct mail, and telemarketing efforts to publicize upcoming events.
- Represented employer during a televised interview with local stations.
- Provided daily support in the production of cable TV content.

EXPERIENCE

AUTHOR C. PUBLISHING, Potomac, Maryland   2007 – Present

Marketing Manager, 2010 – Present
- Launched marketing campaigns to retain membership base of 120,000 subscribers for 2 alternative health publications circulated nationwide and internationally.
- Developed consumer tests and analyzed results to formulate effective strategic marketing plans and new programs.
- Coordinated special events, e-mail broadcasts, and mass mailings, resulting in as much as 16% rise in subscriber retention.
- Achieved 104% of corporate goals for gross annual revenues in FY 2014.
- Collaborate with group publishers to evaluate and improve existing renewal programs.
- Conducted extensive Internet research to facilitate development of marketing strategies.

Customer Service Manager/Group Manager/Team Leader, 2007 –2010

- Co-led Event Planning Committee for the Annual Customer Service Week, which entailed coordination of an event series that hosted key leaders and internal employees.
- Directed up to 22 customer service representatives for all 5 health newsletters, which supported a subscription base of 500,000.
- Increased annual sales as much as 30% by coaching and motivating sales representatives.

GLADINDALES, Kensington, Maryland   2004 – 2007

Assistant Cosmetics Buyer/Department Manager

- Procured merchandise from 30+ vendors based on analyses of inventory needs, market conditions, and seasonal trends.
- Traveled to headquarters in Manhattan, New York to participate in vendors' marketing launches, special events, and presentations.
- Worked with the Public Relations Department and vendors to set up training sessions and new product launches, which included logistics such as space planning, thematic displays, and guest appearances.
- Interviewed, hired, trained, and motivated as many as 50 sales associates while managing departmental operations.
- Planned and coordinated fashion shows in collaboration with team of department managers to introduce and promote seasonal merchandise.

ITS COMMUNICATIONS AGENCY, Pittsburgh, Pennsylvania   2002 – 2004

Public Relations Consultant

- Provided consulting services on informational research and event planning for the agency.
- Doubled the number of events from 5 to 10 within first year.
- Wrote press releases for commercial clients; coordinated celebrity guests; and placed print and radio advertising for events hosting as many as 500 attendees.

MONIS RESTAURANT & NIGHT CLUB, Pittsburgh, Pennsylvania   2001

Marketing and Promotions Manager

- Coordinated all club promotions and events such as Secretary's Day parties and St. Patrick's Day celebrations.
- Secured sponsorship of community events from local organizations and the media.

STATESIDE MARATHON, INC., Pittsburgh, Pennsylvania   2000

Special Events Coordinator
Co-Chaired Children's Marathon

- Assisted in scheduling and coordinating 8 events, including races, award ceremonies, pep rallies, and night parties for the Stateside Marathon Event, which attracted 20,000 participants and 100,000 spectators.
- Collaborated with local television stations by giving a live interview on special events and by coordinating local guest celebrity appearances.

EDUCATION

Duquesne University Pittsburgh
B.A. in Journalism, Concentration in Public Relations, Minor in Sociology, 2000

CORY SCHULMAN

12003 Events Planner Avenue
Silver Spring, MD 20910

Cell: 240-338-0050
eventsplanner@gmail.com

OBJECTIVE

To maximize logistical coordination, communication, and problem resolution as a Project Manager or Events Planner.

HIGHLIGHTS

- Highly organized Events Manager with extensive experience coordinating corporate meetings, seminars, festivals, and multi-million dollar annual conferences for AARP.
- Manage several projects concurrently, including vendor analyses, printing, 300,000-piece mass mailings, space reservations, audio-visual/telecommunications, and related logistics.
- Adept at using APOLLO and SABRE systems for domestic and international travel.

EXPERIENCE

AARP, Washington, DC   July 2006 – Present
Specialist Events Manager, 2010 – Present

Project/Events Management:
- Coordinate logistics for promotional events, including a $5 million annual conference.
- Determined layout of events held in a convention center spanning 250,000 square feet and hosting 20,000 attendees.
- Gather promotional information from 15 sponsors and coordinate marketing collateral, including 4-color brochures and packets.
- Organize 300,000-piece mass mailings to past event attendees and current registrants.
- Cut costs of printing and mass mailings, resulting in a $180,000 savings per annum.

Management:
- Manage staff to effectively solicit advertising and booth space, which resulted in increased revenues.
- Participate on a panel that interviews prospective candidates.
- Interface with personnel from purchasing, legal, creative services, warehousing, and related departments.

Writing:
- Write RFPs, review proposals, and conduct cost analyses to determine vendors.
- Compose letters of agreement in accordance with association standards and budget.
- Revamped a 200-page events manual used by department directors and general contractors.

Meeting Planner, 2008 – 2010
- Coordinated events such as retreats, luncheons, boiler room meetings, seminars, and internal festivities held at hotels throughout the Washington Metropolitan region.
- Conducted cost analyses for internal meetings, and audited invoices.

In-house Travel Agent, 2006 – 2008
- Booked domestic and international business travel in support of 1,000 AARP professionals.
- Used APOLLO and SABRE computer systems to reserve hotels and transportation.

EDUCATION

Facilitative Training and Business Writing, AARP Learning Center, Washington, DC
Certificate of International and Domestic Travel, International Travel Institute, Washington, DC

CORY SCHULMAN

3005 CFO Drive
North Potomac, Maryland 20878

Work: 240-338-0050
Home: 240-338-0050
E-mail: cfo@yahoo.com

HIGHLIGHTS

- Corporate Executive with expertise in corporate financing, investment banking, financial planning, and business development. Revitalized troubled corporations through business acumen and innovative financial management.
- Coordinated more than $100 million in corporate financing.
- Appointed to the U.S. Small Business Administration's Washington, DC Advisory Council.

EXPERIENCE

Chief Operating Officer, Citi Group Companies, Rockville, Maryland   2013 – Present

- Manage an 8-figure investment portfolio consisting of 120 active clients.
- Led a three-fold increase in company revenues for the corporate finance division, which provided corporate and personal financial planning services to the small to middle market.
- Achieved nearly 100% success in securing corporate financing for clients as a result of due diligence and settling more than $100 million in corporate financing.
- Negotiated 30% discount on a $900,000 corporate loan held by FDIC, which had seized the client's bank. Prevented certain bankruptcy of a supply house while also increasing the client's investment portfolio from $500,000 to $750,000. Eliminated a client's $100,000 credit card debt while improving his credit rating from C to A.
- Achieved rapid expansion of the client base, repeat business, and referral-driven growth by establishing relationships with key personnel across industries (software development, telecommunications, transportation, government contracting, law, and accounting).
- Prevented litigation and corporate/personal bankruptcy for numerous clients by executing successful liquidations, refinancings, and other financial management strategies.
- Originated more than $15 million per year in residential mortgages.
- Authored contents of the company's next generation web site, which commanded a domineering presence on the Internet.

Vice President, Universal Trust Bank (and affiliates), Chevy Chase, Maryland   2009 – 2013

- Prevented a myriad of seizures of financial institutions by raising capital through public offerings during the savings and loan crisis.
- Arranged financing for non-financial affiliates in high-tech security, restaurant, and government contracting as a defacto Chief Operating Officer.

Senior Commercial Banker, Wellington Bank, Germantown, Maryland   2002 – 2009

- Performed all phases of commercial banking, including business development, due diligence, negotiations, loan structuring, loan committee presentation, loan closing, and client servicing.

EDUCATION & LICENSURE

The George Washington University, School of Government and Business Administration
M.B.A., Finance and Investments, 2000; **B.B.A.**, Finance, 1998
Securities Licenses: Series 7, Series 63, Life and Health Insurance

CORY SCHULMAN
3006 CFO Drive
Harpers Ferry, West Virginia 25425

Home: 240-338-0050
Work: 240-338-0050
E-mail: cfo@gmail.com

OBJECTIVE

To strengthen resource management through effective accounting and economics, complex project coordination, and/or polished communications as an Economist.

SUMMARY

- Financial Management Executive in IT, biotech, and aerospace industries with experience in mergers, acquisitions, corporate re-engineering, employee ownership plans, and international project finance.
- Facilitated growth of Financial Broker Associates, Inc., an aerospace and engineering firm, from $88 million to $200 million in annual revenues as a result of economic analysis and cost accounting.
- Prevented bankruptcy of troubled corporation by playing a key role in a $55 million divestiture and successful restructuring of senior debt. Analyzed short/long term investment strategies.
- Established and fostered relationships with 250 shareholders during a corporate reorganization.
- Adept in cash management, complex project management and financing, pricing, credit and banking relationships, budgeting/forecasting, risk management, investor relations, tax/retirement planning, benefit plan and employee communications, equity plan administration, and all facets of government contracting.
- Managed as many as 16 accounting/finance, human resources, contracting, and MIS professionals, which entailed clear communications with executives, Board of Directors, investors, and staff.

EXPERIENCE

FBA, Inc. (Financial Broker Associates, Inc.), Rockville, Maryland   2006 – Present
Chief Financial Officer, 2011 – Present; **Director of Treasury Management**, 2006 – 2011

Financial Management:
- Devised and implemented strategic financial plans that facilitated a rise in gross annual revenues from $88 million to $200 million within 6 years.
- Coordinated the acquisition of four companies as the finance team leader which enhanced strategic entrances into key markets.
- Generated an infusion of $55 million, which eliminated the need for long term capital investments, as a key player on the divestiture team negotiating the sale of a satellite manufacturing subsidiary $7 million above goal and book value.
- Developed comprehensive cash management plans on a daily, weekly, and monthly basis.
- Negotiated and secured $45 million in senior and junior debt through investment banking firms.
- Cultivated relationships with 250 shareholders during dramatic downsizing from 1,400 to 190 employees.
- Enabled the capture of $25+ million in new business by obtaining Errors and Omissions insurance coverage, which was typically excluded from Y2K contractors.
- Participated in the selection process to replace the LAN to a nationwide WAN.

- Substantiated the company's image as an employee owned company and retained engineers by implementing equity plans, which supported as many as 1,400 employees.
- Revamped the 401K plan, which provided new fund options and increased returns above market trends.

International Experience:
- Provided project management and risk management expertise for bids in international markets, resulting in a $167 million award for an Indonesian broadcast and satellite TV system.
- Led the development of an international project finance proposal and gave polished in-person presentations to import/export banks, which resulted in securing preliminary approval for a Russian broadcast satellite system having a projected value of $110 million.
- Obtained Russian government commitments, which involved interaction with European and American financial institutions. Developed cost of project finance for delivery of satellites.

Cost Savings:
- Right-sized the human resources department from 30 to 5 employees while maintaining efficient production and performance.
- Saved the company approximately $1.2 million per annum with potential of administering benefits for thousands of employees by successfully instituting a paperless benefits administration system, an employee self-service concept via the Web.
- Restructured company's indirect expenses. Reduced fringe benefit costs 25% without employee attrition. Saved the company roughly $500,000 per annum as a result of reduction in lease obligations and improved space utilization.
- Researched and selected a new headquarters site, a 24,000 square foot facility. Managed a seamless relocation, which involved reviewing architectural design, negotiating a 7-year lease, moving 105 employees, and setting up an IT network without downtime.

ELECTRONIC NETWORK GROUP, Fairfax, Virginia   2000 – 2006

Manager, Group Financial Analysis and Planning
- Led financial analysis and planning for a billion dollar segment while serving as a CAS coordinator and liaison between the DCAS Baltimore and the DCAA.
- Earned the Chairman's Award for capital planning and financing for facility and equipment acquisitions. Devised a creative model for a $75 million asset purchase, which saved the company $10 million after taxes.
- Developed economic analysis and presented business recommendation for two acquisitions.
- Instrumental in designing and implementing a new engineering services labor-rate bid strategy that led to $500 million in new business.
- Drafted a brief on a disputed $300,000 idle facility cost resulting in a favorable government determination.
- Directed the Quality Assurance Team to monitor the labor reporting and timekeeping system.

SUPPLEMENT

Education: Certificate Government Contracts Management (ENG) University of Virginia
MBA, 2001, University of Cincinnati
BBA, 2000, Accounting, University of Cincinnati

Affiliations: Foundation for Enterprise Institute; National Association of Accountants

CORY SCHULMAN

3007 Finance Terrace
Rockville, Maryland 20850
240-338-0050
cfo@gmail.com

OBJECTIVE

To maximize corporate profitability, client satisfaction, and referrals in a Consultative Sales position within the financial services field.

HIGHLIGHTS

- *Licenses:* Series 7, 63, 65, and Life in the State of Maryland.
- Achiever award winner with expertise in Money Management, Insurance, Mutual Funds, Bonds, and Transfer of Assets.
- Closed approximately $330 million in aggregate sales of financial services since FY 2008.
- Emerged as one of the top sales performers among a 100-member peer group and periodically ranked #1 sales producer within the Bethesda Investor Center.

EXPERIENCE

STELLAR INVESTMENTS AND ASSOCIATES, Bethesda, Maryland   2009 – Present
Financial Representative

- Provide primary financial planning and consultation to affluent clientele concerning a broad array of financial services: money management, asset allocation, estate planning, portfolio construction, and life insurance.
- Increased annual sales volume of money management vehicles from $8 million to approximately
$12 million with aggregate sales reaching $27 million since FY 2011.
- Achieved 25% annual growth in mutual fund sales and generated aggregate sales of $130 million since FY 2010.
- Generated $20+ million in insurance sales production (fixed/deferred annuities; life insurance, and income streams/pensions).
- Secured new business consisting of client assets in excess of $160 million.
- Averaged $55,000 in annual concessions from bond sales.
- Perform in-depth needs analyses to ascertain investors' goals, risk tolerance, philosophy, and current investment status.
- Conducted seminars on money management and allocation techniques to professional associations, resulting in $4 million in new managed money and numerous referrals.

Mutual Fund Coordinator

- Research, evaluate, and articulate mutual funds; create performance hypotheticals; and track cutting-edge mutual fund performance and industry developments.
- Train and develop new Financial Representatives I's and II's in consultative sales techniques, client relations, and investment strategies.
- Appointed by the Branch Manager to assist in the hiring process by conducting interviews.

SUNCOAST BANK, Tysons Corner, Virginia   2008 – 2009
Financial Consultant

- Advised individual and corporate clients in stocks, funds, managed money, and other investment vehicles at five branches.
- Grew assets under management from $40 million to $60 million within first year by revamping training of mortgage consultants, tellers, and other staff members.
- Established a book of 125 clients totaling $18 million in assets under management.
- Ranked within the top quarter for revenue production among a 350-member rookie class.

EDUCATION

B.A. Criminology, Minor: Health, 2008, University of Maryland, College Park, Maryland

CORY SCHULMAN

3008 Finance Drive
Bethesda, Maryland 20817

240-338-0050
finance@gmail.com

EXPERIENCE

FRUGAL INVESTMENTS GROUP, Washington, DC   7/2009 – Present

Insurance Specialist, Washington, DC, 2014 – Present
- Advise high net-worth clients on income, retirement, and life insurance planning as a distribution link between the Investor Center and Frugal Investments.
- Promote sales of various insurance products such as deferred/immediate annuities and term/permanent life insurance. Expanded the client base by conducting financial seminars.
- Facilitated a dramatic rise in gross annual revenues from $17 million in FY 2013 to $26 million in FY 2015 and projected revenue of $36 million in FY 2018.
- Direct all 6 brokers who manage high net-worth clients with a portfolio valued in excess of $2.4 billion.
- Provide broker training, resulting in increased insurance sales of approximately 32%.
- Expanded branch territory and market presence from the local Washington, DC area to include Richmond and Alexandria, Virginia.

Financial Advisor, Bethesda, Maryland; Dallas, Texas
- Provided financial advice to high net-worth clients in support of a book of business in excess of $750 million.
- Conducted needs assessment and risk analysis for estate and retirement income planning.
- Maximized return-on-investments in accordance with financial plans, goals, and philosophies of individual and corporate accounts.
- Collaborated with CPAs, attorneys, third-party administrators, and other trusted advisors to ensure integrated financial plans.
- Executed timely and error-free trades for stocks, mutual funds, and bonds, which facilitated a rise in new business valued approximately $250 million.
- Exceeded FY 2012 corporate goals approximately 40% for managed accounts; 66% for fixed income sales concessions; 37% for mutual funds; and 28% for insurance sales in FY 2013.
- Increased the asset base more than $100 million as a result of polished consultation on portfolio construction, wealth replacement strategies, and trust planning.
- Earned an achievement award for sales excellence and #3 ranking among 106 peer representatives throughout the Mid-Atlantic region.

GLOBAL INVESTMENTS NETWORK, Norwell, Massachusetts   2/2006 – 7/2009

Japan Fund Specialist/Scudder Investor Relations
- Served as a Southeast Asia fund Specialist for the Massachusetts and California offices consisting of 130 employees. Provided specialized service to Japan fund shareholders and institutional clients.
- Kept shareholders and Scudder Investments' employees abreast of Southeast Asia's economic and political outlook and related trends. Gained knowledge of Pacific Rim affairs by attending conferences sponsored by the Harvard Asia Business Association.
- Drafted summary reports through consultations with portfolio managers, research teams, and independent data collection.

SUPPLEMENT

NASD Licenses: **Series 6, 7, 63, 66**; *Insurance Licenses:* **MD, DC, PA, VA**

Education: Plymouth State College, Plymouth, New Hampshire
             B.S., 2005, Economics, Business Management, and Political Science

Military: U.S. Marine Corps, 1999 – 2001

Cory Schulman

1000 Firefighter Way
Germantown, MD 20874
240-338-0050
Firefighter@gmail.com

EXPERIENCE

NATIONAL MEDICAL CENTER, Germantown, Maryland
Firefighter/Driver Operator, 2010 – Present

- Served as an Acting Firefighter Crew Chief for the Germantown Fire Department three to five times per month during the Captain's leave or absence.
- Led up to six firefighters in response to Class A, B, C, and D fires, train derailments, plane accidents, auto accidents, emergency medical situations, and other rescue calls in the Bethesda and surrounding Montgomery County area.
- Responded to 814 calls last year, many of which required use of water, foam, and ABC powder to extinguish various types of fires such as ordinary combustible, flammable liquids, energized electrical, and combustible metals.
- Directed crew members to prepare and use various apparatus including ambulances, brush trucks, rescue pumpers, pumper trucks ranging from 500 gallons per minute to 1,250 gallons per minute, ladder trucks, and twin agent units.
- Provided emergency medical assistance to persons in life threatening situations including extrications from vehicles, elevators, and other entrapments. Applied CPR and other medical procedures to resuscitate persons suffering from smoke inhalation, heart attacks, and other states of unconsciousness as a Certified EMT in the state of Maryland,
- Dealt directly with the public when controlling crowds and when obtaining vital information about the nature of the incident.
- Established a command post if first on the scene for major incidences.

WASHINGTON FIRE STATION, NW, Washington, DC
Firefighter/Driver Operator, 2006 – 2010

- Responded to emergency calls to protect life and property by extinguishing fires using chemicals, foams, axes, bars, hooks, and other firefighting equipment.
- Served as hoseman, nozzleman, ladderman, hydrantman, rescueman, salvageman, and hand lineman.
- Evacuated and extricated occupants of vehicles and facilities. Stabilized victims, stopped external bleeding, took vital signs, and recorded data. Assisted persons in overcoming smoke inhalation, shock, and other serious conditions. Administered emergency medical intervention to resuscitate individuals who were unconscious or in need of treatment.
- Conveyed critical information to local paramedics enroute to the scene through radio contact.

- Drove various firefighting vehicles and operated an array of component equipment such as two-way radios, pumps, valves, ladders, etc.
- Applied knowledge of local, Army, OSHA, and National Fire Protection Codes and regulations, as well as, fire protection and prevention theory, techniques, and practices.
- Trained firefighters in driving and operating vehicles/equipment; unreeling and connecting hoses, laying hose lines, operating charged lines, placing and raising ladders, operating portable or stationary firefighting apparatus; using breathing apparatus/protective clothing; and ventilating buildings. Covered subjects such as the theory and chemistry of fire, fire flow hydraulics, and medical first aid.

ROCKVILLE STATION FIRE DEPARTMENT, Rockville, Maryland
Firefighter/Driver Operator, 2001 – 2006

- Provided responsive firefighting protection against all classes of fires, including emergency conditions involving radioactive materials and hazardous chemicals.
- Performed routine functions on the scene such as unreeling and connecting fire hoses, laying hose lines, operating charged hose lines, assisting in directing foam, carbon dioxide, dry chemical, and water streams, setting-up and assisting in operating portable and stationary heavy stream appliances, foam generators, electric generators, etc.
- Operated 750 and 1,000 GPM pumpers to emergency scenes, taking into account fastest and safest routes as well as the source of water. Determined proper pressure based on the distance necessary for effective pumping and the number of lines used.

OTHER QUALIFICATIONS

Job Related Training:
- Montgomery County: Firefigher I, Firefigher II, Firefighter III, Incident Command, Hazardous Materials, Wildland Firefighting, EEO & The Law, Blood Born Pathogens, Flashover Class/Flashover Simulator

- MFRI-MD Fire/Rescue Institute: Confined Space Rescue Training, Basic Fire Fighting, Fire Inspector Course, Air Craft Fire/Rescue, Hazardous Materials (Technician), Weapons of Mass Destruction (WMD), Firefighter IV - Crash Rescue, Wildland Firefighting

Affiliations:
Member; Seneca Valley Park Volunteer Fire Department
Associate Member; Leadership Fire Association of Rockville, Maryland

Awards:
Achievement Medal for Civilian Service, August 2015

Education:
Gaithersburg Senior High School, Diploma, June 2000, Gaithersburg, Maryland

CORY SCHULMAN

16003 Food & Beverage Terrace
Gaithersburg, MD 20878
240-338-0050
beverage@gmail.com

HIGHLIGHTS

- Managed award-winning food and beverage operations with special talent in growing membership, enhancing customer satisfaction, improving training techniques, and increasing gross annual profits.

- Experienced in planning and directing catering operations for such prestigious events as the Pebble Beach AT&T Golf Tournament, the Concours de Elegance Auto Show, and Kemper Open for as many as 5,000 attendees.

- Directed award dinners for internationally acclaimed dignitaries, including former British Prime Minister Tony Blair and former Presidents George W. Bush and Bill Clinton.

- Hired, trained, and supervised up to 245 professionals. Developed policies, procedures, and budgets. Skilled in cost control, inventory audits, decor/theme design, and purchasing.

EXPERIENCE

PGA TOUR, INC., Tournament Players Club at Avenel, Potomac, Maryland
Director of Food and Beverage, 2008 – Present
- Oversee restaurant operations, 55 member staff, and catering services.
- Increased gross annual revenues from $1.6 million to $2 million within first year.
- Instituted new internal controls that upgraded the food quality, presentation, and staff professionalism in a restaurant that serves 350 guests per day.
- Directed food and beverage operations in support of 1,900 guests per day at the Kemper Open, which included 4 sky boxes, the CBS sports tent, the media tent, 144 PGA players, and dining rooms.
- Designed and created a "prepared foods" menu, which increased food sales and accommodated a dramatic increase of patrons.

THE PEBBLE INN BAY, Pebble Beach, California, *[5 Star, 5 Diamond]*
Food and Beverage Manager, 2004 – 2008
- Promoted in 2004 from Banquet Manager to direct a $12 million food and beverage operation, which was voted the number one mainland resort by *Conde Nast Magazine* for 2004 and 2005.
- Supervised 15 managers and 230 support personnel for the room service, banquet, and beverage departments; three dining rooms; and three lounges.

- Managed operations for 16 corporate chalets at the Pebble Beach AT&T Pro-Am Golf Tournaments 2004, 2005, 2006, and 2007.
- Closed and re-opened the dining room in a joint venture with world renowned chef, Roy Yamiguchi of Hawaii. Increased gross annual revenues of food and beverage from $1.8 million to $4.5 million within the first year.

THE RESIDENTIAL RESORT, Scottsdale, Arizona
Banquet Manager, 2003 – 2004
- Managed all catered and food/beverage operations, which generated approximately $8 million per year. Oversaw staff of more than 80 support personnel.
- Planned and directed Chaine de Rotisseur, bar/bat mitzvahs, political fundraisers, and award dinners for Fortune 500 companies.
- Directed a 7 course dinner for 800 guests in honor of former British Prime Minister Tony Blair.
- Planned and implemented 16 food stations and 20 bars for the Barrett-Jackson Auto Auction, which attracted 5,000 attendees.

THE WALTON HOTEL, Scottsdale, Arizona, *[4 Star, 4 Diamond]*
Banquet Manager/Convention Services Coordinator, 2000 – 2003
- Supervised an 80 member banquet staff.
- Planned and directed a dinner for former Presidents George W. Bush and Bill Clinton.

THE WALTON ALBUQUERQUE - CONVENTION CENTER, Albuquerque, New Mexico
Assistant Food and Beverage Director, 1998 – 2000
- Facilitated the opening of a 400 room hotel and opened a 200 seat restaurant.
- Hired, trained, and supervised staff and assisted in managing five departments: banquets, two lounges, room service, dining room, and beverage department.

THE HENSLEY RESORT AND CLUB, Carefree, Arizona, *[4 Star, 5 Diamond]*
Clubhouse Manager, 1995 – 1998
- Managed a renovation project of a 4 star, 5 diamond club, consisting of 300 members.
- Participated in architectural meetings and helped design kitchen/dining room space, furnishings, wall fixtures, and interior design.
- Supervised a 200 seat restaurant, fitness center, and lounge.
- Processed memberships of affluent clientele, which entailed orienting and acclimating new members to the club.

EDUCATION

B.A. in Business Management, 2000, University of Maryland, Adelphi, Maryland

CORY SCHULMAN

15002 Helpdesk Court
Mt. Airy, Maryland 21771
240-338-0050
helpdesk@gmail.com

OBJECTIVE

To maximize uptime, data integrity, system performance, and user satisfaction as a Help Desk Specialist or a related IT career opportunity.

HIGHLIGHTS

Help Desk Applications: Remedy, Brimir, Cherwell, Request Tracker, InfoSys, Solve, Peregrine

Operating Systems: Windows, Citrix, Linux, Novell, Unix, Android

Hardware: Configured, installed, and maintained mainframes, servers, workstations, tape drives, and peripherals.

Software: Microsoft Office, Visual Studio.NET, Python Software, IBM SPSS, Adobe Acrobat

EXPERIENCE

COMPUTER TECHNOLOGIES, INC., Rockville, Maryland   2008 – Present

Computer Operator, 1st Shift Supervisor of Data Center

- Provide technical leadership and oversight in support of government contracts having a combined value of $16 million with the U.S. Department of Education (ED) and the U.S. Department of Housing and Urban Development (HUD).
- Ensure uptime and proper functioning of 2 LANs running on SYR 2 and Windows consisting of 5 mainframes, 20+ servers, and 35 nodes throughout 3 facilities.
- Oversee technical personnel: Lead Supervisor of the Production Center and the Senior Monitor.
- Decreased downtime approximately 50% by effectively identifying and rectifying technical issues concerning glitches, conflicts, viruses, incompatibility, defective components, and memory limitations.
- Improved response time for technical support roughly 60%.
- Updated procedural manual for operating systems and help desk operations, which addressed IPO systems, help desk responses, HUD and ED practices, application procedures, and forms.
- Collaborated with Computer Lead to establish the company's first help desk providing technical support to 50+ internal and external users in local and national facilities.
- Supervised 5 co-workers to successfully relocate 50,000 MVS tapes and 5 mainframes from Rockville, Maryland to Pittsburgh, Pennsylvania within 72 hours.
- Created inventory spreadsheets in support of the disaster recovery program.
- Reformatted 50+ procedures and 100+ forms into ISO 9000 templates.

SUPPLEMENT

Clearance: Held a **Secret Security Clearance** (Currently expired).
Military: **Supply Technician**, U.S. Army, Fort Belvoir, Virginia, 2002
Education: Computer Science, Affiliated Computer Services, 2003 – 2004
      General Education, Montgomery College, Rockville, Maryland, 2005 – 2007

CORY SCHULMAN

16001 Hotel Management Court
Rockville, Maryland 20852
240-338-0050
hotel@gmail.com

OBJECTIVE

To maximize patron satisfaction, occupancy, and corporate profitability as a manager within the hospitality industry.

EXPERIENCE

HENSON CORP, Jacksonville, Florida, February 2007 – Present
Director of Operations, Residence Inn

- Oversaw an extended-stay hotel consisting of 100 suites, which entailed supervision of 22 employees in the guest services, front desk, and housekeeping departments.
- Maintained 100% occupancy by upgrading guest services.
- Analyzed profit and loss statements and curtailed budgetary expenses 60%.
- Cut overtime 50% while increasing employee productivity. Reduced the time taken to clean the rooms from 50 minutes to 30 minutes (40% reduction) by training employees in time management skills.
- Improved guest services department by upgrading employees' professionalism, dress code, and guest relations skills.
- Assist General Manager in devising and conveying strategic sales plans, using MARSHA inventory control, KRS reports, and other forecasting tools. Familiar with the Marriott benefits, and use of the MARTIE system.
- Rally and motivate staff by successfully implementing incentive programs and holding regular reward and recognition meetings.
- Certified in food handling within 60 days of assignment by an approved state of Florida trainer.

HAYWARD INN, Baymeadows, Jacksonville, Florida, November 2005 – February 2007
Quality Assurance Manager

- Reported directly to the General Manager, ensuring highest quality performance of all departments of this 250-room, full-service hotel consisting of 150 employees.
- Managed all departments and oversaw quality control of an on-site sports bar.

THE LITTLE INN, Beaver Falls, Pennsylvania, April 2004 – August 2005
General Manager

- Managed daily operations of this 70-room motor lodge and the adjoining restaurant and lounge, including recruiting, hiring, and training of approximately 30 employees.
- Handled ordering, purchasing, vendor price negotiations, shrinkage, and inventory control as well as strict budget management.
- Performed extensive sales marketing activities including networking among private coach companies, golfing, and sport organizations, plus active solicitation of local corporations for banquet catering events.

EDUCATION

A.A. Degree Program, Hotel/Motel Management, 2003, Community College of Allegheny

CORY SCHULMAN
16002 Hotel Management Circle
Urbana, Maryland 21704
240-338-0050
hotelmanagement@gmail.com

OBJECTIVE

To maximize guest satisfaction, employee productivity, and operational efficiency in a managerial position or a related career opportunity.

HIGHLIGHTS

Management Experience:
- Sixteen years' experience developing, supervising, and motivating housekeeping staffs. Allocated daily assignments to supervisors and crew members. Inspected crew performances in high-end dormitory rooms, conference rooms, and public areas.
- Trained personnel in preparatory procedures, cleaning techniques, and quality control, which improved guest satisfaction from 60% to 98%, based on the guest survey response indexes.
- Achieved 100% room quality scores from corporate Walton inspections in 2009 and 2010; and 100% for public areas in 2013 at the Executive Inn.
- Earned Director-of-the-Year, 2011 and Employee-of-the-Quarter, 1997. Received several letters of commendation from the General Manager.
- Increased productivity of a 30-member crew approximately 20% within 3 months.

Bilingual Skills:
- Applied fluency in English and Spanish as a translator for all departments at the Walton Hotel, Potomac Corporation, and Guest Quarters Suite Hotel.

EXPERIENCE

THE EXECUTIVE INN, Gaithersburg, Maryland   7/2010 – Present
Director of Housekeeping
- Direct the Housekeeping Department consisting of 16 – 20 employees and manage human resource functions for 36 employees.
- Revitalized guest services, employee productivity, and overall hotel appearance, evidenced by increased inspection scores from a failing grade below 60% to a passing grade of 85% for rooms and 100% for public areas.
- Reduced rampant 60% employee turnover and extended average employee longevity from 3 months to more than 7 months.
- Eliminated excessive chemical redundancies, waste, and cost by consolidating cleaning agent purchasing and monitoring usage.
- Increased guest satisfaction from 60% to 98% within 4 months based on guest comment card surveys.

- Prepared annual performance evaluations for 18 employees; ensured accurate and timely completion of W2, personal action, INS, and insurance forms and related employment documentation. Prescreened employees for housekeeping and front desk positions.

WALTON HOTEL, Gaithersburg, Maryland   11/1998 – 7/2010
Executive Housekeeper
- Managed the Housekeeping Department to maintain 301 rooms and public areas, which included floor and carpet care.
- Increased efficiency 50% and improved the quality of maintenance while understaffed.
- Instituted retraining program resulting in greater productivity and quality control.
- Hired, trained, and directed a 35-member housekeeping crew, including assistant management and supervisors.
- Reduced employee turnover from 58%, the highest among all departments, to 10%.
- Achieved immaculate results within stringent time constraints while ensuring compliance with accident/loss prevention SOPs and health/sanitation standards.
- Reduced costs approximately 25% by conducting cost analyses among vendors and negotiating lower purchasing contracts without compromising on adequate coverage and supply shortages.
- Prepared payroll, disciplinary actions, evaluations, and incident reports.
- Coordinated an overhaul of the decorum in all 301 rooms in support of a hotel-wide renovation.

POTOMAC CORPORATION, Potomac, Maryland   4/1996 – 11/1998
Housekeeping Supervisor/Assistant Manager
- Directed the Housekeeping Department and supervised a 30-member housekeeping crew during the absence of the manager.
- Prepared inspection and disciplinary action reports.
- Reduced inventory expenses by strengthening accurate documentation and reorganizing the supply room, which eliminated purchase overages.
- Conducted cost and quality analyses as well as negotiated cost reductions with vendors when ordering supplies.

EDUCATION

- **Degree in Business Management**, 1995, Inteco College, El Salvador
- CPR Certification, Hilton, Washington, DC/North Gaithersburg, 2002
- Management Training, Xerox Corporation, 1997
- Management Training Seminars at Guest Quarters: Time Management, Progressive Discipline, Interviewing, Problem Solving, Stress Management, and Performance Appraisals, 1997

CORY SCHULMAN

16008 Hotel Avenue, Revere, MA 02151   240-338-0050   hotel@gmail.com

OBJECTIVE

To maximize corporate profits, operational efficiency, and guest satisfaction as an experienced and accomplished General Manager in the hospitality field.

HIGHLIGHTS

Increased occupancy, REVPAR, and guest satisfaction throughout 15-year managerial background in various hotel environments, ranging from 2 to 5-Star hotels, including resorts, city-center, and suburban hotels. Supervised as many as 275 employees; improved occupancy and revenues up to 20%.

EXPERIENCE

WALTON HOTEL CORPORATION, 2007 – Present
General Manager, Embassy Suites, Palm Beach Gardens, FL
- Spearheaded dramatic increases in market share, guest satisfaction, and revenues as the recipient of the 2015 Walton Hotel-of-the-Year Award.
- Achieved 185% market share, the highest market penetration percentage in the hotel's history.
- Earned the Blue Chip Award for exceeding financial goals for 5 consecutive quarters.
- Improved hotel's ranking for guest satisfaction from the top 50th to the top 25th percentile out of 138 Embassy Suites.
- Optimized revenues from both leisure and corporate segments by anticipating and reacting to market fluctuations and overflow demand from conventions.
- Promoted from the Ramsey Hotel to the Embassy Suites.

Assistant General Manager, Hensley Hotel City Centre, Indianapolis, IN
- Implemented Remington policies and processes to transition the 800-room Sheraton World Resort, Orlando, FL into a Remington Hotel as a Senior Manager of a 16-member task force.
- Managed a 200-room Holiday Inn in Brooklyn Center, MN as an Interim General Manager.

THE FLAGANS COMPANY, Acquired by Winston Hotels 2005 – 2007
Director of Operations, River Bend Hotel, Braintree, MA, Lake Bend Hotel, Stamford, CT
- Revamped 80% of the managerial staff, strengthened management controls, improved guest satisfaction, and increased REVPAR. Fostered productive relationships with the union representative.
- Increased the number of rooms within the Lake Bend Stamford Hotel (Acquired by Flagans) from 360 to 480 by converting 100+ office suites into guestrooms.

ADDITIONAL EXPERIENCE, 2001 – 2005
- Promoted four times culminating to General Manager of Vive la Viva Hotels, 2003 – 2005.
- Promoted to Night Audit Supervisor of the 5-Star, 5-Diamond Coco Loman Hotel, 2002 – 2003.
- Promoted from Night Auditor to Relief Night Manager of a 5-Star, 5-Diamond, 330-room hotel, The Winston Court Hotel, 2001 – 2002.

EDUCATION

- **Bachelor of Science Degree**, 2000, Finance, Northeastern University, Boston, MA

CORY SCHULMAN

13001 Recruiting Street
Maplewood, MN 55117

(H) 240-338-0050
(W) 240-338-0050
recruiting@gmail.com

HIGHLIGHTS

- Revitalized organizational design, systemic processes, and strategic plans for major corporations as a Senior Staffing Specialist.
- Recruited, trained, and managed 400+ employees. Developed and conducted workshops, clinics, and lectures. Produced a videotape for recruitment.
- Possess expertise in human resources management, staffing and recruitment, employment law and labor relations, diversity education training, employee benefits, and compensation.
- Possess extensive knowledge and ensure compliance with state and federal regulations, especially EEO, FLSA, FMLA, Section 125, COBRA, and ADA.
- Traveled 30,000 miles per year to establish and/or strengthen ties with clients as a Senior Staffing Specialist for the largest Section 125 and COBRA administrator in the country.
- Gave dynamic presentations to small businesses through Fortune 500 companies, associations, hospitals, universities, and public schools.

EXPERIENCE

ACE STAFFING CORPORATION, Shoreview, MN
Senior Staffing Specialist   2007 – Present

- Saved the company roughly $750,000 per annum by re-engineering the infrastructure of the human resource division of a $1.3 billion corporation.
- Facilitated downsizing through change management and transition planning. Overhauled the employee handbook, which was the first revision since 2000.
- Streamlined all staffing processes to a web-based system. Reduced average time to fill vacant exempt and non-exempt positions from 180 days to 87 days.
- Collaborated with computer programmers to convert a human resource database from an obsolete system to a faster, cutting-edge program in Microsoft Access.
- Direct recruiting and staffing initiatives for a 9,000 employee business unit. Develop and implement policies and administrate programs pertaining to recruitment, organizational design/development, performance management, job analysis/evaluation, documentation, compensation and benefits, staff training, and labor/employee relations. Established vendor relationships and negotiated contracts for applicant tracking system background investigations, drug testing, search firms, and temporary agencies.
- Develop and implement coaching workshops for managers, and provide training to associates in dispute resolution, diversity, and corporate culture.
- Reduced attrition among employees by mediating conflicts and strengthening team collaboration and company unity. Decreased employee disputes approximately 60% by setting up a payroll discrepancy system that streamlined resolutions.
- Developed talent sourcing strategies that built a diverse employee base. Established minority internship program and employee referral program.

EDUCATION

Bachelor of Science Degree, May 2007, Southern Connecticut State University, New Haven, CT
Received Human Relations Award, August 2008, Dale Carnegie Sales Course

CORY SCHULMAN, SPHR
13002 Human Resources Way
Rockville, MD 20852-5409

Work: 240-338-0050
Cell: 240-338-0050
humanresources@gmail.com

HIGHLIGHTS

- SPHR Certified with an M.S. in Human Resources Management and 16 years' experience managing human resource functions during periods of corporate expansion, downsizing, and reorganization.
- Enhanced productivity and cost effectiveness throughout tenure by developing new policies, procedures, and systems impacting as many as 7,000 employees.
- Possess knowledge of FMLA, ADA, ERISA, COBRA, EEO and related laws and regulations.
- Improved compensation competitiveness, benefits administration, recruitment/hiring practices, employee relations, professional development, and Web functions for large-scale employers.

EXPERIENCE

PHARM LABORATORIES, INC., Rockville, Maryland   2011 – Present
Senior Manager Human Resources (Promoted from HR Manager)
- Manage staff and report directly to the CEO of this global pharmaceutical research company.
- Oversee human resources functions: policy development, recruitment initiatives, employee development, performance appraisals, salary surveys, and benefits administration for a 125 employee division.
- Participate in a 10-member Global Human Resources Team to co-develop policies for implementation throughout 14 sites worldwide impacting 1,800 employees.
- Conducted focus groups and reported on key points to the Global Vice President of Human Resources regarding performance management, intranet rollout, and corporate code of ethics.
- Developed salary structures and pay grades based on outside pay surveys.
- Harmonized U.S. benefits among five sites that had divergent packages.
- Planned and devised a supervisory boot camp involving six modules to enhance leadership and team building skills. Coordinated mid-year retreats for executive managers.
- Represented and defended the company during legal investigation as a point-of-contact with outside legal counsel. Gave and coordinated witness testimony, and formulated a written response to EEOC resulting in a dismissal of the case.

COMPUTER ELEMENTS, INC. (CE), Bethesda, Maryland   2005 – 2011
Human Resources Director, 2008 – 2011
- Managed the Technical Recruiter, HR Representatives, HRIS Specialist, and HR Assistant.
- Facilitated organizational restructuring in addition to duties of Manager, Corporate Benefits.
- Re-engineered workflow to maintain high-level quality service during a dramatic reduction of operational staff from 900 to 650 employees.
- Reduced operating expenses by transitioning from contracted headhunters to in-house recruiting.
- Instituted a tracking mechanism designed to curtail internal theft of costly high-tech equipment.
- Devised and implemented new policies, procedures, and internal controls, including 90-day performance reviews, E-mail/Internet usage protocols, orientations, and exit surveys.
- Examined incentives, benefits, salary structures, turnover, labor requirements, and review practices to identify potential for improvements in quality and cost effectiveness.
- Provided counsel and guidance on Employee Relations issues maintaining an appropriate balance between organization and employee interests.
- Assisted in the development and implementation of Affirmative Action Plans.

Manager, Corporate Benefits, 2006 – 2008
- Administered health and welfare plans for employees at multi-state locations, including enrollment and claim resolution/assistance. Applied knowledge of FMLA, ADA, ERISA, and COBRA laws.
- Researched and analyzed issues effecting employees' satisfaction of CE's benefit plans, and compare trends with external organizations. Ascertained salary trends based on comparative analyses of competitors within the IT industry.
- Attracted and retained employees in part by expanding employee benefits to include retirement, health, and medical benefits; life and disability insurance; flex accounts; EAP; and work-life benefit initiatives.
- Conducted orientations in California and New York for employees during two acquisitions.
- Facilitated corporate down-sizing by removing 400 employees from payroll and benefits.
- Designed and implemented Web-based interactive channel for human resources functions.
- Overhauled the content and layout of a benefits and policy manual, distributed to 900 employees and new hires, entailing the coordination of the editor, graphic artist, and printer.
- Earned 1999 Business Operations Team Award for Performance Excellence.

Local Personnel Representative, 2005 – 2006
- Delivered and managed human resource services for 400 employees in the Mid-Atlantic and Northeast U.S. regions. Recognized as a subject matter expert on policy interpretation and advisor to both employees and various levels of management.
- Assisted in recruiting by participating in job fairs, placing employment ads, posting job requisitions, screening applicants, tracking resumes, and ensuring compliance with EEO/AAP and FLSA guidelines.

ALAWA AMERICA PHARMACEUTICAL, INC., Rockville, Maryland   2003 – 2005
Human Resource Assistant
- Performed duties related to monitoring confidential records of employment.
- Tracked all new hires and separations, which included new hire orientations and exit interviews.
- Assisted employees with processing all personnel and payroll action forms.
- Researched and solved employee issues relating to benefits and compensation.

BENSON INSURANCE COMPANY, Washington, DC   2003
Human Resource Generalist
- Organized in-house insurance courses for 3,000 corporate employees. Circulated information on courses, managed registration process, ordered and distributed text books, secured instructors, and obtained classroom space.
- Analyzed grades and pass/fail ratios for entire company (7,500 employees) to determine reimbursements and bonuses.
- Conducted various surveys on child care needs and the effectiveness of the performance appraisal.

EDUCATION

Currently pursuing M.B.A., University of Maryland University College
M.S. in Human Resources Management, August 2002, University of Maryland University College
B.A. in Sociology, May 2000, Industrial and Organizational Studies, University of Maryland

CORY SCHULMAN

13003 Human Resources Terrace
Germantown, Maryland 20876
240-338-0050
humanresources@gmail.com

EXPERIENCE

HENLEY'S COMPANY, Bowie, Frederick, Bethesda, Maryland   2003 – Present

Human Resources Manager
- Manage hiring processes, benefits administration, and ongoing personnel matters for a $31 million store in Bowie, Maryland.
- Expanded the employee base from 225 to 275 in 8 months to address an unexpected 130% rise in business. Networked with government agencies and reputable businesses to cultivate referrals for competent new hires.
- Cut turnover of full-time employees from 33% to 8% and part-time employees from 57% to 18%.
- Reduced position vacancies from 3% to 1%, a level far below the chain's 2.6% rate average.
- Trimmed unnecessary overtime approximately 30%, saving the company about $150,000 per year.
- Defended the company at unemployment hearings by providing credible, complete, and accurate testimony that justified employee terminations.
- Eliminated rampant errors in benefits administration and 90-day performance evaluation preparations.
- Administrate worker's compensation and unemployment claims. Strengthened safety enforcement which facilitated a dramatic reduction in worker's compensation claims.
- Curtailed financial discrepancies in payroll by effectively reviewing daily deviation reports.
- Mediated employee grievances regarding interpersonal conflicts, compensation issues, and work conditions.
- Developed and conducted a comprehensive customer service training class, which is currently under consideration for corporate rollout.
- Increased customer satisfaction scores based on responses to customer survey cards.
- Reduced employee turnover in the Frederick store roughly 50% for one of the most transient work forces in the company. Improved team cohesion and employee loyalty by implementing monthly activities that focused on enhancing morale.
- Conducted a competitive analysis among area retailers to reassess the Frederick store's compensation package.

EDUCATION & AFFILIATION

Pennsylvania State University, Major: Labor and Industrial Relations, 2000 – 2003
Member, Society of Human Resource Managers

CORY SCHULMAN

13004 Human Resources Drive
Upper Marlboro, Maryland 20772
H: 240-338-0050
humanresources@gmail.com

EXPERIENCE

COMPUTER ENTERPRISES, INC. (CE), Rockville, Maryland   2008 – Present

Corporate Human Resources Manager

- Earned four promotions for outstanding performance reducing operating expenses, improving caliber of personnel, upgrading benefits coverage, defending the company against lawsuits, and re-engineering workflow.

Human Resources:

- Managed all aspects of human resources during various organizational changes, expansions, and downsizings for this information technology services company.
- Led a dramatic reduction in workforce from 1,500 to 350 within 6 months. Managed exit process by coordinating notifications, re-evaluations, severance packages, and outplacement.
- Examined incentives, benefits, salary structures, turnover, labor requirements, and review practices to identify potential improvements in quality and cost effectiveness.
- Interviewed, hired, and disciplined technical personnel, such as test, systems, and security engineers and software programmers.
- Conducted orientations of new hires; verified legal status, administrated benefits enrollment, and explained corporate policies.
- Provided advocacy for employees regarding health benefits, payroll discrepancies, and job-related conflicts. Ensured a balance between company and employee interests.

Benefits Administration:

- Re-evaluated and negotiated both coverage and rates for health, dental, short/long term disability, and life insurance plans on a quarterly basis.
- Conducted surveys of insurance carriers and analyzed prices, quality, and physician network capacity.
- Served as a liaison between employees and insurance companies to resolve medical claims and related grievances.
- Gave open enrollment presentations at 5 facilities from coast to coast before audiences of up to 40 employees.

Cost Containment:

- Reduced medical insurance premiums 17% and disability insurance premiums 25%, saving the company approximately $200,000 a year.
- Reduced hiring expenses by exercising in-house recruiting instead of subcontracting employment agencies.
- Conducted price analyses for hundreds of computer parts and related engineering supplies and equipment from five vendors. Tracked approximately 20 purchase orders per month for approximately $120 million in procurement per annum.
- Curtailed shrinkage of computer laptops and related devices by instituting security procedures and video cameras.

Regulatory Compliance/Administration:
- Applied knowledge of EEO, FMLA, AA, ADA, VETS 100, FAR, OSHA, HIPAA, COBRA, and related government regulations.
- Supported all out-of-state offices by co-writing Affirmative Action plans, EEO1 reports, and Vet 100 reports to maintain compliance with 4 agencies: FAA, NASA, NOAA, and DOJ.
- Represented the company in their defense in an EEO lawsuit, and successfully negotiated a dismissal of the case with EEO representatives.
- Developed policies and procedures pertaining to time changes, disabilities, leave of absences, family medical leave, separation policy, and new hires.
- Enhanced efficiency for updating personnel information by setting up a network link file of human resource data, resulting in a dramatic 40% reduction in complaints.
- Prepared surveys to document employees' needs and comments.
- Prepared proposals and graphics for mobile computer operations in FEMA trucks.
- Provided administrative assistance to 10 engineers in support of multi-million dollar government contracts with NOAA and NASA.

FORTITHE AUTOMOTIVE GROUP, Silver Spring, Maryland   2004 – 2008
Director of Personnel
- Earned 3 promotions culminating to Director of Personnel for 25 car dealerships consisting of 2,000 employees.
- Recruited 90% of the company's sales and finance management staff. Facilitated 9 consecutive years of increased profits, the expansion of 8 new dealerships, and the emergence onto the *Forbes Magazine* Top 200 highest grossing privately owned businesses in the country.
- Devised help wanted advertisements for print and Internet media, and applied use of applicant tracking systems. Coordinated participation in career fairs. Conducted face to face interviews.
- Recruited higher caliber professionals for various levels and positions, including sales, management, accounting, service, parts, and body shop. Authorized all employee reviews and provided recommendations for promotions and/or disciplinary actions.
- Curtailed a soaring turnover rate from 3% above the national industry average to 10% below it. Introduced and conducted exit interviews to identify and address employee concerns.
- Developed a comprehensive sales training program, which has been packaged in video format and adopted by Chrysler Corporation's 5-Star Training Program for national dealers.
- Prevented litigation through responsive attention and resolution to employee grievances among the 2,000 member work force.
- Presented federal, state, manufacturing, and corporate regulations and related legal compliance issues as a guest speaker at quarterly management meetings.
- Wrote employee handbook, covering conduct, compensation/benefits, dress codes, and harassment; advised the Vice President and owner on personnel issues.

EDUCATION

Certificate of Completion for SHRM PHR
Certificate of Completion for Fundamentals of Affirmative Action Planning
B.A. in Computer Operations, University of Maryland

CORY SCHULMAN
14001 HVAC Terrace
Gaithersburg, MD 20879
Home: 240-338-0050
E-mail: hcac@gmail.com

EXPERIENCE

Air Conditioner Planner/Estimator, 12/2002 – Present
Naval Research Center, Carderock Division, West Bethesda, Maryland

Leadership:
- Manage mechanical, civil, and electrical engineering projects for 3 facilities and provide technical support and maintenance oversight for 60+ buildings on an 89-acre naval research center.
- Charged with emergency response and smooth operations of public works as the Acting Supervisor for the Planning Department. Rectified electrical/mechanical failures and safety/environmental hazards.
- Appointed as a Team Leader of Planning Estimators to facilitate numerous renovations, expansions, buildouts, and remodeling projects. Led installations, replacements, repairs, and maintenance initiatives in compliance with federal regulations.
- Revamped and directed a Preventative Maintenance Inspection (PMI) program as the PMI Manager for HVAC and pipefitting trades.
- Served as Certified Asbestos Inspector since 2003, Designer since 2004, and Management Planner since 2007.
- Coordinate inspection services for the Carderock site and three detachments as a Facility Inspection Coordinator.

Sample Projects:
- Retrofitted 15 to 30-ton chillers and DX air conditioners to meet protocols under the Clean Air Act and EPA regulations. Installed cooling for 15 East Building.
- Planned and designed two 25-ton computer room air conditioner systems in building 15 room 126, building 191 SPARK room, building 15 addition, building 8 computer room, building 19, building 16 penthouse, etc. within stringent budgetary constraints.
- Designed a heat exchange system and layout that satisfied indoor air requirements in accordance with safety regulations.
- Installed heating and air conditioning systems in accordance with various heat and space load requirements.

Cost Containment:
- Apply technical expertise to select appropriate vendor sources, equipment, parts, and controls, saving the research center a minimum of $20,000 per annum.
- Replaced a 5 ton air conditioner with 2 ton system based on heat loss/gain calculations, saving the facility 55% in installation and procurement costs. Reduced recurring energy costs approximately 200% while enhancing energy efficiency.
- Analyze facility requirements and equipment specifications to replace inefficient and/or outmoded equipment.

Regulatory & Technical Knowledge:
- Employ complex mechanical and electrical formulas in the design, repair, and installation of mechanical/electrical systems.
- Apply regulatory and technical knowledge for various projects, such as duct sizing and layout, water pipe sizing, refrigerant piping (fluid flow), psychometrics, heat gain/heat loss calculations (heat transfer theory and principals), valve/equipment selections, wire sizing, circuit/fuse/component sizing, electrical/mechanical troubleshooting, and control system calibration, troubleshooting and design.
- Inspect the condition of electrical, mechanical, structural, roof, fire, and civil aspects of facilities. Write inspection reports, recommend repairs, estimate costs, and coordinate inspection contract services.
- Evaluate facility maintenance and repair projects to ensure compliance with current EPA, MDE, OSHA, NAVY or other applicable codes regarding lead paint, asbestos, ozone, chemical/water drainage, ventilation and exhaust, noise, historic or cultural value, etc.
- Apply intricate knowledge of engineering principles, especially for heat transfer, fluid flow, electrical characteristics, and indoor air quality requirements, to select appropriate equipment and contractors.
- Read schematics, blue prints, and technical drawings, including charts, tables, and formulas.
- Use AutoCAD to design layouts.
- Install, configure, and maintain computer workstations and networks. Provide technical support and training to other users.
- Use Microsoft Word, Excel, MS Access, HazCAD, Outlook, Windows, PWTools, Pulsar, ILSMIS, R&R, Arpeggio, CHVAC, and other peripheral applications, i.e. anti-virus, and compression software.

Communications:
- Addressed customers' requirements, complaints, and concerns as the Facility Liaison and primary point-of-contact for 3+ buildings and secondary point-of-contact for 60+ facilities regarding HVAC related issues.
- Brief managerial and executive level leadership. Consult with engineers on setting/limiting the scope of projects and addressing project needs within budgetary and scheduling constraints.
- Collaborate with manufacturers to select equipment, troubleshoot systems, formulate designs, size heat exchangers, and determine pump flow, pressure drops, and fluid characteristics.
- Plan, estimate, and write material and construction contract specification requirements, in-house packages, and facility condition inspection reports.
- Collaborate with management to prepare annual inspection summaries and outsource facility inspection services for detachments
- Write booklets, procedural/regulatory instructions, and work flow plans for planners.

Financial Experience:
- Authorized to make purchases of up to $100,000 since 2003. Bank Card Buyer/Approver since 2002. Balance and maintain account records, ensure delivery, and quality control for services.
- Apply training in FAR, DAR, NAVFAC, and NAVSUP requirements when procuring services and materials for installations, repairs, and computer upgrades.

Air Conditioning Equipment Mechanic, 8/2001 – 12/2002
Naval South West Center, Bethesda, Maryland

- Installed and repaired various heating, air conditioning, refrigeration, filtration and ventilation equipment. Maintained equipment designed to provide precise climatic conditions in computer rooms and lab areas at buildings 7, 11, 13, 14, and 18.
- Calibrated, tested, and modified pneumatic, electronic and microprocessor controls.
- Worked with complex equipment such as the heat reclaim system at building 17W, variable air volume equipment at buildings 8, 4E and 7 and reheat systems at buildings 15, 17E, and 19. These required unusual piping, design arrangements, and control schemes.
- Repaired lab equipment, including cascade systems used in test experiments. Service equipment as large as 225 ton centrifugal chillers.
- Maintained the central computer facility of building 17E keeping its temperature and humidity within critical limits.
- Made recommendations to the Engineering Department concerning design criteria of new installations.
- Recommended upgrades for obsolete and aging equipment.
- Functioned as Acting Supervisor of the air conditioning and emergency services crew on an intermittent basis.

EDUCATION

1200 hours, Lincoln Technical Institute, Washington, DC, 2000 – 2001

Professional Licenses and Certificates:
Master of Heating, Air Conditioning, Refrigeration, State Board of HVACR Contractors.
EPA Certified Universal Technician for Refrigerant Handling, Environment Training Group, Columbia, Maryland, 2001
Certified Technician, Air Conditioning Refrigerant, IMACA, Fort Worth, Texas, 2000

Cory Schulman
14002 Mechanic Road
Poolesville, MD 20837
Home: 240-338-0050
hvac@gmail.com

EXPERIENCE

Industrial Equipment Mechanic, T.C.A. Equipment Control, Maryland Naval Campus
WG 10 Step 5, September 2001 – Present

- Perform preventable maintenance and repair on all air handlers, return fans, exhaust fans, filtering, HEPA, roll, box, and bay systems.

- Maintain outside pneumatic dampers, smoke alarm systems, freeze stats, temperature transmitters, fan discharge temperatures, air balancing positive and negative air flow rooms, and dental and clinical vacuum systems.

- Repair and maintain diverse compressors, sump pumps, air dryers, water filtering systems, pneumatic controls, motor control units, pneumatic valves (hot and chill water values, gate and ball valve replacements) and plumbing (all size pipes, both iron, copper).

- Replace single and three phase motors, pulleys, fan coil units, T-Stats, powers, Honeywell, Robert Shaw, Barb/Colmens, etc. A/C experience includes maintenance and repair of commercial A/C chill water systems; participate in generator tests; read all meters and gauges.

- Manage a maintenance and repair shop, which services all 27 buildings on campus: including the hospital, training schools, the pharmacy, supply and storage rooms, offices, and labs. Ensure strict compliance with HAZMAT, OSHA, EPA, and related federal regulations.

- Maintain pneumatic, electrical, hydraulic, and facility systems and industrial equipment such as pumps, motors, valves, and HVAC systems. Assemble and install condensate/vacuum pumps, autoclaves, motors, valves, frames, pulleys, bearings, and ice machines.

- Read blue prints on job sites to troubleshoot motor controls, pneumatic lines, water fountains, ice machines, autoclaves, sump pumps, condensate pumps, and underground equipment to locate pipes, gas, and water lines.

- Procure materials, components, parts, and equipment from GSA and distributors within the department's multi-million dollar budget. Reduced expenses by conducting cost analyses among vendors.

- Apply in-depth knowledge of materials, including copper piping, conduit, black iron, schedule 40, electrical wiring, high/low pressure steam, caulking, adhesives, paints, seals, filters, Freon, fluorocarbons, compressor oil, and many others.

- Use a variety of tools: pipe cutter/threader, Freon recovery, vacuum pumps, pipe wrenches, lathe, drill press, punch press, Johnson bar, scaffolding, ladders, and hand tools. Use various measuring instruments, such as air flow meters, pressure gauges, thermostats, Freon digital leak detectors, calculators, micrometers, ohm/volt/amp meters, 3-phase 47480, Amp Pro, high-voltage drills, and others. Operate motorized equipment such as fork lifts, floor jacks, tractors, farm equipment, K-50s, K-60s, 1500 series/sewer drains.

- Implemented a preventative maintenance program on a quarterly basis, resulting in a reduction in customer complaints and cost overruns.

- Participate in approximately 20 work orders per week.

- Improved organization and ensured access to various fact sheets, blue prints, and schematics. Enhanced morale, cooperation, and communications between departments: sheet metal, carpentry, plumbing, A/C, and electrical.

OTHER QUALIFICATIONS

Additional Government Training:
Variable Air Volume Seminar
Pneumatic/Electronic Controls Course
Servicing Pneumatic Controls
AE 5000 and Drives Seminar
Troubleshooting Motor Controls
Programmable Controllers
Coupling Maintenance
Industrial Hydraulics Technology
Basic Bearings
Sexual Harassment Course
HAZMAT Training
Work Hazards, Safety Control

EDUCATION

DeVry Institute of Technology, Phoenix, Arizona, Major: Electronics, 1 year
Tennessee Temple College, Chattanooga, Tennessee, Major: Seminar Studies, 2 years
United States Air Force Jet Engine School, Chonte, Illinois, 1 year

CORY SCHULMAN

14003 HVAC Technician Drive
Orlando, Florida 32828
240-338-0050
hvactechnician@gmail.com

EXPERIENCE

INTERNATIONAL AIR FLOW, INC., Rockville, Maryland   2008 – Present

Lead HVAC Service Technician

- Diagnose, repair, and maintain various HVAC systems such as environmental control equipment; 10-20 ton Liebert DX units; evaporative condensers; glycol circulating pump components; 5-10-20 ton Trane, Carrier, and Command-Air split a/c units; 4-100/150 ton Evapco cooling towers; and a 40 ton Mammoth packaged rooftop heating /cooling unit that support 3 Lockheed Martin buildings.
- Allocate preventative maintenance duties to an HVAC technician.
- Reduced response time to emergencies regarding unit failures and high temperatures in critical rooms that house servers, hubs, routers, switches, and networks. Cut overall systemic downtime by enforcing preventative maintenance and effectively repairing systems upon initial effort.
- Replaced various HVAC parts such as compressors, central components, pumps, fans, and dry coolers. Familiar with diverse brands: Command Air, Trane (5-10-20 ton), American Standard, Carrier, and many others.
- Prepare and organize monthly reports, including monthly Freon usage reports.

Backup High Voltage Electrician

- Participate on the Switch Team to restore high voltage operations of subsystems impacting electrical power of 2 buildings with 500,000 aggregate square feet.
- Perform switching activities in accordance with Pepco isolations.
- Respond to emergency calls to 13 KV switchyard at Lockheed Martin site.

CASIDIA ELECTRICAL CONTRACTORS, Rockville, Maryland   2004 – 2008

Master Electrician

- Provided maintenance services to residential, commercial, and industrial accounts throughout Montgomery County.
- Installed single and three-phase distribution equipment and service wiring.
- Installed and serviced power, lighting, and interior cabling for new construction, remodeling, and retrofit projects.

INTERNATIONAL BUSINESS COPORATION, Gaithersburg, Maryland   2002 – 2004

Journeyman Electrician

- Provided electrical preventive maintenance monitoring for 4 Liebert 1000 KVA single module UPS systems supporting primary computer room floor.

- Monitored 4 Caterpillar 1500 KW Diesel driven generators, via operator control of Allen & Bradley PLC-100 through SWAM paralleling switchgear.
- Monitored and performed required changes of central plant parameters via DDC Building Control System of 3-900 ton; 1-160 ton (Heat Recovery) Chillers in support of facility needs.

| AB&B ELECTRICAL, Capitol Heights, Maryland | 1999 – 2002 |

Journeyman Electrician
- Planned and layed-out installations from blueprints and specifications of power and lighting distribution equipment in commercial and residential applications.

| WASHINGTON MECHANICAL, Weston, Ontario | 1997 – 1999 |

HVAC Technician
- Monitored and maintained operation of 1-600, 1-900 ton chillers under the direction of DDC building control system of plant facility.
- Participated in a monthly PM program for air handling and associated control equipment and circulating pump operations.
- Serviced seals, bearings, and drives as required.
- Air and water cooled condenser and associated control equipment. Performed cooling tower maintenance related to both mechanical and electrical system components.

EDUCATION

- **A.A.S. Degree in HVAC**, 1996, Northern Virginia Community College
- **A.A. Technology Degree equivalent in Electrical Construction and Maintenance**, 1995, George Brown College
- Enrolled in Bachelor of Science degree program, Environmental Control, Ferris State Distance Learning

QUALIFICATIONS

Montgomery County Maryland Master Electrician License
Maryland State Master Electrician License
Maryland State Master HVAC License
Maryland State First Grade Engineer
N.I.U.L.P.E. Third Grade Engineer
Maryland State Master Gasfitters License
District of Columbia Journeyman Electrician License
Virginia Board for Contractors
Master Electrician License
Master HVAC License

CORY SCHULMAN

16007 Import Street
Arlington, VA 22209

import@gmail.com
240-338-0050

OBJECTIVE

To optimize revenues as a Business Consultant within the IT industry through expertise in business process analysis, systems integration, and imports/exports.

HIGHLIGHTS

Direct worldwide import/export operations and technical consulting services in support of 1,400 international accounts. Created multi-million dollar revenues by establishing consulting services, evaluating global business processes, and streamlining automated systems. Facilitated corporate merger which entailed organizational design, system integration, and network architecture. Penetrated and developed markets throughout Asia and Europe. Created alliances with vendors, third-party resellers, and implementation partners. Exceeded corporate revenue targets as much as 47% for 7 years.

EXPERIENCE

EURO-ASIA-AMERICAN BUSINESS, INC., Reston, Virginia   2005 – Present

Director of Worldwide Business Consulting, 2011 – Present

- Direct team of 12 consultants to manage the Europe Asia Pacific Group and America's Group, which generate 20% of the company's $40 million import/export sales per annum.
- Ensured seamless corporate restructuring to facilitate a merger with a $12 million entity.
- Established and cultivated a worldwide business consulting group, which increased revenues from $5.6 million to $8 million.
- Hired, trained, and managed eight professionals; implemented a training program that focused on import/export management, network architecture, and business process analysis.
- Evaluated product lines, which included import, export, and materials compliance management systems.
- Support 1,400 global accounts, which entails initial needs assessment, proposal development, system implementation, testing, employee training, and system performance audits.

Director of Asia Pacific Business Development, Tokyo, Japan, 2008 – 2011

- Penetrated the Asian market and brought annual revenues of sales and business consulting services from zero to $4 million.
- Devised and launched market entry strategies such as product localization, multi-byte operation support, and language translation.
- Earned 2009 Partner-of-the-Year with Oracle Corporation for delivering total business solutions.

Director of Worldwide Alliances, San Francisco, California, 2005 – 2008

- Established alliances and resale agreements with third-party resellers.
- Initiated marketing relationships with partner vendors, third-party resellers, and implementation partnerships. Focused on Enterprise Resource Planning, Transportation Management Systems, and Warehousing Management Systems.

CENTRALIS, New York, New York   2001 – 2005

Consultant

- Provided consultation in import/export management for global clients, resulting in producing $2 million in gross annual revenues.
- Gave in-person sales/implementation presentations and on-site system training.

EDUCATION

BA in International Business, 2000, American University, Washington, DC

CORY SCHULMAN
30003 Journalist Circle
Germantown, Maryland 20874
240-338-0050
journalist@gmail.com

OBJECTIVE

To apply polished verbal, written, and interpersonal skills in a position that is commensurate with experience.

HIGHLIGHTS

Journalism/Media: Experienced in writing on-air scripts for television news anchors and reporting feature articles for a local newspaper. Provided journalistic support during the 2012 Presidential Campaign. Served as an entertainment critic writing on feature films and restaurants. Adept at collecting, verifying, and summarizing significant and relevant facts in support of breaking hard news and features stories.

Communications: Conducted interviews with citizens, public officials, and members of private industry. Interfaced with reporters, anchors, producers, and station managers. Gave public talks before audiences of 130 attendees. Provided communications and marketing support for a 2012 Congressional candidate.

EXPERIENCE

ABC-TV/17, Raleigh, North Carolina   August 2011 – Present
Assistant Intern to News Anchor
- Write scripts for local newscast anchors, which entail reviewing the Associated Press wire and identifying follow-up information for hard news and feature stories.
- Gathered and verified facts of breaking stories by contacting local police stations throughout North Carolina.
- Manned the reporter's desk during the absence of the General Assignment Reporter.
- Provided support during the 2012 Presidential campaign by relaying facts to reporters and the Station Manager.

GAITHERSBURG TRIBUNE, Gaithersburg, Maryland   May – July 2011
Editorial Assistant Intern
- Wrote feature stories based on interviews of people of interest in the community.
- Wrote articles that critiqued new movie releases and local restaurants.

EDUCATION

North Carolina State University, Raleigh, North Carolina
Bachelor of Arts, Mass Communications; Minor: Journalism, 2011, Dean's List

CORY SCHULMAN

2004 Legal Secretary Boulevard
Silver Spring, MD 20902-1965

Home: 240-338-0050
legalsecretary@gmail.com

EXPERIENCE

EXECUTIVE OFFICE OF THE UNITED STATES COURTS   2008 – Present

Legal Secretary, Office of the General Counsel, Washington, DC, 2010 – Present

- Serve as executive legal secretary to the Assistant General Counsels and Paralegal Specialist.
- Provide legal support and advice on laws and legislation to U.S. courts and judges, including the Court of Appeals, district judges, Bankruptcy Court, magistrate judges, and circuit executives.
- Perform legal research for Judicial Branch meetings. Maintain and dispense knowledge of library and legal reference resources, verify legal citations, assist in compiling legal research materials, and locate histories, law periodicals, and other legal documents.
- Type legal memoranda, reports, contracts, legislative articles, and correspondence from written drafts in appropriate format.
- Prepare, organize, and assemble agenda materials, including reports for Judicial Conference Committees and subcommittees. Compile, tabulate, and organize materials for exhibits, reports, and draft legislation.
- Collaborate with the Budget Division to arrange payments for miscellaneous expenses.
- Receive and assist visiting judges, government officials, foreign judges and justices, and other visitors. Address inquiries regarding actions of the Judicial Conference, the status of legislation sponsored by the Conference, the status of litigation involving judges and judicial officers, and reports and studies of various Judicial Conference committees.
- Maintain daily appointment calendar for supervisor and assist attorneys in preparing travel and lodging arrangements.
- Establish and maintain legal files, including precedent files, Judicial Conference Committee files, alphabetical subject files, and daybook and office reading files. Reorganized the physical and electronic filing systems.

Legal Secretary, Bankruptcy Judges Division, Washington, DC, 2008 – 2010

- Organized work flow, located and compiled information for reports and briefings, and word-processed correspondence and reports to support the bankruptcy courts.
- Composed non-technical correspondence to address inquiries regarding procedure and personnel of the bankruptcy courts.
- Maintained mail log and distributed mail throughout the Division.
- Planned itineraries, secured transportation/hotel reservations, and prepared travel vouchers.
- Assisted in planning and developing new policies and procedures for the secretarial staff.
- Ordered and procured office supplies from vendors and the local GSA store.

CITY OF GAITHERSBURG MUNICIPAL COURT   2001 – 2007

Court/Ministerial Recorder, Gaithersburg, Maryland

- Possessed authority to sign arrest and search warrants to be served.
- Administered oaths to officers and citizens filing complaints.
- Prepared bond, jail release, and drivers' license forms for citizens.
- Processed payments for parking tickets, criminal fines, traffic tickets, and miscellaneous fees.
- Answered public inquiries concerning jail sentences, court cases, and general information.
- Entered data such as traffic tickets, booking reports, and receipts into the court database.

SUPPLEMENT

Education: **Criminal Justice**, Southern University, Charleston, South Carolina
Affiliations: President, Alpha Kappa Alpha Sorority, Inc., Delegate for American Baptist Churches

CORY SCHULMAN

3009 Loan Officer Road
Germantown, Maryland 20876

240-338-0050
loanofficer@gmail.com

EXPERIENCE

MARYLAND TEACHERS FEDERAL CREDIT UNION, Gaithersburg, Maryland   2011 – Present

Consumer Loan Officer

- Originated more than $70 million for the Maryland Teachers Federal Credit Union, which entailed an expertise in underwriting, loan request extensions, insurance adjustments/change in terms, cross-selling of financial products/services, and member counseling/service.
- Reviewed approximately 65% – 75% of the credit union's consumer loans, which amounted to roughly $30 million per annum. Authorized unsecured and secured loans.
- Exceeded credit union's monthly goals for loan originations by as much as 45%.
- Processed 25 – 30 consumer loan applications per day from 4 branches, the Internet, incoming calls, and indirect lending dealers.
- Increased loan production 35% by helping introduce risk-based lending, indirect lending, and enhanced computer automation.

UNIVERSAL TRUST HOME MORTGAGE, INC., Frederick, Maryland   2008 – 2011

Mortgage Closer

- Retained on staff despite three corporate-wide layoffs. Promoted from Processor as a result of managing a 120 loan pipeline, which exceeded corporate volume requirements 37%.
- Closed 250 loans per month, which doubled the industry average volume and represented approximately $56 million per month.
- Earned Service Excellence Awards the first and third quarters of 2008 and consistently ranked within the top producing closers among 23 in the office.
- Verified information involving appraisals, titles, and outstanding liens.
- Ordered funds from Treasury Department for disbursement; scheduled closings; ensured delivery of legal documents to closing agent; and updated real estate tax homeowners' insurance information.

MARYLAND HOME MORTGAGE, Rockville, Maryland   2006 – 2008

Senior Loan Officer

- Processed government, conventional, and jumbo loans from application through closing in compliance with Fannie Mae and FHA/VA guidelines.
- Closed $5 – $7 million in streamlined loans per month, which exceeded monthly corporate quotas as much as 40%.
- Ordered and cleared titles; scheduled settlement closings with various title companies and law firms across the country, and negotiated subordination loans.
- Cleared judgments and liens from titles by negotiating settlements with the IRS, collection agencies, state governments, and mortgage companies.
- Established and cultivated cooperative relationships with real estate agents, settlement attorneys, inspectors, loan officers, and underwriters.
- Maintained high closing success based on effective pre-qualification of customers per income/debt ratios and other major contributing variables.
- Processed loans for self-employed applicants. Adept at analyzing 1040s, 1120s, and related corporate tax returns.
- Assessed applicants' financial viability, credit worthiness, and social integrity through background verifications with references, employers, and credit bureaus.

EDUCATION

Bachelor of Arts, Honors, 2005, GPA: 3.5, University of Maryland, Adelphi, Maryland

CORY SCHULMAN

21001 Lobbyist Street
Takoma Park, MD 20912
240-338-0050
lobbyist@gmail.com

SUMMARY

Business Consultant with extensive background coordinating high-profile fundraising events and grass roots community efforts in support of corporate, civic, and political campaigns. Skilled in project management, administration, budgeting, meeting planning, public affairs, lobbying, and international marketing. Experienced in establishing, managing, and growing businesses in consulting. Coordinated catering events for as many as 1,500 attendees.

EXPERIENCE

Lobbyist, Fundraiser, Consultant, Independent Contractor   2000 – Present

Fundraising:

- Managed solicitation efforts throughout 18 states to raise money for candidates supporting civil justice. Participated in fundraising campaigns to successfully raise $1 million for the Democratic Congressional Campaign Committee and the Democratic Senate Campaign Committee.
- Helped organize the first annual Capital Canine Fundraiser for the Capital Children's Museum.
- Planned fundraising efforts as a member of the Executive Committee of Multiple Sclerosis Ambassador's Ball.
- Facilitated a fundraiser in support of UNIFEM.

Consulting:

- Provided consulting services to the American Trial Lawyers' Association.
- Advised the Chairman of the House Administration Committee and his legal counsel on appropriate procedures to modernize operations and procedures in all seven House of Representatives' restaurants. Co-developed plans to gather political and media support.

Special Events:

- Invited by EPA Administrator to introduce Vice President Joe Biden as the Champion of Public Health during a press conference at the White House, which was televised on C-SPAN.
- Coordinated logistics for annual receptions on Capitol Hill for the Pacific Basin Council.
- Arranged for victims of dangerous products on behalf of Public Citizen to participate in press conferences and lobbying efforts against tort reform legislation.
- Appointed by high-level association consultants to take charge of coordinating the OSAP conference after an abrupt resignation of the former meeting planner 4 weeks before the event. Revitalized efforts to meet all logistical demands and direct a successful event catering to 1,500 attendees in support of prenatal drug abuse prevention.

Government Relations/Regional Sales Manager, TourAmerica, Inc.   1997 – 2000

- Collaborated with a Protocol Officer to coordinate award dinners honoring former British Prime Minister John Major, the Philippine President Fidel Ramos, and the Pakistani Prime Minister Malik Khalid. Held responsibility for securing in-kind donations.
- Conceived and implemented a 2-day tourism summit that enabled U.S Senators and U.S. House Representatives to meet international tour wholesalers in an effort to increase tourism in the United States. Hired and supervised media relations staff to write press releases. Edited press releases and secured media coverage.

EDUCATION

B.S. Degree, Government/History, 1996, Florida International University

CORY SCHULMAN

17001 Marketing Street
Chevy Chase, MD 20815
240-338-0050
marketing@gmail.com

OBJECTIVE

To drive business development in a position involving account management, marketing, and/or public relations.

HIGHLIGHTS

Public Relations/Marketing:
- Devised and launched marketing campaigns for Isley, an upscale entrepreneurial company, and achieved a dramatic 12.5% rise in revenues, new accounts, and new orders.
- Secured network coverage on CBS affiliate as a guest interviewee introducing new brand products with a consumer reporter.
- Promoted Isley through a feature article published in *The Washington Post* Style Section.
- Networked with celebrities such as Tommy Lee Jones to coordinate advertising sponsorships, including the televised Celebrity Polo Classic in Palm Beach.
- Captured greater market share by writing press releases, advertising copy, and marketing literature.
- Coordinated advertising in Isley's prestigious catalog, *the book*.

Account Development/Networking:
- Established Fortune 500 accounts, including Neiman Marcus, Nordstroms, and Overton's, the world's largest watersports company.
- Popularized Isley's UV resistant sportswear for children by giving dynamic presentations to senior buyers at tradeshows, fashion expos, trunk events, and retail outlets across the nation. Networked throughout major hubs such as Malibu, Palm Beach, Brentwood, Southampton, and other affluent locations.
- Cultivated relationships with key manufacturers, venders, retailers, and media contacts.

Management:
- Supervised 20+ subcontractors to ensure compliance with stringent manufacturing specifications. Hired and trained support personnel.
- Achieved exponential growth in gross revenues for Isley within first year.
- Coordinated warehousing, manufacturing, material acquisitions, and vendor agreements. Negotiated and closed sales contracts. Cut manufacturing expenses without compromising high-quality standards. Protected revenue potential by patenting swimwear feature.

EXPERIENCE

ISLEY, LLC, Washington, DC   2009 – Present
Marketing Executive
- Marketed an entrepreneurial company specializing in upscale UV protective wear by establishing accounts with industry-leading retailers.

CRIMSTON, INC., Dulles, Virginia   2005 – 2009
Senior Public Relations Writer
- Promoted new computer and telephonic systems by writing press releases, brochures and advertising copy for this international telecommunications company.

EDUCATION

M.A. in English Literature, 2004, Summa Cum Laude, Georgetown University, Washington, DC
B.A. in English Literature, 2002, Trinity College, Washington, DC

145

CORY SCHULMAN

17002 Marketing Lane
Bethesda, MD 20817

240-338-0050
marketing@gmail.com

EXPERIENCE

International Senior Citizens Education and Research Center (ISCERC)   2008 – Present
Manager, Program and Product Development

Program Development:
- Developed and marketed career training and placement programs for older workers in support of a $40 million federal grant.
- Negotiated and established a contract with the Montgomery County Career Transition Center to develop and implement 10 seminars in job readiness for mature workers.
- Established a partnership between ISCERC and the University of Maryland Flagship television channel to air a series on senior employment.
- Developed a proposal to institute a research and development division for evaluating the effectiveness of ISCERC programs.

Media Production:
- Wrote, produced, and anchored live television series promoting senior service community employment programs. Tapes were nationally distributed to 100 Senior Community Service Employment Projects (SCSEP) and all local cable channels in Maryland.
- Wrote and co-produced 60 minute public service announcements distributed to 145 CSCEP projects nationwide.
- Edited 9 hours of NASA footage into a 5 minute video tape to open the national conference of ISCERC.

Marketing/Promotions:
- Developed the Older Worker Week poster featuring Senator John Glenn, which required negotiations with NASA.
- Wrote copy and designed poster for the International Year-of-the-Older-Person.
- Developed business and marketing plans for the Mature Staffing Systems Agency within ISCERC. Produced three 4-color brochures to attract new funding and facilitate lobbying efforts as well as to expand enrollees among non-profit and private sectors.

The Lutheran Village (local ISCERC sub-grantee for SCSEP)   2003 – 2008
Director of Title V Programs

Program Development:
- Developed, marketed, and managed SCSEP, ABLE (Ability Based on Life Experience), and VESL (Volunteers Enhancing Seniors' Lives) programs. Secured funding from AT&T.
- Wrote grants for the annual implementation of programs, resulting in an increase in funding from $100,000 to $500,000 while expanding program participation 4-fold.
- Conducted workshops to train hundreds of project directors and assistants in support of SCSEP, which focused on strategies for employing the older work force.

- Established partnerships with high-profile government agencies such as the IRS, NIH, NOAA, etc. Established alliances with Montgomery College and non-profit organizations that supported computer training programs.

Marketing and Media Production:
- Generated publicity for programs on radio and cable television shows and as a guest speaker to state legislatures, county councils, various panels, and Fortune 500 companies.

The Learning Center Services   2000 – 2003
Director

- Led professional consulting team to provide educational services on grantsmanship skills for acquisition of funding from government agencies.
- Established contracts with U.S. Office of Personnel Management, U.S. Office of Education, National Career and Counseling Services, Applied Management Science, State Education Agencies in Georgia, Ohio, Arkansas, Louisiana, New York, Maryland, and Virginia.

Program Transitions, Inc.   1995 – 2000
Director of Title V Programs

- Developed diverse programs, seminars, and resource materials for public and private organizations targeting workers facing life transitions, displacement, and retirement.

The Education Management Association   1993 – 1995
Education Director

- Developed and produced a multi-media career advancement program for high ranking military professionals engaged in contract management. Produced a series of interactive learning packages that were distributed nationally.

Diagnostic-Teaching Center, Inc.   1988 – 1993
Founder/Director

- Provided psycho-educational assessment and counseling for children with disabilities and their parents. Partnered with George Mason University.

EDUCATION

Ph.D. in Education and Psychology, The American University
M.A. in Marketing, University of Maryland
B.S. in Business, New York University

SUPPLEMENT

Member, The United Business Marketing Association
Earned the Marketer-of-the-Year Award, 2015, ISCERC
Gave inspiring speeches in college auditoriums as a paid public speaker of career issues, including the experiences of executive women working in a male dominated industry.

CORY SCHULMAN

17003 Marketing Avenue
Washington, DC 20016

240-338-0050
marketing@gmail.com

EXPERIENCE

ADVANCED MEDICAL, Gaithersburg, Maryland 2005 – Present

Product Marketing Manager

- Promote sales of virtual reality software, which have generated approximately $3 million per annum.
- Direct launches for software products by developing marketing collateral and press releases.
- Manage booths at industry tradeshows held throughout the United States and Europe.
- Target various markets, including the medical community, academic institutions, government agencies, and the corporate sector. Expanded the medical school market 100% within the first year. Increased overall accounts from 200 to 550 within 2 years.
- Give product demonstrations to CEOs, directors, and staff; negotiate terms and conditions; convert objections into closed sales agreements for products valued up to $80,000 per unit.
- Collaborate with interactive design and advertising agencies to produce promotional CD-ROMs.
- Develop content and design of the company Web site, e-newsletter, and customer Internet forum.
- Write scripts, facilitate story boarding, and produce/edit videos.
- Advise software development staff in product enhancements based on assessment of client needs.
- Create marketing tools by analyzing and summarizing validation studies and industry literature.
- Lead sales meetings and give presentations on target markets, product attributes, and sales techniques.

Project Manager

- Led team of nine technical, content, marketing, and engineering professionals.
- Oversaw the product development process, which entailed scheduling milestones from initial concept development through manufacturing. Wrote, starred-in, edited, and produced video products.

STENTON INTERACTIVE, Alexandria, Virginia 2005

Multi-Media Project Manager

- Produced educational training videos and CD-ROMs for corporations' human resources departments and the Space Center. Coordinated focus groups that led to changes in the training product.

ADDITIONAL EXPERIENCE

Writer/Researcher, *The Washington Tribune*, Washington, DC 2003 – 2004
- Clients included National Film Institute, Meridian Productions, and Dialogue Productions.
Producer/Project Coordinator, Institute For Health Management, Washington, DC 2002 – 2003
- Produced videotapes of national conferences; edited journal articles and proposals; vendor relations.
Art Coordinator, *Washington Magazine*, Washington, DC 1999 – 2001
- Coordinated graphics production and story development; managed departmental budget.

EDUCATION

MBA program, 2015 – Present, Johns Hopkins University, Baltimore, Maryland
BA, Art History, 1998, University of Pennsylvania, Philadelphia, Pennsylvania
Annenberg School for Communications ABC & CBS TV News Internships, 1994 – 1996

Professional Development:
Sales Presentations, American Management Association, 2000
Information Design with Edward Tufte of Yale University, 1998
Budget & Schedule Estimation for Software Development, School of Engineering, UCLA, 1997
Macromaedia Director Class, Gestalt Systems, 1997
Screenwriting, Creative Writing, Feature Article Writing Classes, The Writer's Center, 1994 – 1997

CORY SCHULMAN

17004 Marketing Court	Fax: 240-338-0050
Gaithersburg, MD 20877	Work: 240-338-0050
marketing@gmai.com	Home: 240-338-0050

OBJECTIVE

To maximize lead generation, market penetration, and revenue growth as a highly experienced and successful Marketing and Production Manager.

EXPERIENCE

ESSENTIAL TECHNOLOGIES, INC., Rockville, Maryland   2007 – Present

Direct Marketing Manager

- Manage the marketing communications section and support staff for a $16 million software publishing company rated within the top 50 fastest growing companies by *Washington Technology.*
- Promote sustainability software by managing integrated-channel marketing campaigns.
- Facilitated double-digit growth in annual company revenues which are projected to reach $23 million for FY 2017.
- Cut production costs from $2.3 million to $1.5 million through leadership in transitioning hard-copy product sales to on-line subscription sales.
- Manage the events coordinator for tradeshows, seminars, and conferences held at major hubs throughout the nation.

Website Management:
- Developed the structure, navigational strategy, and design of 5 interlinked web sites with 3 additional websites on schedule for release, comprising more than 400 viewable pages.
- Generated 125 highly-qualified leads per week from users' hits.
- Ensured a commanding presence on the net through clear content, refreshing graphics, rapid down-load speed, user-friendly search capabilities, and user-feedback forms.

Mail Campaigns:
- Tripled lead generation from less than 1 percent to 3 percent by creating testimonial text for monthly e-mail and quarterly direct mail campaigns that reached approximately 400,000 workstations per year.

Database Management & Profiling:
- Established procedures for capturing lead information from various channels, including website user forms, advertising, and e-mail/direct mail.
- Analyzed the effectiveness of integrated campaigns to determine cost-effectiveness of various channels, including press releases, on-line newsletter, e-mail/direct mail, special events, business alliances, advertising, and telemarketing.
- Prepared comprehensive PowerPoint presentations based on Excel spreadsheet data to profile and target both government and corporate customers.
- Created follow-up and cross-selling programs in the database system.

Production and Related Responsibilities:

- Planned and executed all direct marketing and print production activities, including all printed materials; direct mail lettershop and postage; fulfillment development and processing; e-mail and list serv; and research, rental, and management activities.
- Created telephony structure, which is projected to reduce the length of sale from 6 to 3 months.
- Supervised graphic designer, copywriter, lead administrator, and marketing assistant in addition to contracted associates.
- Developed product packaging to achieve consistency in corporate identity.

THE NATIONAL AFFAIRS ADMINISTRATION, Washington, DC   2003 – 2007

Marketing Creative Coordinator

- Contracted and coordinated printing services for promotional materials, including direct mail campaigns, corporate materials, conference presentations, and product packaging in support of tax management/accounting software publisher and video training producer.
- Developed budgets with an aggregate sum in excess of $3 million per annum.
- Supervised a graphic designer and junior copywriter.
- Developed print and CD-ROM catalogs; performed copywriting; and developed the company website.

Copywriter/Creative Coordinator/Webmaster

- Performed the following responsibilities: creating strategy; writing, editing, designing direct mail campaigns and web pages; supervising others, analyzing promotions; buying media and print; reviewing scripts; product development; budgeting; developing catalogs; creating and analyzing surveys and marketing research.

INSURANCE ONE, Washington, DC   1996 – 2003

Copywriter/Production Coordinator

- Created strategies for business to consumer direct mail campaigns involving 15 million pieces per year for the 8th largest mailer in the country.
- Performed copywriting, design, print purchases, distribution, and reports evaluation.

SUPPLEMENTAL INFORMATION

Education:

- Bachelor of Arts, Graphic Arts, 1995, University of Wisconsin, Madison, Wisconsin

Technical Skills:

- Complete knowledge of the direct response marketing, multi-media, e-mail, list serv, website development, and postal industries.
- Thorough knowledge of QuarkXpress, Excel, PowerPoint, Microsoft Word, Access, Onyx, InDesign, PhotoShop, Illustrator, Microsoft Project, Paint Shop Pro, HTML, Astound, Macros, Corel, FrontPage, cc: mail, Outlook, and other software.

Professional Memberships/Accomplishments:

- General Chairperson for 2006 DMAW Conference and Expo
- 2004 Maxi Award Winner for B to B Catalog Category

CORY SCHULMAN

15001 Network Way
Montgomery Village, MD 20886

240-338-0050
network@gmail.com

HIGHLIGHTS

- **MCNE, MCSE, MCP + Internet, CCNA, CCA** with expertise in Microsoft, Cisco, Citrix, and Novell technologies. Former Director of Information Systems.

- Seventeen years of experience in LANs/WANs, client/server hardware/software, data security/backup/disaster-recovery systems, Internet/intranet connectivity, technology integration, compatibility, fault tolerance, infrastructure design, remote management, Website administration, and training. Familiar with Interactive Voice Response (IVR) units and telephony installations.

OS:	Windows 2010/NT/XT/XP; Novell 2.15 – 5.1, Linux, Unix, Oracle
Languages:	Java, JavaScript, HTML, C, C++, C#, Perl, SQL Server, ActiveX, Visual Basic
Hardware:	Installed and configured AutoCAD, Microstation, bridges, routers, hubs, switches, servers, workstations. Experienced with IBM, Dell, Compaq, HP, and many other manufacturers.
Applications:	MS Office Professional Suite, Dreamweaver, FrontPage, ColdFusion, Flash, Oracle

EXPERIENCE

NETWORK TECHNOLOGIES, Gaithersburg, Maryland   2007 – Present
Senior Network Consultant

- Provide network solutions, crisis management, and technical consulting to 60+ corporate and government clients such as Charles E. Smith, Department of Energy, and many others.
- Support various industries: property management, hospitality, medical/legal firms, telecommunications, and technology.
- Revamp equipment, operating systems, security, and Internet connectivity. Update servers; install firewall, backup and disaster recovery protocols; and provide training and technical support onsite and from remote locations.
- Manage 16 servers running on Citrix metaframe 1.8/XP, 4 Windows 2010, Novell, and Linux that support e-mail, Web site, application, and database services.
- Maintain Cisco PIX 515 firewall for more than 10 sites.
- Manage facilities consisting of 32 Novell and Windows servers and voice response units in central offices for XO Communications in Dallas, Texas.
- Support 20-user Windows network, including dial-in sales staff, configuration of routing, Internet services, and connections of satellite locations.

Sample Projects:

- Administrated LAN running on Novell servers and protected by BorderManager firewall for Carlyle and Savoy hotels. Established connectivity throughout 150 rooms. Designed and established cyber café with Wyse terminals using Citrix metaframe for Internet access.
- Installed 10 Compaq ProLiant 2500 servers running Microsoft Windows server with 100 gigabytes.
- Assisted IBM with the design of an 80,000-user, 2000-domain roll out of Microsoft System Management Server for Lucent Technologies.

- Redesigned a dial-in network for the Department of Energy that decreased application load and start-up time from 3 minutes to less than 30 seconds for users.
- Planned and implemented the Lakeforest Library Connection, a first-of-its-kind state-sponsored branch consisting of a PC and Mac network running on Novell and Appletalk with a full-time fiber-optic connection to the Internet.
- Designed network migration and disaster contingency plans based on Microsoft Windows for the Federal Aviation Administration (FAA). Minimized downtime in the event of hardware failure.

Projects for Primary Client, Charles E. Smith:
- Built, installed, and maintained 15+ servers that supported 1,000 users.
- Provide on-site and remote technical consultation for eight satellite offices, which involves switches, cable backbones, connectivity issues, Novell firewalls (border management), and system conversions.
- Reconfigured Novell directory for 13 servers, resulting in a dramatic reduction in traffic and log-in failures.
- Eliminated chronic crashes/locking among 30+ servers by building and installing 12+ HP and 6+ Dell servers, while retiring unreliable servers.
- Troubleshot connectivity among application servers using Citrix Winframe, Metaframe, and Windows.
- Collaborated with a network design firm to migrate to Cisco 6500 series multilayer switch.
- Converted T-1 to Worldcom in 11 satellite offices throughout the East Coast, which entailed phasing out frame relay, ISDN, and fractional T-1 technology.
- Reconfigured routers; tested connectivity for more than 70 ISDN lines.

SUPPLEMENT

Extensive educational achievements and community service experiences shall be supplied on supplemental sheets if pertinent.

2009:   Vinca Standby Server for Novell, 2/2009; Novell Small Business Suite; X10 Tech Storage System; Certified Novell Salesperson 5/09

2008:   NetWare 5.0 Boot Camp – Global Knowledge Network; PSINet 2-Day Internet Training – PSINet, New York, New York, 6/26; Microsoft Transaction Server 6/16 – Microsoft Seminars; Novell BorderManager; Netware for Small Business 10/21, Novell Seminars; Integrating NT into a NetWare Environment TechShare Encore!; FOSE

2007:   3D Concept in MicroStation 2005 MicroStation Forum and Exhibition; Enabling the Intranet 3Com; Inside Windows Seminar Series (Win95) Mastering Computers; NDS and Server Troubleshooting; Web Server; ManageWise and Advanced GroupWise Novell techShare 97

2006:   Engineering Your Future Seminar SoftDesk 7.5; Inside Windows Seminar Series (WinNT 4.0); Mastering Computers

2005:   CNE Boot Camp NetWare Users International; GroupWise 4.1 Administration; NetWare 4.1; NDS and Remote Access; NetWare Users International MicroStation 5.0 HM Systems

CORY SCHULMAN

15003 Networking Lane
Germantown, Maryland 20874

240-338-0050
networking@gmail.com

OBJECTIVE

To enhance LAN/WAN performance, security, and infrastructure as a Network or Systems Engineer.

HIGHLIGHTS

Network Engineering: Network Engineer with extensive IT experience designing, configuring, and implementing network infrastructure and architecture for large scale commercial and governmental projects involving LANs/WANs with as many as 10,000 workstations. Designed backup, disaster recovery, and restoration systems. Built and repaired network infrastructures, including cabling, hubs, switches, routers, and NICs.

Network Technology: TCP/IP (DNS, DHCP, WINS, FTP, Telnet, HTTP, SSL, etc.); IPX/SPX (SAP); incendiary protocols (NetBEUI, etc.) and routing topologies.

Servers: Microsoft Exchange Server 5.5 and 2000, Windows 2010, NT4, Microsoft SQL Server 6.5, 7.0, and 2000, Microsoft Internet Security and Acceleration Server.

Operating Systems/Applications: Backup Exec 8.6 Veritas, MS Back Office Suite (Exchange 2010, SQL 2010, and Host Integration 2010); MS Meta Directory Services (MMS), and Windows Office/Outlook   (95 – 2010) workstation.

Certifications: **MCSE 2010**, Orange Technologies
A+, ECPI College of Technology
CNA 4.11, ECPI College of Technology

EXPERIENCE

TRISTATE ENGINEERING, INC., Arlington, Virginia   2012 – Present

Network/Systems Engineering:
- Design, configure, and implement Microsoft technologies and network infrastructure in support of federal clients such as the U.S. Army and the National Guard.
- Completed the design of global infrastructure for the National Guard Bureau to implement Active Directory and Microsoft Exchange 2010 in 54 territories throughout the United States.
- Determine forests and domains to effectively design a Microsoft framework that encompasses operations, support, optimization, and change management.
- Designed and configured Microsoft Active Directory, Microsoft Windows 2010, and Sun One LDAP servers for cross-platform user account management in a shared data warehouse. Implemented 12 Dell server class COTS systems for LDAP, Oracle, and SQL applications.
- Enable co-existence between Sun ONE and Active Directory servers in lab and road show environments.
- Enable secure web site access by designing and configuring Internet Information Server (IIS) 4.0/5.0 and Sun ONE Web.
- Prepare discovery and draft reports detailing design of infrastructure architecture.
- Assess network security vulnerabilities and implemented security solutions, including firewall status, intrusion detection devices, virtual private networks (VPNs), and Public Key Infrastructures (PKIs).
- Develop disaster recovery plans for Enterprise networks.
- Evaluate performance monitors such as HP Openview, Net IQ, and Netcool and provide recommendations to executive staff.

BOLLING, INC., Bethesda, Maryland   2011 – 2012

Systems Engineering:

- Completed a 7-month engagement on-time for Montgomery County, which entailed implementing Active Directory and Exchange 2000. Designed co-existence of Windows 2010 and Novell proprietary systems on a 10,000 user WAN.
- Presented design and status of infrastructure and test results from pilot operations.
- Designed backup disaster recovery and restoration systems using Veritas.
- Designed and implemented a training lab consisting of classrooms that supported 50 users.
- Streamlined administration of Active Directory and Exchange 2000 by preparing procedural guides for Systems Administrators, Organizational Unit Administrators, and Power Users.
- Interfaced with various officials from a broad spectrum of county departments, including the Department of Power, Water, and Transportation.
- Designed and tested MS Meta Directory Service on NASA LAN running on Windows 2010 platform to share MS Exchange information.

INTERNATIONAL EXCHANGE, INC., Silver Spring, Maryland   2010 – 2011

Systems Engineering and Architecture:

- Upgraded NT4 to Active Directory and Exchange 2000 on network infrastructure.
- Installed, configured, and maintained Microsoft Backoffice 2010 Suite (Exchange 2000, SQL 2000, and Host Integration Server 2000).
- Installed and configured Windows 2010 DNS, DHCP, and WINS in a TCP/IP environment.
- Designed and implemented a backup schema using Veritas Backup Exec 8.6 for disaster recovery and restoration of the Active Directory infrastructure.
- Evaluated, recommended, and procured all server and desktop related hardware and software throughout the organization.
- Improved capacity, domain control, and network stability and increased reception of agents' daily downloads 50% from 2,000 to 3,000 by improving infrastructure.
- Upgraded and rebuilt 50 PCs from low to mid class Pentiums. Implemented TCP/IP functions and created fault tolerances and redundancies within the infrastructure. Configured routers, switches, hubs, and bridges.
- Planned, documented, and implemented migration strategy from Windows to Windows 2010.
- Provided on-site and remote technical support for network, server, workstation, peripheral, and software issues. Supported more than 75 users in multiple locations.

WORLD CABLE TELEVISION, Charlotte, North Carolina   2009 – 2010

Tier III Technical Support:

- Provided tier III technical support to Internet subscribers throughout Mecklenberg County to ensure Internet connectivity and resolve conflicts and misconfigurations.
- Performed on-site technical support involving Microsoft Internet Explorer, Outlook Express, Microsoft Outlook, Windows 95 – 2010, and Apple Macintosh systems.
- Replaced network interface cards, cable connectors/splitters, CAT5/RG6 cabling, and conducted Internet connectivity tests in a TCP/IP environment.
- Used Trilithic meters to test forward and return signals across RG6 cabling to troubleshoot faulty cable modem installations.

EDUCATION

Strayer University, **Bachelor of Science in Computer Networking**, 2014
Orange Technologies, Inc., **Microsoft Certified Windows 2010 Systems Engineer**, 2011
ECPI College of Technology, **CNA and A+ Certifications; PC Technician**, 2008 – 2009

CORY S. SCHULMAN, BSN, RN

18001 Clinical Nurse Boulevard • Rockville, Maryland 20852 • 240-338-0050 • nurse@gmail.com

SUMMARY

Provided nursing care and leadership in critical care and general medicine units as a Clinical Staff Nurse, Charge Nurse, and Team Leader. Operated EKG machines, defibrillators, temporary and permanent pacemakers, mechanical ventilators. Intra-aortic balloon pumps, hemodynamic, and cardiac telemetry monitoring equipment. First Lieutenant in U.S. Army, 2005 – Present.

Licensure: State of Wisconsin, Department of Regulation and Licensing: 847325
Certifications: BLS, ACLS, TNCC

EXPERIENCE

ST. JUDE MEDICAL CENTER, Washington, DC, 2005 – Present
Clinical Staff Nurse, Coronary Care Unit, 2007 – Present
- Coordinate and provide holistic nursing care for acute MI, cardiac catheterization, electro physiologic study, PTCA, intubated, and pacemaker patients in a 10-bed Intensive Care Unit.
- Assess, plan, implement, and evaluate nursing care for critically ill coronary patients.
- Take and interpret vital signs, ABGs, laboratory values, and cardiac dysrhythmias. Record neurological, cardiovascular, gastrointestinal, respiratory, and integumentary conditions on patient charts and assessment sheets.
- Administer medications such as antihypertensive, anticoagulants, diuretics, vasodilators, beta-adrenergic blocking agents, calcium channel blockers, (ACE) inhibitors, cardiac glycosides (digitalis), and IV sedation per physicians' orders.
- Serve as an advocate assuring education/resource support, emotional comfort, and confidentiality.
- Orient, train, and supervise Registered Nurses and Licensed Practical Nurses. Match staff skill levels with patient acuity.
- Observed coronary artery bypass surgery to become sensitized to patients' surgical experience.

Clinical Staff Nurse, General Medicine Ward, 2005 – 2007
- Rendered direct care to an average of 25 high acuity, complex patients on a 32-bed General Medicine unit in the U.S. Army's largest medical treatment facility and teaching institution.
- Charged with monitoring skin care on the ward by providing inservices and developing reference tools that facilitated a hospital-wide reduction in nosocomial decubitus ulcers. Educated the staff on skin care techniques.
- Developed a storyboard on Peripherally Inserted Central Catheter line management, which was adopted by other units in the hospital.
- Contributed to the development of the Section's SOPs in accordance with JCAHO criteria as a member of the Medical Nursing Section's Standardization Committee.
- Precepted incoming registered nurses in the General Medicine Unit.

EDUCATION - CERTIFICATES - AFFILIATIONS

School of Nursing University of Wisconsin, Madison, Wisconsin
Bachelor of Science degree in Nursing, May 2005, GPA: 3.6/4.0, Graduated with Distinction

St. Jude Medical Center, Washington, DC
Certificate, Intensive Care Nursing Course, 2007

Member, American Association of Critical-Care Nurses, May 2007 – Present
Member, Sigma Theta Tau, April 2005 – Present
Member, American Heart Association Council on Cardiopulmonary and Critical Care, 2007 – Present

CORY S. SCHULMAN, RN

18002 Nursing Road
Rockville, Maryland 20853

240-338-0050
nursing@gmail.com

EXPERIENCE

MARYLAND ADVENTIST HOSPITAL, Rockville, Maryland   2012 – Present
Staff Nurse
- Assess, prioritize, and render quality nursing care to acutely-ill patients on a 39-bed Medical Surgical Unit specializing in gynecology, urology, and nephrology.
- Provide care to patients with diverse diagnoses, including sickle cell anemia, HIV, hematological disorders, chemical dependency, fetal demise, and many other conditions.
- Perform routine nursing duties such as taking patient histories and vital signs; administering IVs, injections, and medications; and assisting physicians with procedures on patients diagnosed with multiple complications.
- Develop treatment plans and coordinate communications among five specialty doctors in preparation for the discharge of patients.
- Adapted to dramatic changes in the delivery of medicines, which involved decentralizing medicine inventories, new charting procedures, and use of computerized entry-order systems.
- Provide pre/post-operative education to patients and family members.

Committee, Team & Leadership Experience:
- Participate on a multi-disciplinary medication task force to improve the delivery of quality care, efficiency, cost-effectiveness, communications, and accuracy.
- Serve on the Cultural Diversity Committee and the unit's Leadership Committee.
- Serve as a liaison between patients and physicians.
- Direct as many as 10 staff nurses as a Charge Nurse on a periodic basis.

PSYCHIATRIC INSTITUTE OF MARYLAND, Rockville, Maryland   2007 – 2012
Staff Nurse
- Provided short-term, acute care on a 30-patient Adult Psychiatric unit.
- Held therapeutic and educational sessions in both one-on-one and group capacities for patients typically diagnosed with bi-polar conditions, OCD, behavioral/personality disorders, and schizophrenia.
- Wrote progress reports indicating medication intake, behavioral changes, and related information. Maintained treatment plans. Acquired knowledge of drug interactions.
- Supported NIH psychiatrists who were conducting research on anti-psychotic drugs for schizophrenia.

SUPPLEMENT

Education: **Bachelor of Arts,** Chemistry, University of Maryland, College Park, Maryland
Associate of Arts, Nursing, Montgomery College, Takoma Park, Maryland
Critical Care Certification, Maryland Adventist Hospital, Rockville, Maryland
Transplant Care Training, Symposium

Licensure: Registered Nurse – State of Maryland

CORY SCHULMAN

18003 Nursing Trail Way
Beltsville, Maryland 20705
240-338-0050
nurse@gmail.com

HIGHLIGHTS

Licensure & Education:
- Licensed registered nurse in Washington, DC
- **B.S. degree in Nursing**, 2008, The University of Maryland at Baltimore
- **A.A.S. degree in Nursing**, 2006, Norfolk State University

Clinical Experience:
- Provide nursing care to orthopedic, neurological, gastrointestinal, and pre/postoperative patients.
- Identify current and potential complex conditions; analyze trends and changes in patient statuses; prepare, deliver, and delegate care plans to patients ranging from simple needs through complications with chronic medical disorders: AIDS, diabetes, congestive heart failure, and end-stage renal disease.
- Assess effectiveness of treatments and pain management interventions. Collaborate with nurse manager and clinical nurse IV to develop standards of care. Identify and evaluate short and long-range goals of nursing care.
- Appropriate intravenous tubing to decrease waste and risk of accidental needle sticks.
- Functioned as patient controlled analgesic resource coordinator for nurses.

Written & Verbal Communications:
- Co-authored a self-learning patient education packet on Enteral Nutrition.
- Document patient information to facilitate integration of nursing assessment data, pathophysiology of disease processes, and the therapeutic regimen into an appropriate evaluation of the patient status.
- Serve as a patient advocate by communicating clinical concerns to other members of the healthcare team and by providing patient education on medical conditions, medication intake, wound care, and post discharge treatment procedures. Allay anxieties and address concerns of both patients and their family members.
- Mentor new nurses in facility protocols, patient care, charting, and equipment operations.

Informatics/Administration:
- Research lab test results and x-rays to identify abnormalities in post-operative patients and convey relevant research findings to staff.
- Develop, conduct, and evaluate unit-based inservice education programs.
- Participate in formulating, implementing, maintaining, and evaluating departmental goals, objectives, policies, and procedures.
- Implement and evaluate unit assessments and audits, including quality assurance and patient classification.

EXPERIENCE

Staff Nurse, Post Anesthesia Care Unit, Washington Medical, Washington, DC, 2015 – Present
Staff Nurse, Medical Unit, Washington Adventist Hospital, Washington, DC, 2013 – 2015
Staff Nurse, Surgical/Telemetry, Washington Medical Center, Washington, DC, 2012 – 2013
Surgical Nurse, Rockville Hospital, Rockville, Maryland, 2008 – 2012
Staff Nurse, Orthopedic Unit, Hagerstown Hospital, Hagerstown, Maryland, 2006 – 2008

CORY SCHULMAN
18004 Nursing Terrace
Germantown, Maryland 20876
240-338-0050
nurse@gmail.com

OBJECTIVE

To obtain a position that requires in-depth experience in the nursing process, patient education, and overall team leadership.

EXPERIENCE

MEDICAL ONE, Marlow Heights, Maryland   2010 – Present
Clinical Nurse/Advice Nurse
- Oversee daily activities of the OB/GYN clinic, which treats approximately 240 patients per day.
- Direct 4 medical assistants and support a 12-member medical team.
- Perform follow-up communications with patients regarding abnormal lab results and provide patient education covering prenatal classes, diabetic management, and HIV counseling.
- Teach all aspects of diabetes management, including symptoms, insulin instruction, glucose monitoring, hypo/hyperglycemia, and non-stress testing for pregnant mothers.
- Ensure proper operations of the diabetic monitor in accordance with QA standards.
- Triage telephone calls using the nursing process and protocols at the North Capital Center.
- Perform PAP-tracking duties.
- Schedule appointments for procedures such as LEEPs, cryosurgeries, colposcopies, etc.
- Perform patient histories, assessments, injections, IV therapy, intramuscular/IV medications, EKGs (as needed for pre-op and diabetic patients), and related nursing functions.

WILSON VALLEY NEIGHBORHOOD HEALTH CLINIC, Washington, DC   2009 – 2010
Clinical Nurse
- Oversaw daily activities of an OB/GYN clinic in conjunction with a multidisciplinary team. Performed assessments, patient histories, patient education, intravenous medications, and lab follow-up. Relief Nurse in the internal medicine and pediatric clinics. Taught prenatal classes.

ADDITIONAL EXPERIENCE

Intern Team Leader, Orthopedic/General Surgery, Neonatal, Rockville Hospital, 2008 – 2009
- Provided nursing care to patients with total hip replacements, fractures, dislocations, amputees, laminectomy, concussion and head trauma, hernia repairs, thyroidectomy, cholecystectomy, etc. Taught diabetic and post-partum classes.

Intern Nurse, ENT, Head and Neck/Oral Surgery, Shady Grove Hospital, 2006 – 2007
- Provided nursing care to patients undergoing radical neck dissection, laryngectomy, septorhinoplasty, and related ENT, head, neck, and oral surgeries. Taught tracheotomy care to patients and families. Performed venipuncture, IV chemotherapy, and 12-lead EKGs.

Intern Nurse, Hemodialysis, Washington Medical Hospital, 2005 – 2006
- Initiated, monitored, and terminated peritoneal and hemodialysis.

EDUCATION

Bachelor of Science in Nursing, 2005, Howard University, College of Nursing
Clinical Research, 2006 – 2009, Georgetown University
Ambulatory OB/GYN Nursing, Contemporary Forums
High-Risk OB Patients, Washington Hospital Center

CORY S. SCHULMAN, RN

18005 Nursing Hill Court
Gaithersburg, Maryland 20878
240-338-0050
nurse@gmail.com

EXPERIENCE

ROCKVILLE ADVENTIST HOSPITAL, Rockville, Maryland   2011 – Present

Staff RN
- Managed two to six patients in the ER depending on the patients' acuity.
- Applied the nursing process for patients with such conditions as congestive heart failure; renal and respiratory dysfunctions; orthopedic and gynecological abnormalities; psychiatric emergencies, and non-critical pediatric illnesses.
- Performed assessments and nursing diagnoses, planned and implemented interventions, administered medications (PO, IM, SC, IV), performed phlebotomy, started peripheral IVs, dressed central lines, and evaluated and documented patient outcomes.
- Used various equipment, including EKGs, heart monitors, IVs, Accucheck, oxygen tanks, nebulizers, gastrostomy tubes, nasogastric tubes, urinary catheters, and bear-huggers. Assisted physicians with chest-tube set ups.
- Interfaced with multidisciplinary teams, laboratories, and patients' families.

WASHINGTON MEDICAL HOSPITAL, Washington, DC   2009 – 2011

Staff RN
- Rendered care to as many as 10 patients in the Medicine Diabetes Unit.
- Provided direct care to patients diagnosed with diabetes, renal failure, AIDS, gastrointestinal ailments, and other serious conditions.
- Inserted and managed IVs; operated PCA pumps; administered blood and blood products; used oxygen tanks, oxygen flow meters, nasal cannulas, masks, and pulse oximeters; inserted ng-tubes; suctioned naso/oropharyngeal areas and tracheostomies; administered tube feedings; performed wound care; applied aseptic techniques, monitored I&O; and reported pertinent lab results.

PREFERRED MEDICAL, INC., Crofton, Maryland   2008 – 2009

Agency RN
- Provided acute care to adult and geriatric patients in Med-Surg and ER units at hospitals throughout the Washington Metropolitan region.

SUPPLEMENT

Licensure: Registered Nurse in the State of Maryland and Washington, DC

Certifications: Basic Life Support (BLS); Advance Clinical Life Support (ACLS)

Additional Experience: Performed nursing rotations through University College caring for psychiatric patients (bipolar conditions, psychosis, schizophrenia, and substance abuse) at Shady Grove Hospital; Med-Surg patients at Medical Center Hospital and Suburban Hospital; and obstetric patients at Washington Adventist Hospital, 2008 – 2009.

Education: Associate of Science Degree, Spring 2008, Licensed Registered Nurse (Maryland and Washington, DC), GPA: 3.39, Montgomery College, Takoma Park, Maryland
German Abitur (equivalent to AP work), Spring 2006, Klosterschule, Hamburg, Germany
Critical Care Consortium Course, 2011, Rockville Hospital, Rockville, Maryland
Basic Dysrhythmia Interpretation, Washington Medical Hospital, 2012

Affiliation: Member of the Emergency Nurses Association

CORY SCHULMAN

19001 Office Manager Place
Montgomery Village, MD 20886

240-338-0050
officemanager@gmail.com

EXPERIENCE

WILLIARD STONE, INC., Damascus, Maryland   2012 – Present
Office Manager
- Manage the central office of a mid-sized tile installation company and perform accounting functions, including accounts payable, invoicing, accounts receivable, general ledger, end-of-month reconciliations, and financial reports.
- Develop a $600,000 annual operating budget with more than 25 line items based on historical trends and projected needs.
- Reallocate budget line items to facilitate the reduction in procurement expenses.
- Assist management team in writing the company's first standard operating procedures, employee manuals, forms, and templates.
- Draft business correspondence that typically addresses client requests for price quotes.
- Organize archives of digital images used for installation projects and marketing.
- Research new products to identify potential acquisition of materials and applications.

MULTIMEDIA SOLUTIONS, INC., Gaithersburg, Maryland   2008 – 2012
Project Manager/Rental Administrator
- Hired/contracted technicians for as many as 30 corporate events per month such as annual stock holder meetings, new product demonstrations, multi-city satellite links, and live entertainment.
- Coordinated all travel arrangements, prepared itineraries, handled purchase orders, and produced requests for labor and related requirements for assignments.
- Increased profit margins from 10% to 25% within the first year.
- Interfaced with CEO, CFO, Accounting, Director of Production Management, and sales representatives on a daily basis.
- Analyzed, updated, and expanded the database of subcontractors. Ordered office supplies.
- Updated spreadsheets for freelancer's profit-and-loss reports.
- Prepared all invoices, credit card charges, and reports for the Accounting Department.
- Reconciled and approved timesheets for accuracy of job costs.

MEDICAL INTERNATIONAL, Rio de Janeiro   2005 – 2008
Account Analyst
- Advised CFO on budgetary and account matters, including general ledger, journal entries, end of the month reconciliations, financial and investment statements.
- Submitted monthly financial reports to the Comptroller.

SUPPLEMENT

Education: **Bachelor of Science, Accounting**, 2005, Saint Ursula University

Computer Skills: Peachtree, Microsoft Office (MS Word, Excel, Access) Lotus Notes

Language: Fluent in Portuguese

CORY SCHULMAN

19002 Office Manager Way
Germantown, MD 20874
240-338-0050
officemanager@gmail.com

EXPERIENCE

LUPUS FOUNDATION OF AMERICA, INC., Rockville, Maryland   2010 – Present

Office Administrator

- Manage daily operations of a national non-profit healthcare organization and report to the President and CEO. Interface with the Board of Directors, government and institutional executives, and senior management regarding lupus initiatives. Arrange all business meetings, travel, presentations, and registrations.
- Hire, train, and supervise office staff comprising six clerical, administrative, and accounting personnel. Administer human resources benefits.
- Distribute correspondence, financial reports, chapter criteria, and special events information to 58 chapters throughout the nation and at various annual, committee, and Board meetings.
- Coordinate printing of brochures, annual reports, and mailings with a circulation as much as 50,000. Reduced expenses by effectively conducting cost analyses and negotiating lower prices among vendors.
- Facilitate the organization of fundraising efforts by preparing and disseminating foundation literature to 7,000 prospective donors.
- Assist in setting-up and managing Internet connectivity, LAN installations, and database management. Perform daily backup of LAN consisting of 12 workstations. Maintain various databases of donors, memorials, patient information, and outside inquiries.
- Manage daily cash donations as much as $80,000.

HIGHLAND MORTGAGE, INC., Frederick, Maryland   2006 – 2010

Norwest acquired Prudential Home Mortgage in 2006

Administrative Assistant

- Provided Senior Vice President/Site Manager with administrative support, which included preparing correspondence and reports, scheduling appointments and meetings, preparing presentations, setting up travel and conferences, monitoring costs, serving as a liaison to other departments, and performing special projects as assigned.
- Earned two performance awards and one joint effort award.

WARREN HOME MORTGAGE INC., Frederick, Maryland   1998 – 2006

Business Coordinator

- Provided Senior Vice President/Site Manager with daily support, which included preparing management reports, correspondence, spreadsheets, and graphics.
- Set up video meetings with other sites across the country. Interfaced with internal communications group on special projects.
- Facilitated a smooth transition for Warren Mortgage, Inc.'s acquisition of Prudential as a member of the Acquisition Team.
- Earned performance bonuses every quarter for 4 consecutive years.

EDUCATION

B.A. Degree in Journalism, 2001, American University, Washington, DC

COMPUTER SKILLS

Proficient in MS Office (Word, Excel, PowerPoint, Access, Outlook), ACT, GiftMaker Pro.

CORY SCHULMAN
19003 Office Manager Road
Boyds, Maryland 20841
240-338-0050
officemanager@gmail.com

OBJECTIVE

To maximize operational efficiency and productivity as an Office Manager or a related administrative position.

EXPERIENCE

ADVERTISING INTERNATIONAL, Potomac, Maryland   2014 – Present
Office Manager
- Manage a client base of 400 – 500 consisting of corporate accounts, universities, non-profit organizations, and individuals. Coordinate order fulfillment of promotional products as a liaison between clients and manufacturers in support of approximately $250,000 in gross annual revenues.
- Coordinate 12 – 18 projects concurrently with single jobs requiring as many as 5 manufacturers for diverse products such as awards, uniforms, signage, desk accessories, and hand-held items.
- Define client needs and research appropriate pricing among 2,500 manufacturers in the U.S. and Canada.
- Conduct cost analyses of manufacturing services based on product lines, quantities, production quality, and delivery schedules. Negotiate pricing and prepare proposals.
- Resolve emerging production issues, resulting in dramatic turnaround efficiency and client satisfaction.
- Use Quicken to process accounts payable and accounts receivable; collect receivables as much as 120 days delinquent.
- Prepare internal administrative documents, such as proposals, order confirmations, invoices, client directory, and general correspondence using Microsoft Office.

THE HANSON SCHOOL, Gaithersburg, Maryland   2013 – 2014
Office Manager
- Supported the Principal, School Board Chair, and 30 faculty. Prepared faculty contracts and files. Performed payroll, purchasing, accounts receivable, and accounts payable. Maintained personnel files. Set up and maintained database. Reception, customer service, and sales.

SUPER K FOOD, Landover, Maryland   2011 – 2013
Management Assistant
- Supervised 60 to 100 employees, coordinating operations. Handled a wide variety of tasks and responsibilities simultaneously and efficiently, often in a stressful environment. Performed daily reconciliation and deposits, personnel management and scheduling, customer relations, payroll processing, and training of new employees.

EDUCATION & LICENSE

Real Estate License, 2013, State of Maryland
University of Maryland, University College, College Park, Maryland, 2010 – 2012, Accounting

CORY SCHULMAN

19004 Office Manager Road
Olney, Maryland 20832
240-338-0050
officemanager@gmail.com

OBJECTIVE

To maximize patient relations and operational efficiency in an administrative or managerial position.

EXPERIENCE

WINSTON PEARL, D.D.S., Bethesda, Maryland   2010 – Present
Patient Coordinator/Office Manager

Operations Management:
- Earned a promotion from New Patient Coordinator to manage front desk operations for a dental practice that generated more than $1 million per annum and employed two dentists and three hygienists.
- Facilitated a rapid increase of the patient base from approximately 2,000 to 3,300 by providing leadership in public relations, follow through, and organizational management.
- Devised strategies to quickly book openings resulting from last-minute cancellations and missed appointments.

Administration & Financial Management:
- Contributed in the development of a manual on updated HIPAA policies and procedures.
- Created a system to administer HIPAA procedures.
- Assisted in converting manual operations to computerized systems, involving industry-specific software that automated appointment confirmation practices, scheduled appointments, and processed insurance information.
- Reduced outstanding account receivables that were as much as 90 days overdue.
- Performed daily bank reconciliations, transfers, and deposits.

Public Relations & Personnel Management:
- Registered new patients and documented their medical histories. Enrolled new employees into insurance plans. Assisted patients in preparing and submitting insurance forms.
- Optimized patient volumes and revenue by coordinating temporary personnel to ensure coverage for all positions.
- Trained administrative assistants in customer service, scheduling techniques, and information management.

EDUCATION

University of New Hampshire, Durham, New Hampshire
Bachelor of Arts in Business Administration, 2009, Minor: French
Summa Cum Laude

CORY SCHULMAN
1006 Payroll Road
Wheaton, Maryland 20906

H: 240-338-0050
W: 240-338-0050
payroll@gmail.com

SUMMARY

Payroll Administration:

- Experienced in performing payroll administration for 7,000+ worldwide employees for such employers as AlliedSignal Technical Service Corporation (ATSC) and MCI.
- Administrate accounting functions, such as general ledger, journal entries, adjustments, and intercompany transactions. Skilled in processing payroll taxes, unemployment claims/taxes, and garnishment payments. Ensured timely and accurate processing of local, state, and federal tax filings.
- Prepare reports, plans, and recommendations on payroll activities related to PeopleSoft and Ceridian systems.

Leadership Roles:

- Consultant to Fiscal Administrators regarding payroll processing and problem resolution at ATSC.
- Acted as the Interim Cash Management Administrator and verified proper balance of daily deposits amounting up to $400,000 in paid invoices at CTA.
- Served as an Arbitrator between employees and bargaining units at ATSC.
- Manage staff and provide training to ensure compliance with payroll laws and regulations.
- Implement and enforce policies and procedures to maintain internal and system control.

Computer Skills:

- Ceridian Source 100/Source Empowerment/Repertoire, Deltek CostPoint, Deltek System 1, PeopleSoft, Quickbooks, Quicken, Excel, Outlook, PowerPoint, ADP, Impromptu, Monarch.

EXPERIENCE

Computer Technology And Development (CTAD), Rockville, Maryland   2012 – Present

Payroll Manager

- Manage up to $1.2 million in payroll processing for as many as 800 employees.
- Direct staff of administrators to process timesheets, leave modules, termination orders, new hires, and short-term disability forms.
- Review, analyze, and approve state withholdings and payroll/unemployment tax reports, including 941s and 940s.
- Enter journal entries and rectify financial discrepancies using the CostPoint system.
- Prepare utilization reports comprising all overhead expenses such as employees' direct/indirect charges.
- Conduct quarterly audits; prepare spreadsheets on year-to-date earnings, and initiate corrective actions when necessary.
- Eliminated a severe deficiency in incomplete and inaccurate information within the direct deposits file.

- Established a labor schedule and defined positions, which curtailed unnecessary labor and eliminated overtime abuses. Conduct manual research on employees' missing hours.
- Retrain staff in advanced accounting skills such as journal entries and labor corrections.

ABD Investment Technology Group, Rockville, Maryland   2008 – 2012

Payroll Administrator

- Streamlined payroll processing by introducing and implementing the Ceridian system, which enabled electronic fund transfers and reduced cash deposit cycle times as much as 2 weeks.
- Reduced chronic employee complaints by revising policies regarding submission of travel expenses for reimbursements.
- Eliminated credit card abuses by changing credit liability from the company to the employee, which saved the company approximately $200,000 a year.
- Initiated the application process for American Express credit. Issued corporate American Express cards and reviewed accounts on a monthly basis.
- Served as the point-of-contact with employees regarding 401(K) plans.
- Set up deductions, new hires, terminations, overtime, direct deposits, hours, and earnings.
- Received and downloaded biweekly master reports from Ceridian.
- Processed monthly payroll journal entries in PeopleSoft, wire transfers, and 401(K) plan.
- Reviewed and processed all employee travel reimbursements.
- Handled levies and wage attachments.
- Reconciled state and federal taxes with quarterly Ceridian tax filing service.
- Reconciled 401(K), Flexible Medical, Dependent Care, and Vision Services for payment.
- Maintained and reconciled employee leave records.
- Generated payable and receivable reports for accountants, managers, and human resources personnel.

ATSC Corporation, Columbia, Maryland   2005 – 2008

Payroll Accountant/Leader

- Supervised a 6-member staff to process biweekly payroll for 7,500 employees.
- Reviewed all edits from in-house data processing and coordinated the collection of timed documents.
- Prepared checks for signature and authorized distribution.
- Processed payroll file for EFT transfers and made all payments before payday.
- Planned, developed, and implemented EFT direct deposits, which reduced processing time 1-day per pay cycle.
- Reconciled all state tax accounts and labor correction processes.
- Improved the process of check distribution of terminated employees, which resulted in cycle time reduction and cost savings.
- Documented and flow-charted 60% of the payroll desk procedures in the department.
- Served as one of the key leaders in the successful conversion of the in-house payroll system to the MSA system in the financial office in Tempe, Arizona.

EDUCATION

B.A. Business Administration, 2004, Strayer College, Washington, DC

CORY SCHULMAN

20002 Law Enforcement Boulevard
Laurel, MD 20724
240-338-0050
police@gmail.com

SUMMARY

Decorated Maryland Police Sergeant with expertise in conducting hundreds of overt and covert criminal investigations throughout tenure. Directed department operations and mobilized as many as 50 officers, resulting in multi-million dollar seizures and convictions of kingpins as well as other high-level offenders. Spearheaded 30% reduction in crime in targeted jurisdictions. Former U.S. Marine and Retail Security Manager.

EXPERIENCE

MARYLAND STATE POLICE, College Park, Maryland   2005 – Present

Sergeant, 2008 - Present; Promoted twice from Corporal and Uniformed Road Trooper.

Management:

- Charged with managing police operations and as many as 50 police officers in Prince George's County during the absence of the Lieutenant.
- Direct troopers in response to homicide, assault, high-speed chases, theft, crowd control, disabled vehicles, and related law enforcement matters.
- Organize and supervise manpower, local police department, helicopters, and canines to serve warrants and lead raids.

Criminal Investigations:

- Led majority of investigations, including undercover and overt operations in Baltimore City and other jurisdictions (Virginia, Pennsylvania, and New York).
- Successfully infiltrated tight-knit rural operations, suburban communities, urban gangs, and commercial environments (BWI Airport, etc.), resulting in a dramatic 30% to 75% reduction in illegal activity in high-crime areas within 4 to 6 weeks.
- Led drug investigations that resulted in convictions of street-level dealers through high-level kingpins.
- Recovered millions of dollars of illegally acquired currency, jewelry, cars, homes, and controlled dangerous substances.
- Coordinated covert investigations of murder-for-hire cases, homicides, and illegal fire-arm sales.
- Convictions of murder-for-hire suspects were based on successful adherence to legal investigative and arrest practices, effective evidence collection, positive identification, and clarity of court testimony.
- Identified Jamaican and New York gang related criminal activity.

Written and Verbal Communications:
- Provided court testimony against indicted offenders in approximately 500 jury trials since 2005, resulting in 92% conviction rate.
- Write search and seizure warrants on homes and individuals.
- Prepare evaluations on subordinates and delegate specific police assignments such as road blocks and DWI enforcement.
- Improved department morale and doubled officers' productivity as evidenced by the sharp increase in arrests and approximately 70% reduction in crime throughout Frederick, the Eastern Shore, and several other counties.
- Established contacts within local police departments throughout the Washington Metropolitan area.
- Interface routinely with the States Attorney's Office, the U.S. Attorney's Office, and the Attorney General's Office.

Recognition:
- Earned awards by the Drug Enforcement Agency and the Maryland State Police for exemplary performance during covert drug investigations.
- Received numerous letters of commendation from the State's Attorney, U.S. Attorney, and immediate supervisors.

DELLS RETAIL STORE, Lake Success, Queens, New York   2002 – 2005
Security Manager

MILITARY

UNITED STATES MARINE CORP.   1999 – 2002
Communication and Radio Technician
- Managed the Communications Unit consisting of 12 subordinates to maintain radio communications among the tank platoon during 2 world tours.
- Directed 25 marines in the second marine division.
- Honorably discharged.

SUPPLEMENT

Education: MSP, FBI, DEA, and ATF
Criminal investigation school: interviewing and interrogation, drug enforcement and investigation, covert investigations, chemical intoximeter, officer survival, master qualified marksman, employee relations, employee sensitivity, supervisor school, drug detection and identification, criminal and investigative law, and speed enforcement.

Volunteerism: Troubled Youth of Washington, DC

Affiliation: Fraternal Order of Police

CORY SCHULMAN

20003 Police Officer Terrace
Damascus, MD 20872
240-338-0050
police@gmail.com

OBJECTIVE

To obtain a position within the Central Intelligence Agency (CIA), whereby experience from the Montgomery County Police Department, CIA, and U.S. Army will have valuable application.

EXPERIENCE

MONTGOMERY COUNTY POLICE DEPARTMENT, Silver Spring, Maryland   2015 – Present

Police Officer

- Patrol approximately 16 square miles within a highly populated urban/suburban beat near Washington, DC, and respond to medical, fire, and law enforcement emergencies.
- Conduct surveillances of suspected drug dealers and organized-crime networks, resulting in numerous arrests.
- Facilitate investigations of bomb threats, homicides, grand larceny, arson, armed robbery, and other illegal activities. Secure crime scenes, collect evidence, interview witnesses/involved parties, interrogate suspects, and write initial reports.
- Collaborate with HAZMAT teams to investigate potential illegal use of hazardous materials. Use chemical agent monitors (CAM), RADIAC meters, and personal denominators.
- Participate in the preparation for an upcoming IMF demonstration, which entails crowd control and identification of radical protesters.
- Co-coordinated logistics of Emergency Response to secure the Public Service Training Academy in Washington, DC.

CENTRAL INTELLIGENCE AGENCY, McLean, Virginia   2009 – 2015

Federal Police Office

- Protected CIA personnel and property in addition to enforcing federal, state, and local laws by responding to medical emergencies, fire/vault alarms, and criminal activity.
- Performed counter surveillance and mobile patrol at commercial and government buildings.
- Earned above average performance appraisal reviews (PARs).

UNITED STATES ARMY, Fort Bragg, North Carolina   2004 – 2008

E-5; Sergeant

- Planned, coordinated, and executed security and maintenance activities for a large military battalion.
- Oversaw work performed by 10 soldiers; prioritized and delegated job assignments; trained new personnel in daily activities including equipment operation and repair, field procedures, and military policies.
- Coordinated security efforts; secured field positions during numerous tactical exercises to optimize personnel and equipment safety; and maintained a wide variety of military weaponry.
- Received exceptional performance reviews; earned numerous medals, awards and letters of commendation.

SUPPLEMENT

Clearance: Held Top Secret Security Clearance
Designations: Certified Emergency Medical Technician and Maryland First Responder
Education: Graduated in upper 10%, 2010, Montgomery County Police, Training Academy
Graduated, 2009, Mixed Basic Police Training Academy, FLETC
Norwich University, Northfield, VT, completed 72 semester hours in Liberal Arts
Completed a wide variety of courses, including Federal Law Enforcement and Training; Nuclear, Biological and Chemical Weapons

SERGEANT CORY S. SCHULMAN

20005 Police Way
Germantown, Maryland 20876
240-338-0050
police@gmail.com

EXPERIENCE

MONTGOMERY COUNTY POLICE DEPARTMENT   2002 – Present

Police Sergeant, Field Services Bureau

Investigative Services Bureau:

- Coordinated the investigations of numerous multi-jurisdictional and complex felonies, including homicides, organized crime, assaults, missing persons, drug trafficking, armed robberies, and burglaries. Employed patrol tactics, evidence collection/analysis, and interview and interrogation techniques.
- Notable investigations include the following:
  - The investigation of serial murderer Mitchell Moore, whose prosecution set court precedents in Maryland for the introduction of previous crime convictions in subsequent trials to show progression of violence.
  - The investigation of a missing person, which developed into a homicide, and successfully prosecuted without a body.
- Member of an Asian Organized Crime Task Force in the Washington, DC Metropolitan area (local, state, and federal), which assisted the FBI's development of its Asian Organized Crime Report.

Trainer:

- Certified as a Training Instructor by the Maryland Training Commission.
- Certified as a Field Training Officer by MCPD.
- Member of the Field Training and Evaluation Program Steering Committee, which oversees FTO program and maintains its success as a nationally recognized program for the training of new officers.
- Established the Hostage Negotiations Program for the department in 2002 and served as the sole negotiator for 2 years.
- Assisted in implementing the department's current hostage negotiating teams and served on them for 5 years.
- Developed training programs and instructed at our own police academy and outside the department for hostage negotiations, homicide investigation, robbery investigation, burglary investigation, patrol tactics, and interview and interrogation techniques.

EDUCATION

Master of Arts, Forensic Criminology, 2001, Nova University, Washington, DC
Bachelor of Arts, Administration of Justice, 1999, American University, Washington, DC
Associates Degree, Administration, 1997, American University, Washington, DC

CORY SCHULMAN

20006 Police Drive
Clarksburg, Maryland 20871

240-338-0050
police@gmail.com

HIGHLIGHTS

Possess **Top Secret Security Clearance** with varied experience in investigative, security, and law enforcement positions as a Federal Air Marshal, Secret Service Officer, Correctional Officer, and First-Emergency Responder. Skilled in emergency planning and escape routing with knowledge of chemical, biological, and radiological response plans. Highly accurate sharpshooter experienced in using such firearms as Uzis, shotguns, 9 mms, M-14s, M-16s, 38s, and 357s. Adept at crowd control, witness interviewing, evidence collection/analysis, close quarter combat, incident investigation and reporting, and computer maintenance and repair.

EXPERIENCE

TRANSPORTATION SECURITY ADMINISTRATION, Herndon, Virginia   2014 – Present
Civil Aviation Security Specialist

- Provide armed, undercover security on commercial flights for domestic and international destinations.
- Prepare flight reports covering incidents, intervening actions, and air crew/passenger information.
- Give briefings to pilots and flight attendants; maintain communications with upper management.

UNITED STATES SECRET SERVICE, Washington, DC   2010 – 2014
Officer, 2012 – 2015

- Performed numerous high-profile, VIP security details, including protection of the President and Vice President of the United States, foreign dignitaries, and heads of state. Facilitated protection of the Pope in New York, which involved screening persons among 500,000 attendees. Safeguarded the President of Korea in San Francisco without incident.
- Patrolled and conducted surveillance of the White House compound. Collected evidence and interviewed witnesses of a shooter in front of the White House. Collected evidence and witnesses for a firearms incident on the south-side of the White House and secured and analyzed the crime scene.
- Arrested persons for various unlawful actions, including DWI, assault/battery, theft/grand larceny, and related offenses. Secured, analyzed, and reported on various homicide sites.

Emergency Response Procedure Officer, 2011 – 2012

- Developed emergency procedures regarding hostage negotiations, sniper positioning, rescue and fire fighter safe points, equipment placement, and traffic/person control points.
- Responded to a high-volume of emergency calls as a first responder to suspected anthrax contamination and related alarms at foreign embassies.

MARYLAND DEPARTMENT OF CORRECTIONS, Brockbridge, Maryland   2008 – 2010
Correctional Officer

- Maintained security and prevented prisoner escapes within a medium security prison, consisting of 6 dormitories all open concurrently resulting in a 300 to 1 ratio of offenders to officers. Intervened to control rioting and other disturbances. Conducted prison escorts to medical facilities.

UNITED STATES DEPARTMENT OF THE NAVY, Norfolk, Virginia   2003 – 2007
Electronic Warfare Technician/Seaman, USS Preble DDG 46, Honorable Discharge

- Monitored and analyzed electronic magnetic frequencies throughout the Mediterranean and performed electronic countermeasures to prevent radar detection.

SUPPLEMENT

Education: B.S., 2002, Federal Law Enforcement Training Center, Glynco, Georgia
Awards: Department of Navy and Secret Service, Outstanding Performance Awards

CORY SCHULMAN
21002 Politics Place
Rockville, Maryland 20852
240-338-0050
government@gmail.com

HIGHLIGHTS

Government/Politics:
- Campaigned for Jamie Raskin, candidate for the Eighth Congressional District, against third-term incumbent, Chris Van Hollen Jr.
- Experienced in polling, canvassing, media/community relations, and reporting.
- Introduced, defended, and addressed the candidate's stance on traditional issues, such as economic conditions/job growth, budget management, law enforcement, traffic/development control, environmental protection, and specific legislation.
- Majored in Government and Politics with completed relevant courses in American Social Policy, Law and Society, Philosophy of Law, The 3rd World, Principles of Government, American Government, Genocide and Violence, Economics of War, Comparative Politics, and many others from the University of Maryland.
- Participated in group academic research involving data analysis and event coding to identify patterns of military actions during the conflict in Rwanda. Conducted campus surveys; wrote website content on the Rwandan genocide of 1994 and presented data analysis.
- Traveled throughout the Middle East and Europe with strong cross-cultural understanding. Bilingual in English and Farsi; conversant in French.

EXPERIENCE

JAMIE RASKIN CONGRESSIONAL CAMPAIGN, Bethesda, Maryland 2014 – Present
GOTV Coordinator
- Oversaw the operations of five voting booths throughout the District to register new voters, disseminate political literature, and tabulate/report on election results.
- Promoted the candidate's platform through community canvassing and telephone flushing, which involved polling and information dissemination.
- Expanded the base of supporters by co-creating a Democratic Student Union and recruiting volunteers to participate in grassroots efforts. Supervised and trained up to 12 volunteers.
- Addressed the media during a community festival through a televised interview.

EDUCATION

University of Maryland, College Park, Maryland
B.A. in Government and Politics, minor in Philosophy, 2013

CORY SCHULMAN

22001 Property Management Place
Gaithersburg, MD 20878

240-338-0050
propertymanagement@gmail.com

OBJECTIVE

To maximize occupancy, positive tenant relations, and corporate profits as a Property Manager or a related position.

EXPERIENCE

ALLISTON PROPERTIES, Gaithersburg, Maryland   2009 – Present
Landlord Agent

Sales and Management:
- Manage 500 units that generate more than $1 million in gross annual rents and consist of condominiums, townhomes, and detached houses.
- Expanded the inventory of listings 8-fold and doubled the number of clients as the #1 renting agent for 5 consecutive years.
- Increased occupancy from 75% to nearly 100% by launching effective advertising campaigns, negotiating tenant leases, and improving curb appeal of properties.
- Reduced expenses by implementing preventative maintenance, scheduling agents, qualifying prospects, selecting contractors, and conducting inspections.

Technical Skills:
- Serve as the company's computer expert. Established and updated the company's computerized tracking and reporting system that documents rental payments, provides on-line credit reports, and networks with the MLS.
- Installed Windows, Office software package, MLS, Internet browsers, Adobe Acrobat, Norton Utilities, and many other applications.

Tenant Relations:
- Foster positive tenant relations by coordinating smooth move-ins/outs as a liaison between tenants and maintenance crews.
- Close long-term leases and sustain longevity of tenants by securing renewals.
- Conduct move out and interim inspections and report damages to owner.

Risk Management:
- Strengthened adherence to pre-qualification procedures for screening prospective tenants. Run and evaluate credit reports, verify tenant income and housing references, and conduct criminal background checks.
- Apply knowledge of HUD standards and local, state, and federal laws, including fair housing laws.

MORRISON REALTY, Gaithersburg, Maryland   2006 – 2009
Real Estate Agent
- Emerged as a Million Dollar agent for 3 consecutive years by listing and selling detached homes, townhouses, and condominiums in Montgomery County.
- Coordinated marketing seminars that attracted prospective buyers.

CORY SCHULMAN

22002 Leasing Circle
Olney, Maryland 20832

240-338-0050
lease@gmail.com

EXPERIENCE

REAL PROPERTIES DEVELOPMENT COMPANY, Wheaton, Maryland   2009 – Present

President
- Provide leasing services to 30+ local and national developers for an accumulated 3 million square feet.
- Render additional services in architectural design, financing, lease administration, and property management.
- Lease various commercial retail properties such as community shopping centers, power centers, entertainment shopping centers, and manufacturers' outlets.
- Cultivated loyal relationships with off-price, outlet, and regional mall retailers, including Giant Food, Bed, Bath & Beyond, Liz Claiborne, Barnes & Noble, AMC Theatres, Dress Barn, Fashion Bug, and many others.
- Devised and launched leasing campaigns, which involved dynamic in-person presentations to as many as 40+ developers.
- Negotiated and successfully closed long-term leases ranging from $150,000 to $10 million.
- Increased combined lease values per year from $2 million to approximately $50 million.
- Grew staff from 2 assistants to 30 full-time employees and increased gross annual revenues 8-fold within first 3 years.

LEASE MANAGEMENT COMPANIES, Springfield, Virginia   2007 – 2009

President of Leasing
- Established and managed an in-house leasing department, which provided pre-development, leasing, and re-leasing of 2 million square feet of community shopping centers.
- Increased occupancy from 65% to 97% within the first year.
- Secured higher caliber tenants while reducing vacant time from 12 to 6 months.

MOORES CORPORATION, Washington, DC   2004 – 2007

Senior Leasing Executive
- Emerged as a top producing leasing agent among 20 others for the last 2 years.
- Leased specialty stores, food courts, and 20,000 square feet anchors.
- Participated in the pre-development and leasing of Potomac Mills in Woodbridge, Virginia consisting of 1.2 million square feet and Franklin Mills in Philadelphia, Pennsylvania consisting of 1.8 million feet.
- Facilitated the pre-development and merchandising stages of Sawgrass Mills, a 2 million square foot specialty retail mall in Sunrise, Florida.
- Conducted and analyzed feasibility studies, which examined critical mass, demographics, and traffic patterns.

SUPPLEMENT

Affiliations: International Council of Shopping Centers, 2007 – Present
                    Value Retail News Advisory Board Member, 2007 – 2008
                    Value Retail News Advisory Board Sustaining Member, 2007 – Present
Education: Business Administration, American University, Washington, DC, 2014 – Present

CORY SCHULMAN

22003 Property Management Terrace
Rockville, MD 20855

240-338-0050
leasing@gmail.com

EXPERIENCE

Property Manager, WELLINGTON CONSTRUCTION CO., Washington, DC   1999 – Present

Property Management:

- Established the Property Management Division and led the rapid expansion of managed properties from 2 to 35+ complexes having an aggregate value of approximately $400 million in Maryland.
- Opened 12 new office buildings and coordinated seamless tenant move-ins.
- Oversee 50 major properties consisting of 2 million square feet of office space and 200 thousand square feet of retail shopping centers, warehouses, and residential properties.
- Increased the value of a 120 unit garden apartment 50% by improving management of services, rentals, and collections. Eliminated a 25% vacancy rate and minimized tenant turnover of low to middle income occupants by instituting stricter screening procedures, enhancing curb appeal, and strengthening tenant relations.
- Selected and direct 25 building engineers and subcontractors for all aspects of property management: facility maintenance, grounds, construction/renovation, etc.

Professional and Tenant Relations:

- Cultivated strong tenant relations by providing reliable and expedient responses to tenant issues. Ensured repairs were completed timely and in a workman-like manner.
- Ensured a safe and convenient working environment for 600 tenants during a major renovation in a 100,000 square foot building, which entailed intricate planning and coordination of carpentry, finish work, and furniture.
- Foster strong professional relationships through collaborative efforts with interior designers, space planners, architects, engineers, and site planners.

Project Management:

- Manage 50 – 60 projects per year with single projects valued up to $300,000. Direct construction from excavation through punch-out; retrofits, and interior renovations, which includes plumbing, mechanical systems, electrical layout, trim, decor, and furniture layout.
- Cut operating costs through effective bid solicitation for services, contracts, and tenant work while achieving the highest quality in the shortest available time.
- Increased revenues $750,000 per year by conceiving and spearheading the construction of a fee-based parking lot with 1,500 spaces. Streamlined billing, which eliminated costly invoicing and collection efforts for all 1,500 occupants.

Fiscal Management and Administration:

- Oversee rent collection of approximately $15 million per annum.
- Formulate annual budgets for each property and achieved budget projections within 2 – 3% every year.
- Negotiate service contracts valued up to $350,000.
- Standardized rent increase schedules, budget projections, and operating cost pass throughs.
- Negotiate unit pricing agreements with federal agencies such as NOAA, NIH, and GSA.

Media Relations:

- Serve as the company spokesman to deter or defend against litigation and negative media coverage. Preserved the company's reputation and prevented monetary losses from litigation regarding landlord and tenant affairs, sexual harassment, and liability cases. Represented the company during intense media interviews concerning bomb threats, environmental issues, and controversial parking policies.

EDUCATION

A.A. Degree, 1998, Montgomery College, Rockville, Maryland

CORY S. SCHULMAN, Ph.D.

23001 Psychology Trail, Centreville, Virginia 20120   240-338-0050   psychology@aol.com

OBJECTIVE

To optimize corporate and employee effectiveness and development as an Industrial-Organizational Psychologist or a related position.

HIGHLIGHTS

Profile: Industrial-Organizational Psychologist with 15 years of experience. Skilled in designing and directing national/regional initiatives to research organizational effectiveness and development. Possess Ph.D.'s in Industrial-Organizational Psychology and Clinical Psychology. Applied knowledge of psychometrics, human resource selection practices, and both individual and organizational performance models.

Large-Scale Research/Analysis: Designed national research impacting the American public, 80 offices, and up to 1,400 internal employees. Performed qualitative and quantitative statistical analyses. Defined qualitative variables, customized surveys and other measurement research tools, and provided systemic solutions. Planned and developed enhanced business practices pertaining to personnel, administrative, and managerial issues.

Communications: Provided executive consultation, coaching, PowerPoint presentations, and strategic plans to address such issues as leadership styles, empowerment, change management, total quality control, performance measures, internal effectiveness, human resource systems, and customer satisfaction. Former Compliance Specialist providing consultation on Federal labor laws including FLSA, FMLA, EPPA, CCPA, MSPA, INA, and government contracts.

EXPERIENCE

U.S. DEPARTMENT OF LABOR, Washington, DC   2007 – Present

Senior Program Specialist, *8/12 – Present, Wage & Hour Division, Office of External Affairs*
- Develop, manage, and assess national initiatives regarding outreach, recidivism, and customer satisfaction. Write press releases and present campaign results to executive staff. Lead field staff, internal/external agencies, and contractors in organizational development practices.

Industrial-Organizational Psychologist, *[Detail 3/10 – 7/12], Office of Workforce Security*
- Evaluated effectiveness of the Office of Workforce Security, consisting of 16 nationwide offices and 316 employees operating within a multi-billion dollar fiscal budget.
- Proposed, created, and implemented the first internal assessment in the office's history. Assessed empowerment on organizational effectiveness based on leadership styles.
- Devised customized internal measures for 16 different offices by using focus groups to research and define effectiveness measures, such as high performance, service quality, customer satisfaction, and public accountability. Utilized various measurement instruments such as MLQ-5X, empowerment, and PANAS.
- Produced executive summaries and conducted PowerPoint presentations before the executive staff (eight division chiefs, eight regional administrators) regarding research protocols, findings, and recommended solutions to organizational effectiveness.

Quality and Human Resource Specialist, *10/07 – 9/10, Office of Quality and HR Development*
- Developed national action plans pertaining to the Wage and Hour Division's organizational development and improvement of 80 offices across the country.
- Headed several teams for national initiatives that provided strategic planning, Total Quality Management, communications, and training to 1,400 internal employees.
- Devised several surveys for internal employees and the U.S. workforce regarding customer satisfaction and quality of services rendered by the Division's field staff.
- Directed up to five team members and six support personnel. Managed as many as eight projects concurrently, which involved researching raw/archival data, developing measurement tools, coordinating resources, scheduling milestones, allocating personnel, writing reports, and giving presentations.
- Gauged annual effectiveness which rose from baselines of 60% employer satisfaction and 40% employee satisfaction to 5% increases in each category for 5 consecutive years.
- Provided executive coaching to the Director of Quality & Human Resources Division in the presentation process and for national program planning.

CLINICAL EXPERIENCE

HUMAN SERVICES CENTER, Falls Church, Virginia   2005 – 2007
Doctoral Intern
- Pre-doctoral training experience in multidisciplinary psychiatric patient care.
- Conducted psychological testing and compiled psychological reports.
- Conducted outpatient therapy and group therapy for adults and children.
- Led workshop training on strategies in developing effective treatment interventions.

UNIVERSITY OF ROCHESTER, Medical Center   2000 – 2005
Clinical Practicum
- Conducted psychological testing, neuropsychiatric exams, outpatient and group therapy.
- Tested and counseled in-patients diagnosed with schizophrenia and personality disorders.

EDUCATION

California School of Professional Psychology, San Diego, California
Ph.D. Industrial-Organizational Psychology, 12/2005
Ph.D. Clinical Psychology, 06/2003
- Dissertation: *The Effect of Psychological Suppression on Workplace Productivity.*

The University of Texas at El Paso, El Paso, Texas
B.A. Psychology, minor: Journalism/Advertising, graduated with honors, 5/2000

SUPPLEMENT

Affiliations: Member of the American Psychological Association (APA)

Awards: U.S. DOL, Wage & Hour Division Vision Award, Western Region, 2007
Public Service Ambassador's Award Nominee, 2002

CORY S. SCHULMAN, PSY. D.

23002 Psychology Drive
Gaithersburg, Maryland 20886
240-338-0050
psychology@gmail.com

EDUCATION

Psy. D. in Clinical Psychology, September 2002, Miami Institute of Psychology, APA Accredited, Renamed Carlos Albizu University, Miami, Florida
MS in Counseling Psychology, 1994, University of Baltimore, Baltimore, Maryland
BS in Psychology, 1992, University of Maryland, College Park, Maryland

HIGHLIGHTS

Psychotherapy Experience:
- Licensed Psychologist in the State of Maryland experienced in conducting short/long-term psychotherapy, psycho-social intake/case management, and psycho-educational counseling to self-referred and court-ordered patients.
- Led individual, couple's, family, and group sessions for patients facing severe maladies, including bipolar conditions, schizophrenia, psychosis, anxiety, paranoia, depression, and obsessive/compulsive disorders.
- Counseled geriatric, adult, adolescent, and pediatric populations.
- Administered formal psychological assessments using standardized tests.
- Interfaced with professionals from diverse institutions: mental health centers, hospitals, clinics, private practices, protection/justice agencies, courts, insurance companies, and educational systems.

Program Development:
- Devised a stimulating lecture series and gave dynamic presentations to audiences of 200.
- Focused on topics pertaining to intimacy, gender, and seniors.
- Coordinated guest speakers and collaborated with a licensed psychologist to develop corporate training programs.

Cross-Cultural Experience:
- Lived in Iran, Germany, and various parts of the United States, including immersion in a Spanish community. Traveled extensively throughout the Middle East and Europe.
- Trilingual in German, Farsi, and English.

EXPERIENCE

KAISER PERMANENTE, Marlo Heights, Maryland   2005 – Present
The largest managed care organization in the United States with 8.7 million health plan members, 156,000 employees, and $34.4 billion in annual operating revenues.
Program Psychologist
- Provided cognitive behavioral therapy for a 200 patient case load, comprising children ages 4 to 11, adolescents, and parents. Led individual and group sessions.

- Diagnosed and counseled patients inflicted with depression, suicidal ideation/attempts, eating disorders, child abuse, sleep disturbances, self-injurious behavior, conduct disorders, ADHD, and many other mental health conditions. Provided therapeutic intervention for wide ranging issues, including sexual orientation, teen pregnancy, broken families, academic performance, and social skill development.
- Provided consults, crises management, and psycho-therapy for the Pediatric Department at the Camp Springs facility. Developed treatment plans with clear objectives, including measurable and attainable goals.
- Wrote clear and insightful session progress notes, initial evaluations, discharge summaries, and documentation in support of Individual Education Plans and other student needs.
- Collaborated with in-network and out-of-network psychiatrists, social workers, parole officers, academic officials, legal guardians, parents, and hospital staff. Worked with case managers to coordinate third party resources for patients suffering from abuse and eating disorders.
- Cultivated productive and respectful relationships with parents despite initial resistance to psycho-therapy.

MSA-THE CHILD AND ADOLESCENT CENTER, Columbia, Maryland   2002 – 2004
A private mental health agency.
Psychologist, Program Therapist
- Managed a caseload of approximately 12 pediatric and adolescent patients diagnosed with schizophrenia, depression, anxiety, and psycho-social issues.
- Conducted individual, group, and family therapy, which entailed psychological evaluations, psycho-social interviews, medical record reviews, case conceptualization, and treatment planning for social, cognitive, and behavioral interventions.
- Co-developed an intensive children's outpatient program, which generated a new revenue stream and facilitated a 29% increase in new patients.
- Developed and implemented parenting skills training and psycho-educational sessions.
- Focused on developing patients' life skills: effective communication, stress/anger management, medication management, assertiveness, social skills, problem solving, and conflict resolution.
- Wrote various reports, such as treatment update summaries, discharge summaries, school placement recommendations, and assessments/reviews/referrals.
- Consulted interdisciplinary professionals, including psychiatric specialists, academic counselors, medical care providers, and guardian ad litems.

CENTER FOR GROUP COUNSELING, Boca Raton, Florida   2000 – 2001
A non-profit community health center specializing in group therapy.
Pre-Doctoral Psychology Intern
- Performed individual, family, group, and couples' therapy for on-site patients. Assisted in the development of a "Caregivers' Program" and led support groups for caregivers of chronically-ill family members/friends.

SYLVESTER COMPREHENSIVE CANCER CENTER, Miami, Florida   1999 – 2000
A leading medical center affiliated with the National Institutes of Health and The University of Miami. The Center specialized in the treatment, diagnosis, prevention, detection, and supportive care of cancer patients.
Certified Cancer Information Specialist
- Provided psycho-social support and referral information on publications and studies relating to the prevention, symptomology, detection, diagnosis, and treatment of various cancers.

Cory Schulman

30002 Radiology Terrace
Montgomery Village, Maryland 20886
240-338-0050
radiology@gmail.com

EXPERIENCE

UNITED STATES ARMY   **2002 – Present**

HOUSER ARMY COMMUNITY HOSPITAL, 2008 – Present

Lead Radiology Technician

- Ensure quality assurance and quality control of x-ray films and equipment such as portable x-ray machines, processors, and C-ARMs.
- Perform fluoroscopy and routine diagnostic procedures as well as bone density and computer tomography (CT) for in/out patients.
- Implemented a system to track film logs, which eliminated a backlog of 6,000 unread films.
- Instituted a monthly reconciliation system for unread films.
- Direct a team of 5 x-ray technicians, schedule 1,000+ labor hours per month for 3 shifts, and coordinate radiologic exams in various departments: OR, ER, ICU, CCU, and Bone Density.
- Spearheaded the preventative maintenance program, which reduced equipment downtime approximately 30% while curtailing repair costs.
- Flag malfunctions and submit work orders for prompt repairs.
- Write standard operating procedures approved by the Chief Radiologist regarding scrub uniforms.
- Minimize radiation exposure to patients and cost of film processing by achieving a high rate of successful first time filming.
- Participate in weekly NCO meetings to review departmental issues and solutions.
- Promoted from Specialist to Corporal.

Staff Technician, 2006 – 2008

- Worked all three shifts in Diagnostic Radiology, including CAT scan and Bone Density departments providing general patient care; shooting and processing x-rays; and starting IVs for CAT scan procedures.

FT. MEADE, 2004 – 2006

Head of Radiology Clinic

- Managed and operated field x-ray clinics as the sole technician at Camp McCarthy performing quality assurance, quality control, and 24/7 on-call support.
- Collaborated with an AID station to coordinate patient care for all 1,000+ soldiers and civilian emergencies.
- Maintained authority on all equipment valued approximately $100,000.
- Ordered all supplies such as x-ray film and chemicals.

ST. FRANCIS HOSPITAL, 2002 – 2004

PRN X-ray Technician

- Performed diagnostic x-rays on a high patient load with class one wounds from gunshots, stabbings, car accidents, and other conditions such as cardiac infarctions, and aneurysms.

EDUCATION

University of Phoenix, Major: Hospital Management, Internet, 2015 – Present
Walter Reed Army Medical Center, Academy of Health Sciences, United States Army, 2002

CORY SCHULMAN

31003 Radio Engineer Terrace
Montgomery Village, Maryland 20886

240-338-0050
producer@gmail.com

OBJECTIVE

To maximize station ratings through high-quality representation as an On-Air Personality or other career opportunity commensurate with experience as a Staff Engineer.

HIGHLIGHTS

Broadened listening audiences for 9 years as an On-Air Personality for several FM stations. Read news, announced music, and performed voice overs for WASH, WDON, WAVA, and WEZR. Experienced in directing, production, commercial writing, news casting, and traffic. Trained and supervised engineers in studio operation of tape decks, control boards, CD/mini-disc recorders/players, and computers. Possess 20 plus years as a Staff Engineer for KVM and served as one of the principal night engineers for the Larry King Show.

EXPERIENCE

KVM NETWORKS, Washington, DC   2011 – Present

Staff Engineer – Earned numerous awards for outstanding performances.

Technical Experience:
- Maintain audio levels and quality of music and speech for worldwide broadcasts.
- Supply nationwide sound periodically for TV and radio networks. Feed audio to CBS, NBC, ABC, CNN, Mutual, and VOA for speeches, briefings, hearings, and press conferences. Set up and operate audio equipment for Congressional hearings.
- Manage control boards with up to 30 channels for digital productions.
- Equalize substandard audio and use Harrison broadcast console and Dalet computer programs to enhance sibilants and to program sequences of broadcasting events.
- Perform technical interventions, such as soldering, voltage checks, and schematic interpretations.
- Provide stand-in directing when necessary, which entails transliterating talents' on-air needs, especially audio quality control.

Foreign Language Experience:
- Coordinate director's talent to create live and recorded news/entertainment shows in any language.
- Pre-record segments for upcoming shows in various languages, resulting in minimal post production editing.
- Interface with non-technical foreign language studio directors to prepare broadcasts and recordings.

INTERNATIONAL BROADCASTING SYSTEM, Washington, DC/Virginia   2005 – 2011

Master Control Engineer
- Operated control board for mults, newscasts, feature shows, network sports events, and remote coverage of Capitol Hill hearings and State Department briefings.
- Edited Capitol Hill and State Departments' press conferences, briefings, speeches, and network programming.
- Trained incoming engineers in studio operations, which included loading commercials in the master control and operating associated equipment in three studios.

EDUCATION

National Academy of Broadcasting, Washington, DC
Grantham Electronics, Washington, DC, Broadcast Electronics, FCC License, 2005

CORY SCHULMAN

31004 Radio Producer Terrace   producer@gmail.com
Montgomery Village, Maryland 20886   240-338-0050

OBJECTIVE

To ensure quality production of live and pre-recorded broadcasts as a program manager, producer, or related assistant position.

EXPERIENCE

PACIFIC RADIO, Washington, DC   2007 – Present

Studio & Recording Operations Supervisor, 2013 – Present
Purchase Order Reader of Special English, 2009 – 2013
Broadcast Technician/Producer, 2007 – 2009

Production Management:
- Produce and supervise hundreds of international radio broadcasts for over 50 countries.
- Supervise operations of the Central Recording Department, which entails overseeing proper functions of 10 computers that record and play airshows.
- Record and air up to 8 informational and/or entertainment shows per shift in 50 different languages.
- Manage more than 20 studios. Reduced recording wait time about 18%, 7 minutes per service, through effective management of multi-studio operations, production time, and equipment.
- Train new technicians in studio operations, which include recording and airing language shows and communicating with multi-language radio broadcasts.

Technical Skills:
- Operate broadcast consoles, tape recording and playback equipment, duplication devices, CD players, mini discs, digital audio tape (DAT), tape cartridges, equalizers, digital delay units, telephone hybrids, and remote line equipment.

Awards and Quality Control:
- Won two awards from Pacific Radio for Excellence in Programming of Pre-recorded Shows, "Jazz Beat" and "It Was 50 Years Ago Today – Beatles."
- Achieved high-quality shows by ensuring tapes were properly labeled and aired in designed sequence without loss of air time. Ensure programs end at sign-off. Rectify operational errors of the Dalet automated recording and playback system.
- Prevent dead-time by effectively interfacing with 200+ international radio broadcasters and by anticipating unusual circumstances such as short-timed tapes, cartridge failures, defective CDs, etc.

WNTR (AM-FM), Washington, DC   2006 – 2007

News Director
- Reported, wrote, and anchored hard news and feature stories. Produced a 1-hour financial advice program. Wrote and produced promo announcements. Introduced a fresh, provocative reporting style that gained a strong listener following.

- Determined an array of stories relating to the African American community, especially police actions, employment, civic issues, religion, and race relations.
- Represented the station at promotional special events.

KVOL, Ft. Collins, Colorado   2004 – 2006

Program Manager
- Transitioned the station's format to news talk.
- Developed marketing campaigns which dramatically increased listenership.
- Supervised and trained interns in gathering sound, writing news stories, and reading police activity logs.

WRMP, Fairfax, Virginia   2002 – 2004

Station Manager
- Managed staff of 40 announcers, engineers, and program manager.
- Led the station to a homogenized sound that captivated the listener base.
- Established the Sports Department, which covered George Mason University's home and away athletic contests.
- Increased radio advertising revenues approximately 20%.

WMRT, Boston, Massachusetts   2000 – 2002

News Anchor and Utility Announcer
- Operated console, anchored newscast, played music as an on-the-air personality, and controlled 50,000 watt AM and 20,000 watt FM transmitters.

WSTE, WKPP, WNDE, New England   1999 – 2000

Programming Consultant
- Revitalized radio stations by instituting modern formats, programming music, writing promotional announcements, and training announcers.

WBAB (AM - FM), Nashua, New Hampshire   1995 – 1999

Station Manager
- Managed 20 staff members and transitioned the station from outdated recording equipment and consoles to modern equipment which eliminated periodic down-time.
- Implemented new CHR format that dramatically raised ratings from 0 to 2.7 within 6 months in Manchester, the state's largest city.
- Developed engineering and operations budgets.
- Sold radio time for advertising. Brought the station from a loss to profitability.

SUPPLEMENT

License: Valid FCC Radiotelephone General Class, Lifetime

Education: **B.S. in Broadcasting and Film**, 1994, Boston University

Cory Schulman
26001 Real Estate Place
Laytonsville, MD 20882
240-338-0050

OBJECTIVE

To close high-volume contracts as a New Home Sales Community Manager.

EXPERIENCE

Community Sales Manager	**1999 – Present**

D.R. Horton; Ryland Homes; and Pulte Home Corporation, Maryland

Performance/Honors:
- Emerged as the #1 ranked producer for D.R. Horton for achieving the highest dollar and sales volumes in FY 2005.
- Generated in excess of $100 million in new custom home sales with $15 million produced in FY 2015 and $57 million since FY 2008.
- Honored as the first recipient of the President's Award in the history of the Maryland Division.

Selected Community Sales Challenges:
- Opened and closed Wildwood Manor, a 44-home community imbedded in a high-decibel area between Rt. 270 and Democracy Blvd., despite the 2008 recession in the real estate market.
- Sold 30 homes within first year of managing the Oak Grove Olney Community as the successor of 3 previous sales managers who sold a combined 20 homes over 4 years.
- Opened and closed in 2 years the Seneca Springs I Laytonsville development, which consisted of 42 custom estate homes loaded with features on 1 – 4 acre lots.

Sales Functions:
- Open and close numerous single-family and townhome communities ranging from 42 to 200 homes with list prices from $500,000 to $1 million in 3 counties.
- Network and cultivate contacts throughout real estate agencies and related industry venues.
- Apply in-depth understanding of creative financing, which has facilitated the prequalification process and brought borderline cases to settlement.
- Conduct needs analyses and provide consultation to buyers regarding unique structural changes and other custom requirements.
- Read blueprints and interface with architects and engineers.
- Instill confidence in home buyers through inspired enthusiasm and extensive knowledge of community attributes, building materials and processes, floor plans, alterations, and financing.
- Trained numerous sales managers and assistants who became award-winning sales producers.

SUPPLEMENT

Education:
- **B.A. Degree in English**, GPA: 3.8, 1998, California State University at Northridge

Affiliations:
- Member of the Major Achievement and Marketing Excellence Association
- Member of the Washington Metropolitan Sales and Marketing Council

183

CORY SCHULMAN
26002 Real Estate Place
Laytonsville, MD 20882
240-338-0050

SUMMARY

- Produced more than $87 million in new home sales as a dynamic Sales Manager with a gift for re-invigorating sales production of planned communities.

- Managed 8 communities concurrently. Successfully opened and closed developments of high-end and custom built homes ranging in value from $250,000 to $1+ million per property.

- Negotiated and closed contracts as much as double the base price.

- Fostered long-term relationships with real estate agents throughout Southern Maryland and with diverse new home builders, such as Toll Brothers, Caruso, Classic, Ryan, Pulte, and D.R. Horton.

EXPERIENCE

HOME PLACE REALTY, Laytonsville, Maryland   2008 – Present
Real Estate Sales Manager

Sales Performance:
- Revitalized sales of a gated community, the Ridges in Brandywine, by generating more than $12 million within the first 8 months, which reversed 3 years of sales dormancy.
- Raised the base price 4 times, starting from the low 400's and reaching the 600's with strong demand.
- Averaged $150,000 to $200,000 in options per home sale, and closed contracts as much as $390,000 above base price for estate homes on 2 – 5 acre lots.
- Achieved the greatest profit margin for base prices and options among the developer's three active home sites.
- Closed challenged communities despite sites involving sharp topography, power lines, industrial sites, composts, rail roads, and zip code stigmas.
- Opened the Woods at Muddy Branch and sold 50% of the 49 sites despite list prices $50,000 above market. Increased the rate of sales 4-fold while sales prices rose 23%.

T. WELLINGTON REALTY, 2007; FIRTHE REALTY, 2008, Laytonsville, Maryland   2007 – 2008
Real Estate Agent

Sales Performance:
- Closed $21.8 million in sales of luxury homes within 18 months. Took over sales management of Winding Ridge, a formerly bankrupt community of 71 homes with small lots and challenging terrain, and closed out the division 7 months ahead of budget.
- Ensured settlement of home sales through effective coordination and communications with title companies, attorneys, lenders, inspectors, appraisers, and contractors.

BARTON HOMES, Owings, Maryland   2003 – 2006
Sales Manager

Management and Sales Production:
- Tripled sales of custom homes ranging in base prices from $250,000 to $500,000 through creative marketing and aggressive networking among real estate agencies.

- Produced $15 million in FY 2003, which accounted for 75% of the company's total sales.
- Closed sales contracts up to $120,000 above base prices by providing extensive consultation to promote upgrades and customize floor plans.
- Achieved more than 300% growth by accelerating sales from 20 to 70 homes per year despite small lots on hilly terrain with well/septic systems.
- Managed eight planned communities in Calvert County; hired and coached sales associates.
- Advised the company president with land acquisitions, plat/price analyses, and development planning.

Public Relations:
- Applied knowledge of 40+ different house plans and customized plans on builder's lots.
- Exuded professionalism and an upbeat atmosphere when greeting and registering prospects. Ensured compliance with Fair Housing laws. Oriented prospects by leading tours of new homes and explaining community issues/construction processes. Presented amenities, lot availability, site plans, model variations, options and upgrades, and prices, etc.
- Prepared and presented material lists, demographics, competition analyses, and other pertinent information to assist buyers in their decisions. Pre-qualified buyers and discussed financing options.

HENSLEY HOMES, INC., Rockville, Maryland; Vienna, Virginia   2000 – 2003
Assistant Manager/Acting Manager

Sales Production:
- Facilitated a 280% increase in sales of condominiums ranging in value from $150,000 to $370,000.
- Wrote 64 new home sales contracts within 6 months and ensured transactions reached settlement as a liaison between the purchaser and the builder.
- Secured as many as six deposits per day. Closed sales contracts as much as $60,000 above base prices and generated more than $18.2 million in aggregate sales.

Public Relations:
- Addressed customer concerns regarding electrical, mechanical, plumbing, flooring, insulation, brick and siding, interior finishing, as well as landscaping issues.
- Represented and promoted the company through participation at new home trade shows.
- Resolved numerous customer complaints inherited from two previous sales managers.

BUILDERS STAFFING RESOURCES, Potomac, Maryland   1999 – 2000
Sales Associate/Manager

Sales Production:
- Provided dynamic sales support to major home builders, including Toll Brothers, Caruso, Classic, Ryan, Pulte, D.R. Horton, Porten, M.I. Homes, etc. resulting in an aggregate sales volume of approximately $35 million.
- Facilitated a dramatic rise in sales of single-family detached homes, townhomes, and condos ranging from $150,000 to $1 million in developments with as many as 300 home sites.
- Coordinated marketing campaigns, including grand opening celebrations that attracted up to 200 attendees.
- Opened and closed divisions in Howard, Montgomery, and Prince George's Counties.
- Focused on the luxury move-up and empty-nester markets averaging prices starting at $400,000.

AFFILIATIONS & EDUCATION

Maryland Association of Realtors, 2002 – Present
B.A. in Business, 2001, University of Maryland, College Park, Maryland

CORY SCHULMAN
19005 Receptionist Street
Rockville, Maryland 20850
240-338-0050
receptionist@gmail.com

EXPERIENCE

ARNOLD TENOR, M.D., Rockville, Maryland   2007 – Present
Head Receptionist
- Facilitated 33% growth in gross annual revenues of this private practice specializing in pulmonology and critical care medicine.
- Maintained medical charts for more than 1,000 active patients.
- Provided a gracious atmosphere as the first point-of-contact via the telephone and when greeting patients.
- Increased scheduling of patient visits from 140 to 340 per month. Optimized physician time with patient by reallocating responsibilities for triage and patient education from physician to medical assistant.
- Scheduled new and follow-up patients for the practice and hospitals; arranged for home nursing care; and scheduled bronchoscopies and other pulmonary procedures.
- Interfaced with healthcare companies, including PPOs, HMOs, IPAs, Medicare/Medicaid, and Workers' Compensation agencies.
- Prepared orders for bloodwork, x-rays, and related medical services.
- Participated in conducting preliminary interviews to screen prospective employees.
- Hired several medical assistants, and provided training in patient relations, equipment operations, data processing, filing, insurance documentation, and telephone etiquette.
- Reduced procurement expenses roughly 15% by performing cost analyses, and ordered all medical and clerical supplies from local and national vendors.
- Compiled industry literature from pharmaceutical companies, associations, and the media.
- Used ICD-9 and CPT codes to secure optimal reimbursements.
- Entered patient information using the ProtoMed/ProtoLogics application.

JANICE PORTLAND, M.D., Bethesda, Maryland   2001 – 2007
Front Desk Receptionist
- Greeted, scheduled, and directed patients for appointments with the internist.
- Assisted in implementing the ProtoMed/ProtoLogics application, the practice's first automated system.
- Initiated a marketing program that improved follow-up visits three fold.
- Provided patient education regarding physician's orders, prescription instructions, and insurance procedures.
- Reconciled all bank accounts, payroll, tax payments, and petty cash.
- Processed insurance billing and collected overdue payments.

EDUCATION

Major: Education, University of Maryland, College Park, Maryland
Major: Accounting, Montgomery College, Rockville, Maryland
Computer Skills: Microsoft Word and Access

CORY SCHULMAN

25001 Restaurant Drive
Darnestown, Maryland 20878
240-338-0050
restaurant@gmail.com

HIGHLIGHTS

- Directed up to 45 employees in various fine dining and casual theme restaurants featured in *The Washingtonian Magazine*, *The Washington Post*, and *The Washington Times*.

- Improved corporate profits as much as 30% and expanded market share through effective management and marketing initiatives. Negotiated contracts valued up to $1 million.

- Successfully cut food, beverage, labor, and related operating costs without compromising quality services. Enhanced operational efficiency, employee productivity, and customer satisfaction for all employers since 2004.

EXPERIENCE

General Manager, Il Primo, Gaithersburg, Maryland   2013 – Present

- Generated robust double-digit annual growth for this 225-seat fine dining Italian restaurant, which received favorable recognition in *The Washingtonian Magazine*.
- Hired, trained, and directed a 30-member crew. Improved employee productivity through motivational leadership and effective recruitment. Cut overtime without compromising service or productivity.
- Enhanced profit margins by cutting food costs roughly 24% and liquor costs 20%; revamping the menu, eliminating shrinkage, and enforcing portion control.
- Negotiated cost reductions with vendors while improving quality of produce, meats, seafood, dry goods, beverages, beer, wine, and liquor.

Manager, Galleys Restaurant, Washington, DC   2008 – 2013

- Directed operations of this 350-seat fine dining and casual theme Italian restaurant, which generated approximately 15% growth per year.
- Maintained Galleys' sterling reputation for quality and service, which was recognized by popular food critics in *The Washington Times* and *The Washington Post*.
- Oversaw managerial staff and crew of 45 employees.
- Established relationships with vendors and negotiated bulk-rate discounts for food, beverages, beer, wine, and liquor.
- Minimized operating expenses in labor, procurement, and inventory/portion control.

Restaurant Manager, Wilson Inn Hotel, Bethesda, Maryland   2004 – 2008

- Managed restaurant operations and 20 employees ensuring timely orders, consistent quality, and courteous relations while cutting expenses.
- Earned nearly perfect marks from Mystery Shopper evaluations and customer satisfaction surveys.

EDUCATION

B.S. in Business, 2003, University of Maryland, College Park, Maryland

CORY SCHULMAN

25002 Restaurant Manager Road
Germantown, Maryland 20874
240-338-0050
restaurantmanager@gmail.com

OBJECTIVE

To maximize corporate profits and apply mutli-location oversight experience as a District or General Manager.

HIGHLIGHTS

- Experienced in exceeding corporate P&L projections in new openings, troubled units, and multiple locations concurrently. Managed up to 200 unit employees and 9 managers. Cut expenses in all areas, including food, liquor, and labor, while improving operational productivity, quality service, and guest relations.

- Winner of more than 10 company awards, including multiple Presidential Gold Stars, Wizard Awards, and the nomination for the 2012 Carlson Fellowship.

EXPERIENCE

BIG CITY GOURMET BURGERS   2012 – Present
General Manager, Germantown, Maryland; Indianapolis/Ft. Wayne, Indiana; Cleveland, Ohio

Indianapolis/Ft. Wayne Locations:
- Managed 2 units in Indianapolis with aggregate revenues of $4.6 million, 140 employees, and 8 managers.
- Reversed a 7% loss in Net Income Before Operating Expenses (NIBO) to a 12% gain despite a poor location and history of declining revenue.
- Exceeded the corporate plan 2 percentage points in NIBO at the Ft. Wayne location by enforcing internal controls, reducing food and liquor costs, and cutting shrinkage.
- Coordinated advertising initiatives with large private and civic entities such as coliseums, the city zoo, and the public school system.

Cleveland, Ohio:
- Appointed for a 6-week term to revitalize a troubled unit operating 11% below NIBO.
- Led 100 employees to improve all aspects of operations, including sanitation and appearance, guest relations, production efficiency, and inventory control of this $3.5 million unit.
- Improved food, liquor, and labor costs 3% points and reduced the NIBO deficit in half, a gain of 6%.

Germantown:
- Opened and manage a 240-seat establishment that generates approximately $3 million per annum, which exceeds projections approximately 9% despite a labor shortage.
- Hired up to 120 employees and provided training in all aspects of front and back of the house operations for a casual theme full-service restaurant.

- Cut operating expenses by curtailing food costs below budget and eliminating 95% of overtime without compromising quality service.
- Improved employee productivity approximately 49%, which exceeded corporate goals 10%.
- Tripled productivity of employees based on guest counts divided by labor hours.
- Promoted community awareness and increased patronage by launching marketing campaigns and successfully negotiating joint programs with public schools.
- Honored in the Quarterly Bonus Celebration as one of the top 10% of General Managers among 186 restaurants nationwide.

DICK CLARK'S AMERICAN BANDSTAND GRILL   2006 – 2012

This unit was designated as the training store for all new managers hired by Dick Clark Restaurants, Inc.

General Manager, 2009 – 2012, Indianapolis, Indiana
- Oversaw an entertainment based, casual-theme restaurant, consisting of the dining area, bar, nightclub, and retail merchandise that generated $4.3 million dollars per annum.
- Marketed the nightclub as a banquet facility during non-peak hours and arranged for guest appearances of bands and celebrities.
- Held responsibility for P&L, budget development and analysis, sales forecasting, vendor relations, purchasing, negotiations, inventory control, scheduling, labor cost control, shrinkage control, marketing, customer relations, payroll, and related functions.
- Recruited, hired, trained, and supervised 9 managers and 120 unit employees.

Special Assignment, 2008
- Led joint venture with Host Marriott Corporation by opening a new-concept bar-restaurant located in the Indianapolis International Airport.

Assistant Manager, 2006 – 2007

BRANDED GRILL   2004 – 2006

General Manager, 2005 – 2006, Indianapolis, Indiana; Columbus, Ohio; Ft. Lauderdale, Florida
- Coordinated high-volume operations with sales of $3.3 million per annum.
- Appointed to open the first new unit in 5 years and exceeded opening budget projections 7%.
- Increased 2005 sales $89,000 (2.8%) and managed an increase in profit of $71,000.
- Nominated for the 2005 Carlson Fellowship.
- Managed the Southeast Regional Training Center.

Assistant General Manager, 2004 – 2005, Nashville, Tennessee; Indianapolis, Indiana
- Coordinated high-volume operations with sales of $3.3 million per annum.

SELENA'S MEXICAN RESTAURANT   1999 – 2004

Kitchen Manager, 2003 – 2004, Indianapolis, Indiana
- Participated in opening 13 units, managed up to 40 kitchen employees and 4 assistant kitchen managers.

General Manager, 2001 – 2003, Clinton, Maryland
- Managed 200 employees, 4 managers, and 3 department heads and daily operations that produced $3.4 million per annum.
- Promoted several times and performed various managerial functions since 1999.

CORY SCHULMAN

25003 General Restaurant Manager Road
Rockville, Maryland 20852

240-338-0050
generalmanager@gmail.com

OBJECTIVE

To maximize corporate profitability, operational productivity, and quality service in a managerial position or in a related capacity.

EXPERIENCE

BRAZILIAN BARBECUE RESTAURANT, Rockville, Maryland   2004 – Present
General Manager, 2008 – Present

Revenue Generation:

- Increased gross annual revenues of a 380 seat, all-you-can-eat Brazilian barbecue/buffet establishment from $2.5 million in FY 2013 to $5 million in FY 2015.
- Exceeded corporate sales goals for 2 consecutive years as the first restaurant among seven predecessors to remain in its location for more than 1 year.
- Raised the Rockville location's corporate ranking from last to second, despite having the smallest seating capacity. Increased the average guest check 20%.

Cost Containment:

- Negotiated food and liquor cost reductions with local vendors, saving $75,000 per annum.
- Curtailed food waste roughly 10% by enforcing strict adherence to portion control.
- Cut labor expenses by eliminating excessive use of overtime throughout 25% of the staff.

Interpersonal Communications:

- Apply fluency in 5 languages to effectively direct diverse crew of 60 employees for both front and back of the house operations.
- Increased employee productivity and longevity through effective recruitment, training, coaching, and team development. Replaced unproductive or problem employees, which eliminated absenteeism, turnover, and service deficiencies.
- Network with large institutions, businesses, and government agencies, including NIH, FDA, NYPD, NY Fire Department, NRC, etc. to attract new patrons.
- Interface extensively with contractors, inspectors, and government officials/agencies, including the Fire & Health Department for complex renovations and expansions.

Innovation, Strategic Planning, & Quality Service:

- Optimized guest capacity by initiating profitable ventures such as live entertainment and sales promotions.
- Oversaw renovations enabling use of space for social and business events, such as weddings, banquets, conferences, and celebrations, etc.
- Improved patron satisfaction and loyalty as a result of timely, accurate, and courteous service as well as visually appealing presentations.
- Built and sustained a strong reputation, which has been featured in glowing reviews by the *Washingtonian Magazine*, *The Washington Post*, and other prominent newsprint.

SUPPLEMENT

Additional Experience:

- General Manager, Los Angeles, 2003, Supervised a $980,000 renovation, which was completed $200,000 under budget. Procured equipment, furnishings, and supplies. Negotiated credit with 10 distributors to establish the company's first location in the West Coast. Recruited 60-member crew and readied the location for its grand opening.

Education: A.A. Business, Apparel Manufacturing Management, Santa Monica College, 2002

CORY SCHULMAN

25004 Restaurant Way
Germantown, Maryland 20874
240-338-0050
retail@gmail.com

OBJECTIVE

To maximize corporate profits, quality service, and operational efficiency in a managerial position within the hospitality industry.

EXPERIENCE

THE SPORTS EDGE, Frederick, Maryland   2011 – Present

MANAGER
- Increased gross annual revenues from $280,000 to approximately $350,000 for this casual-theme restaurant, bar, and billiards establishment.
- Enhanced profit margins from 45% to 73% by cutting food costs while raising menu prices.
- Expanded patronage by improving customer relations and curtailing order processing time more than 60%. Updated the menu to address changes in customer demand.
- Revamped staff of 10 employees and provided hands-on training to overhaul service standards. Reduced staff of servers from eight to four and eliminated overtime without compromising quality of service.
- Led initiatives to repair chronic facility deficiencies, especially air conditioning, refrigeration and facility sanitation.

THE PANCAKE STACK, Alexandria, Virginia, Gaithersburg, Maryland   2008 – 2011

GENERAL MANAGER
- Increased gross annual revenues approximately 8% per annum for 3 consecutive years for this 275-seat, $2.5 million operation.
- Directed as many as 45 employees resulting in improved customer service, including a dramatic 43% reduction in service processing time.
- Decreased food costs from 32% to 28% by reducing overstock, waste, and portion overages.
- Completed training and secured certificates from Pancake Stack training centers in Georgia and California. Certified in Food Service.

LITTLE ITALIAN RESTAURANT, Falls Church, Virginia   2006 – 2008

GENERAL MANAGER
- Improved the store's ranking from #5 to #1 out of 12 stores throughout the Northern Virginian District.
- Maintained gross annual sales while all other 37 corporate stores in the Washington Baltimore market declined 55%.
- Launched aggressive marketing campaigns, which entailed developing relationships with public and private schools and coordinating promotional tours for students.
- Earned a certificate for the 90% Club from sanitation classes.

MILITARY

U.S. Army/Reserves
- Directed kitchen operations to serve 500 military personnel.

CORY SCHULMAN

28003 Retail Manager Place
Montgomery Village, MD 20886
240-338-0050
retailmanager@gmail.com

EXPERIENCE

PHILLIPS HARDWARE, Germantown, Maryland   2012 – Present

Department Manager

- Direct 19 employees and the Lumber and Building Materials Department, which accounts for 28% of the store's $54 million in gross annual revenues.
- Improved all aspects of the department, including sales, gross margins (35%), turns (30%), GMROI (15%), and shrinkage.
- Manage the top 500 commercial contractor accounts, which generate 9% of total sales valued more than $4.5 million per annum.
- Devised a strategic plan dedicated to expand the commercial sector 12% within the first year of implementation.
- Reduced shrinkage by instituting security check-out points, conducting weekly inventory audits, and preventing damaged materials.
- Order 3,000 SKUs valued $125,000 per week. Enhanced receiving operations by improving the accuracy of product type and quantities.
- Prepare report analyses of daily operations, sales, and end-cap plans. Coordinate events, seasonal changes, and merchandising displays.
- Increased employee productivity and floor sales more than $110,000 through effective coaching.
- Minimized employee turnover by improving the hiring process, setting goals, and effectively training teams.
- Developed and conducted product knowledge workshops that educated customers and promoted sales of high-end product lines.

HENSLEY COUNTRY CLUB, Rockville, Maryland   2009 – 2012

Food & Beverage Director

- Managed food and beverage (F&B) operations in 5 club house sections that supported 740 members. Coordinated F&B for both casual and formal events.
- Decreased food costs approximately 16% by consolidating vendors, conducting cost analyses, capitalizing on bulk discounts, and negotiating price reductions.
- Streamlined operations which reduced complaints from 20+ per day to nearly zero.
- Oversaw 35+ employees and scheduled 1,400 labor hours per week.
- Eliminated rampant employee turnover through leadership in interviewing, hiring, and training new resources. Lengthened average longevity from 3 months to several years.

SUPPLEMENT

B.S. in Business Administration, 2008, Candido Mendes University, Rio de Janeiro, Brazil
Certifications: Loss Prevention, Lift Equipment Operator, Physical Security Procedures, Cash Handling, Food Safety Management, Techniques in Alcohol Management
Languages: English, Spanish, and Portuguese
Computer Skills: MS Excel, PowerPoint, Word, Digital Dining POS programming/maintenance

CORY SCHULMAN
16004 Retail Terrace
Potomac, MD 20878
240-338-0050
retailmanager@gmail.com

OBJECTIVE

To enhance corporate profitability as a Director of Sales and Marketing or related upper managerial position.

EXPERIENCE

THE HENSLEY OFFICE, Rockville, Maryland, 2000 – Present
Branch General Manager, Washington, 2010 – Present
- Oversaw sales, service, and administrative departments consisting of 70 employees and generating $16 million per annum as a leading office equipment reseller.
- Led branch to number one ranking in the country in 2006 and won the President's Club award 4 consecutive years by increasing gross annual sales from $11 million in 2004 to $16 million in 2008. Spearheaded high volume sales to local and national federal government accounts.
- Controlled asset inventory of $2 million.
- Slashed operating expenses 15% by re-engineering all three departments which entailed: renegotiating favorable GSA multiple award contracts; relocating the facility; and eliminating non-revenue producing personnel.
- Conducted P&L analysis and prepared bids that successfully won awards from government agencies such as DoT, Social Security, and the U.S. Marines.

Branch General Manager, Dallas, 2006 – 2010
- Reversed $400,000 annual losses in 2006 to $800,000 annual revenue surpluses within 2 years by successfully generating high-volume sales throughout major market, commercial, and federal markets.
- Restructured and grew the sales force, relocated the facility to a centralized locality, and controlled a $1 million inventory.
- Grew net placement and market share approximately 66% within 2 years.

National Training Manager, Atlanta, Georgia, 2005 – 2006
- Revamped a comprehensive, nationwide training program for 800 participants.
- Developed training programs focusing on sales techniques; account development for government, major, and commercial markets; sales management; and interpersonal management skills.
- Traveled throughout the 48 contiguous states to give presentations and launch new products and training programs.

Sales Manager, Washington, DC, 2000 – 2005
- Earned Sales-Manager-of-the-Year 4 consecutive years.
- Emerged as the number one sales producer among 30 local sales associates.

EDUCATION

Business Administration, 1998 – 2000, Virginia Union University, Richmond, Virginia

CORY SCHULMAN

16006 Retail Street
Arlington, VA 22209
240-338-0050
retailmanager@gmail.com

OBJECTIVE

To maximize corporate growth, efficiency, and profitability in a managerial position or a related career opportunity.

EXPERIENCE

ELZALEAS FASHION, Washington, DC   2004 – Present

Operations Manager, 2010 – Present
- Manage operations of 70 stores located throughout the United States that generate $58 million per annum and employ 600 support personnel.
- Reduced shrinkage approximately 50% saving the company roughly $5 million.
- Prevented the closure of three locations in Ohio by revitalizing management controls, which reversed declining sales to robust profits. Revamped staff, instituted aggressive training programs, strengthened documentation of sales/projections, and installed security systems. Increased revenues more than 25% in numerous units.
- Cut operating expenses companywide by centralizing procurement. Reduced purchasing costs by conducting cost analyses, replacing vendors, negotiating price reductions, and capitalizing on bulk rates and pre-payment discounts.
- Initiated and successfully implemented the company's first complete inventory count and drafted a comprehensive operations manual.
- Opened the Pittsburgh, Pennsylvania unit (3,200 square feet), Columbus, Ohio unit (4,200 square feet), and Georgetown, Washington, DC unit (9,500 square feet).
- Coordinated the operational logistics of three acquisitions in Atlanta, Georgia.
- Appointed by the company president to direct the POS system upgrade nation-wide.
- Utilize computer skills to conduct sales and inventory analyses as well as to generate various reports on employee performance, sales projections, and shrinkage.

District Manager, 2008 – 2010
- Exceeded corporate projections for sales, operating expenses, employee productivity, shrinkage, and inventory volume as the manager of the Ohio territory.
- Improved cost per labor hour by effectively training staff to meet rising sales goals.
- Procured inventory for three stores, which entailed revising the product mix to address changing consumer, fashion, and seasonal trends.

Store Manager, 2004 – 2008
- Emerged as a Nominee for One-of-the-Best-Managers in North America among 45+ unit managers in Canada, Mexico, and the United States.
- Achieved the best inventory with the lowest shrinkage in the company.
- Increased gross annual revenues from $370,000 to $470,000 by enhancing product mix, merchandising, customer service, and employee productivity.

EDUCATION

B.A. in International Business, 2003, American University, Washington, DC

CORY SCHULMAN

26008 Account Manager Court • Germantown, MD 20874 • 240-338-0050 • sales@aol.com

EXPERIENCE

NEW HORIZON TECHNOLOGIES, INC., Frederick, Maryland　　　　2013 – Present
Account Manager

Outside Sales:

- Negotiated and closed contracts ranging from $50 million to several hundred million dollars for network security products for Federal agencies and Fortune 500 companies, such as Carillion, Becton & Dickinson, Kennedy Kriegor, NASDAQ, Department of Energy, and the Department of Education.
- Managed commercial and federal end-user accounts throughout the Mid-Atlantic region.
- Gave dynamic in-person presentations to IT professionals and executive management that detailed corporate history; products, services, and technologies; capabilities and benefits; and needs analyses.
- Conducted technical network assessments and security issues, including vulnerability scans, ISS intrusion detection, fire walls, URL blocks/filters, and high availability load balancing systems.
- Tripled sales performance within first 6 months and generated more than $1 million in revenues within first year.
- Spearheaded the company's sales campaign within the commercial market by securing $900,000 within the first year, a 4-fold increase company-wide and the largest expansion in the company's history.

INTERWAVE COMPANIES, Value Added Distributor, Gaithersburg, Maryland　　2006 – 2013
Regional Manager

New Business Development:

- Increased gross annual revenues from $2 million to $5 million within the first year for sales of hardware and software solutions to accounts throughout the Washington Metropolitan region.
- Expanded market share approximately 40% among major value added distributors in the region.
- Penetrated new markets such as the imaging division within federal integrators which doubled the account base and increased revenues $3 million per annum.

Product Knowledge and Service:

- Managed staff of inside sales associates to promote 35 product lines with hundreds of SKUs.
- Applied in-depth knowledge of systems and imaging applications, including DEC, Intel, Kodak, Cofax, image capture software, and storage solutions (Raid, Optical Disk, and CD ROM).
- Coordinated staff of five engineers to perform post-sale follow-up services such as installations, on-site service, testing, burn-in, and integration.

Marketing and Consultative Communications:

- Participated in trade shows by managing booths with VARs. Promoted total solutions to prospective commercial/federal end-users. Coordinated and disseminated letters of supply for GSA schedules.
- Gave highly polished, in-person presentations to resellers, which entailed conducting demonstrations to train personnel in features and benefits.
- Provided consultative sales presentations and recommended solution packages that addressed resellers' unique needs.

EDUCATION

Bachelor of Science, 2005, Economics and Marketing, Maryland University

CORY SCHULMAN

26005 Auto Parts Court
Germantown, MD 20874
240-338-0050
sales@gmail.com

OBJECTIVE

To maximize corporate profits, customer satisfaction, and account growth in an Outside Sales position.

EXPERIENCE

Field Representative, Parklawn, LLC, Monrovia, Maryland   2010 – Present

- Generated $3.8 million in aggregate sales of preventative maintenance vehicular products and equipment in the wholesale market throughout Montgomery County.
- Earned induction into the Diamond Club for 2 consecutive years for exceeding quotas 106% in FY 2014 and 120% in FY 2015.
- Exceeded manufacturer's annual sales goals of $450,000 by closing more than $540,000 per annum.
- Increased annual sales volume from $94,000 in FY 2010 to $436,000 in FY 2012.
- Expanded the number of active clients 57% despite an industry decline in the marketplace.
- Developed numerous existing accounts by introducing new products and services among independent stations and dealerships.
- Conducted seminars to attract new prospects and strengthen a market presence among key industry contacts. Gave in-depth presentations and training to owners, managers, and service advisors, resulting in greater sales and continued loyalty.
- Maintained a product and equipment inventory, which entailed procurement functions based on analysis and forecasting of fluctuating market trends.

Sales Manager, Dale's Auto Parts, Cloverly, Maryland   2007 – 2010

- Managed approximately 300 wholesale accounts that generated more than $3.5 million per annum.
- Achieved a 20% – 30% increase in gross annual revenues by expanding the account base and upselling existing accounts.
- Targeted the wholesale market, which included dealerships, service stations, independent garages, and fleet services.
- Launched a proactive marketing campaign by giving dynamic sales presentations and needs analyses at client sites throughout Montgomery County.
- Elaborated on attributes, benefits, and cost effectiveness of 40 NAPA product lines.
- Revamped team cohesion, which resulted in greater sales production and morale among sales associates.
- Improved delivery efficiency of products from 3 days to a reliable 24-hour turnaround, which eliminated chronic customer complaints and encouraged new business.

Manager/Mechanic, Auto Service, Silver Spring, Maryland   2005 – 2007

- Performed Maryland State inspections for local dealerships and fleet accounts.
- Performed general automotive repairs for domestic and foreign cars and trucks.

CORY SCHULMAN

26003 Car Sales Place, Gaithersburg, MD 20886
carsales@hotmail.com   240-338-0050

OBJECTIVE

To drive corporate profits and unparalleled customer service as a seasoned Pre-Owned Sales Consultant.

HIGHLIGHTS

- *Sales Experience:* Service-driven Pre-Owned Sales Consultant with an award-winning record of achievement as one of the top ranked sales performers in the luxury-car industry. Promote and close sales of Mercedes-Benz, BMW, Audi, and Porsche vehicles by effectively cultivating relationships and productive rapport with affluent, well-educated clients. Experienced as a leading sales producer for dealerships of various sizes including a 150-car lot with a $7 million inventory.

- *Sales Performance:* Achieved #1 ranking for several dealerships in the luxury-car market during varying economic conditions. Sold as many as 26 units in a month and single units retailing as much as $97,000, while maintaining 100% Customer Satisfaction Index scores. Exceeded sales quotas as much as 45% and earned numerous awards, such as Salesman-of-the-Month, Highest Gross Sales, and related accolades throughout sales career.

- *Consumer Relations:* Adept at converting indecisive and inhibited lookers into satisfied buyers. Instill trust and confidence through polished communications, in-depth knowledge, and ability to meet special needs.

EXPERIENCE

LUXURY BMW, Marlow Heights, Maryland   2007 – Present
Pre-Owned Client Advisor
- Emerged as the top advisor, ranking #1 or #2 for 8 consecutive years by leading sales of pre-owned BMWs to an educated and affluent clientele.
- Achieved 100% Customer Satisfaction Index scores by effectively fostering relationships, identifying needs, converting objections into agreements, and instilling confidence in customers who varied in age, temperament, and financial standing.
- Earned Salesman-of-the-Year and the Top Gun award for the highest gross sales at the dealership, 2012 – 2015.
- Sold 12 units per month on average, which exceeded the average sales performance of the dealership by 13%.
- Closed single transactions as much as $97,000.

SHEBLEY PORSCHE, BMW, AUDI, Silver Spring, Maryland   2005 – 2007

Pre-Owned Sales Consultant
- Generated award-winning sales volume of BMW, Porsche, and Audi units as the #1 or #2 ranked consultant. Exceeded the average monthly sales production roughly 45% above the sales performances of all other sales associates.
- Achieved the highest gross sales of the dealership for September 2006.

SPECIALTY AUTOS, INC., Temple Hills, Maryland   2003 – 2005

Sales Representative
- Closed roughly 120 Mercedes-Benz, Land Rover, Audi, and BMW units ranging from $30,000 to $80,000 per transaction.
- Increased personal sales volume approximately 25% by the second month and maintained a performance ranking within the top three every month.

MARC TANZEN MAZDA SOUTH, Austin, Texas   2001 – 2003

Pre-Owned Sales Associate
- Rose to one of the top-performing sales producers by exceeding the average 15 unit sales minimum per month for 14 consecutive months.
- Closed as many as 26 car sales in a single month while generating roughly $200,000 above corporate expectations.

CLASSIC HONDA, TOYOTA, & GMC, Round-Rock, Texas   1999 – 2001

Pre-Owned Sales Associate
- Ranked #10 as a rookie to the automotive sales industry among 22 seasoned sales associates. Emerged as #2 for the month as a result of a stellar sales performance.

TRAINING

- Zig Ziglar Seminar, 2003, Guest appearances by motivational speakers: Brian Billick, Rudolph Guiliani, and Les Brown
- BMW Sales Academy, 2003
  125 Different Closes, Selling in the 21st Century
  Operate and Demonstrate Safety Features in Inclement Weather
- Grant Cardone Sales Training, 2002
- Joe Verde Sales Training, 2002
- Brian Tracy "Cash is King" Sales Training, 2001
- Paul Cummings Sales Training, 2000

EDUCATION

A.A. in Automotive Studies, 1998, Montgomery College, Rockville, Maryland

CORY SCHULMAN
26004 Car Sales Court
Germantown, MD 20874
240-338-0050
sales@gmail.com

EXPERIENCE

VILLAGE AUTOMALLS, Gaithersburg, Maryland
Sales Associate, July 2012 – Present

- Generated approximately $1.5 million in sales of new and used cars as well as leased vehicles. Applied extensive product knowledge of roughly 300 vehicles consisting of 20 models ranging in age from 1989 to the present and ranging in price from $3,000 to $50,000 per car.
- Assessed consumers' needs and concerns about safety, performance, style, features, fuel economy, price, number of passengers, and business use.
- Provided counsel to consumers by explaining new technologies pertaining to suspensions, infrared heating, air conditioning, four-wheel drives, gears, GPS, and video.
- Prepared financial prequalification worksheets to estimate whether prospects can secure financing for a purchase. Submitted credit information to local banks, credit unions, and Chrysler Corporation. Presented reports to financial officers.
- Coordinated delivery of purchased vehicles, oriented new owners to their vehicles, and provided post-sale follow-up.
- Generated 200 leads per month by providing effective e-mail, twitter, and telephone responses to on-line web site inquiries.
- Prepared paperwork to transfer ownership of vehicles.

SUPPLEMENT

Military:
U.S. Armed Forces, U.S. Army, January 2000 – April 2008
Reserves: June 2008 – January 2012

Education:
Graduate, 2007, U.S. Army Armor School, Fort Knox, Kentucky, Basic Noncommissioned Officer Course For Combat Arms

Professional Training:
Customer Relations, Paul Cummings, 2008
Chrysler, Plymouth, and Hyundai certification programs, 2013 – 2014
Product Certification Training: Telephones, computers, audio, video parts, wireless communications, VCRs, January 2012
Seven C's Selling Seminar, 2012

Awards and Certificates:
Outstanding Performance, 2015, Spirit of America

CORY SCHULMAN

16009 Greenhouse Sales Management Road	240-338-0050
Rockville, MD 20711	salesmanagement@hotmail.com

HIGHLIGHTS

- 20 plus years' experience in seasonal crop production specializing in bedding plants, foliage, potted crops, and related vegetative specialty garden liners and plugs.

- Facilitated rapid expansion of a multi-million dollar greenhouse and propagation operation as President of Penske Greenhouses with expertise in greenhouse/propagation management, pest/disease management, local/national distribution, sales, marketing, quality control, service, team development, and financial management.

- Generated a dramatic 40% rise in new business development within a mature market territory in New York. Strengthened ties with wholesale and retail markets, including commercial growers, greenhouse nurseries, suppliers, and brokers.

- Established key contacts in the greenhouse industry including commercial landscape contractors, garden centers, and chain stores throughout the Baltimore-Washington, DC regional market. Secured representation of Penske Greenhouses by top industry brokers.

EXPERIENCE

PENSKE GREENHOUSES, Gaithersburg, Maryland   2012 – Present

A multi-million dollar rooting station and licensed propagator/distributor of North African impatiens and a root-and-sell station for the Cory Schulman Ranch.

President

- Established partnership between Seed Grow and Penske Greenhouses in 2006; increased gross annual revenues from $1.6 million to more than $2.2 million within the first year.
- Broadened the broker base throughout the United States and Canada.
- Oversee production of top-quality specialty garden plant liners, poinsettias, and plotted plants on 55 acres and a 2 acre greenhouse, which is planned for a 2 acre expansion.
- Direct more than 30 laborers and support staff.

SEED GROW, Long Island, New York   2007 – 2012

Sales Representative

- Represented 250 national/international suppliers to promote sales of seed, soil, vegetative cuttings, and hard goods to the commercial greenhouse industry.
- Managed 160 accounts throughout the Long Island - New York Metropolitan region.
- Increased gross annual sales in the Long-Island/New York territory from $3.5 million to $5 million per annum.
- Increased gross annual sales in the Maryland territory from $1.5 million to $2 million within one year.
- Increased the percentage of proprietary exclusive products from 53% of total company sales to 70% in FY 2008.
- Facilitated record-breaking sales for Seed Grow as a top sales producer in the nation.
- Earned the following awards and honors:
  - ◆ Top Field Marketer for Seed Premier Line   ◆ Top Business Manager

♦ Member of the "Original Seed Top Region"
♦ Pan American Seed "Top Field Marketer Award"
♦ Goldsmith Seed "Top Selling Field Marketer"
♦ Top Seller of Proprietary Original FloraPlant Products

♦ Original FloraPlant Topper
♦ Outstanding New Field Marketer

PLANT NURSERY, INC., Crystal City, Virginia   1999 – 2007

Vice President, Director of Production, 2000 – 2007
Vice President, Creative Plantings, (Sister Company 1999 – 2000)

Sales & Service:
- Increased gross sales from $600,000 to $2.5 million, which reversed losses of more than $1 million a year to a profit during a recession.
- Penetrated new markets and cultivated accounts by aggressively networking throughout industry associations and local businesses.
- Maximized sales volume by improving quality control of products and services.
- Implemented a pre-booking system to confirm orders, which enhanced operational efficiency and prevented errors.
- Yielded top dollar for products by ensuring accurate, prompt, and reliable deliveries.
- Established a Special Services Division, which maintained high quality service standards during rapid expansion of the commercial customer base from 600 to 1,000 accounts.
- Re-engineered service capabilities by defining territories and appointing supervisors.

Cost Reduction:
- Reduced overhead expenses approximately 25% by streamlining procurement, renegotiating contractual terms with suppliers, increasing off-season warehousing, and incorporating cost containment programs such as the Integrated Pest Management system, which dramatically slashed pesticide costs 50%.
- Cut unnecessary labor hours while improving service and sales through effective training of a 25 member staff.
- Authorized and supervised roughly $1.5 million worth of facility construction/renovation projects, including reskinning greenhouses, which curtailed heating costs 50%.

Human Resources:
- Recruited and developed a multi-cultural, service-driven and team-oriented staff.
- Held weekly progress meetings to identify opportunities to achieve greatest productivity.
- Provided hands-on training on all facets of service and production, including fertilization, irrigation, planting, shipping, and pest/disease identification.

Professional Affiliations:
- Board of Directors, Long Island Flower Growers Association.
- Board Member of the Maryland Greenhouse Growers Association.
- Member of numerous professional affiliations, including the Landscape Contractors Association, the Poinsettia Growers Association, the Professional Plant Growers Association, the Montgomery College Landscape Technology Advisory Committee, and the Prince George's Community College Landscape/Greenhouse Advisory Committee.
- Promoted industry awareness as a guest lecturer at public schools, colleges, and community organizations; led many tours throughout greenhouses.

CORY SCHULMAN

26005 Medical Sales Court
Germantown, MD 20874
240-338-0050
medicalsales@gmail.com

OBJECTIVE

To penetrate markets, expand account bases, and close high-volume sales as a Sales Representative of medical devices.

HIGHLIGHTS

- Inducted into Dilliards Pharmaceutical's President's Club as one of the top representatives across the country.
- Ranked #14 in the nation among 180 total representatives and #4 in the Southern Region.
- Secured #1 ranking in the nation for Astelin sales in the fourth quarter of FY 2015.
- Emerged as a member of the Over The Top Club for exceeding 1,000 prescription sales.

EXPERIENCE

DILLIARDS PHARMACEUTICALS, Gaithersburg, Maryland   2010 – Present
Medical Sales Representative

Sales Performance – Account Management:
- Generated 129% of corporate sales goals by closing more than $1.7 million in sales of 6 pharmaceutical products for FY 2015.
- Achieved 180% of sales goal for Rynatan; 148% of goal for Soma; and 136% of goal for Astelin.
- Managed more than 200 active accounts across three states by building and sustaining productive relationships with numerous specialty offices, which encompassed family practitioners, internists, pediatricians, ENTs, allergists, pulmonologists, and orthopedists.
- Increased prescription sales of a 3-state territory from 380 to 1,100 within 10 months.
- Led the Southern Region (60 representatives) in prescription sales growth, which exceeded 75% for Astelin in the third quarter of FY 2014.
- Improved personal ranking 53 spots within 3 months; rose from #142 to #12 within 11 months.

Communications – Marketing – Administration:
- Appointed to serve on the Astelin task force and develop a sales model, which was adopted by the company for nationwide implementation.
- Selected to conduct training classes for 150 new hires.
- Strengthen relationships within the medical community by serving as an information resource on formulary coverage, dosing, pathophysiology, and indications.
- Provide polished corporate representation as a Booth Manager at national conventions.
- Plan and coordinate marketing seminars featuring guest speakers to address 100+ attendees from the medical community.
- Devise efficient routing throughout an intricate 200-mile territory.
- Monitor budget and track ROI for business luncheons, marketing incentives, and programs.

EDUCATION

Virginia Polytechnic Institute and State University, Blacksburg, Virginia
B.S. Dairy Science, Science/Biotechnology/Pre-Vet option; Minor: Biology, May 2010
Relevant courses: Biochemistry for Biotechnology, Cell and Molecular Biology, Microbiology, Pathogenic Bacteriology, Animal Physiology & Anatomy, and Organic Chemistry

CORY SCHULMAN

26006 Pharmaceutical Sales Court
Germantown, MD 20874
240-338-0050
medicalsales@gmail.com

OBJECTIVE

To maximize corporate profits and client satisfaction as an effective Sales Representative.

HIGHLIGHTS

- Increased sales of disposable OB/GYN products for 7 consecutive years for Bronson Products, Inc.
- Ranked within the top 10% among 450 sales representatives for highest sales production at Benson & Benson in 2015.
- Earned #1 Sales Representative-of-the-Year for the Southeast region at Baylor Pharmaceuticals and achieved 204% of sales goal for Ditropan XL product in 2011.
- Adept at major product launches, marketing events, and dynamic in-person presentations to promote sales of medical products.
- Established and fostered long-term relationships with a broad network of professionals throughout the medical community in diverse venues: private/military hospitals, clinics, pharmacies, physician's offices, and related medical facilities.

EXPERIENCE

BENSON & BENSON (ORTHO Pharmaceuticals), Raritan, New Jersey   2011 – Present

(Acquired Baylor Pharmaceuticals), Products: Ditropan XL, Elmiron, Levaquin, Ultracet
Executive Professional Sales Representative (Urology Division)
- Emerged within the top 10% of all 450 company sales representatives nationwide for highest sales of pharmaceutical products to surgery centers, clinics, and specialists such as OB/GYNs, urologists, and primary care physicians.
- Targeted the medical community throughout Montgomery County giving dynamic presentations to as many as 15 physicians and support staff. Focused on efficacy, features, and health/cost benefits.
- Achieved more than 100% of sales goals for all three products as a result of effective networking, persuasive presentations, and closing skills.
- Cultivated more than 200 clients through extensive knowledge of products, medical terminology, needs analysis, and relationship building.
- Collaborated with the team to develop and launch marketing programs, including informational seminars, luncheons, and dining events.
- Secured nomination in the Levaquin Contest for acquiring the highest market share for Levaquin sales in the region.

BAYLOR PHARMACEUTICALS, Mountain View, California   2008 – 2011

Executive Sales Specialist, Products: Ditopan XL, Testoderm TTS, Mycelex Troche
- Achieved 148% of quota for sales of Testoderm TTS in 2010.
- Achieved 118% of quota for sales of Ditropan XL in 2010.
- Spearheaded a major launch of three major products throughout a five-county region.

- Earned recognition as #1 Sales Representative-of-the-Year for the Southeast in 2009 out of 150 others.
- Top Sales Performer for Mycelex in 2008.
- Rose in ranking from #19 to #4 among 150 sales representatives nationwide.
- Established and conducted residency training programs at Holy Cross Hospital and Bethesda Naval Hospital.
- Interfaced with department heads of various hospitals and HIV clinics to promote product awareness.
- Trained new representatives in product knowledge and territory management.

VAXCO, INC., Parsippany, New Jersey   2007 – 2008

(Contract Sales Organization)
Specialty Sales Representative
- Achieved or exceeded sales quotas for such products as Lorabid, antibiotic for otitis media and sinusitis; Kadian, morphine sulfate for severe chronic pain; and Ivory Moisture Care.
- Represented Eli Lilly Pharmaceuticals, Zeneca Pharmaceuticals, and Procter & Gamble Company.
- Coordinated dinner/event programs and in-service luncheons to primary care and infectious disease physicians, pediatricians, as well as pain management clinics throughout the Washington Metropolitan region.
- Trained new representatives in sales techniques, marketing strategies, and product knowledge.

BRONSON PRODUCTS, INC., Chicago, Illinois   2000 – 2007

Specialty Sales Representative
- Increased sales for 7 consecutive years for OB/GYN disposable products, stainless steel instruments, and patient education literature.
- Generated a 6-fold rise in territory sales from $25,000 to $160,000 per annum.
- Gave dynamic and persuasive presentations on various OB/GYN products.
- Established more than 200 clients within first 18 months.
- Expanded the territory from one county to four counties and successfully targeted OB/GYNs, fertility specialists, teaching hospitals, military hospitals, HIV clinics, and surgical centers.
- Provided training to medical residents, medical students, and sales representatives.

EDUCATION

Certified Medical Assistant's Program, 2001, Central Pennsylvania Business School, Summerdale, Pennsylvania

Business Major, 2000, State University of New York at Albany

Bachelor of Arts Degree, 1999, The Traphagen School of Design, New York, New York

CORY SCHULMAN

26007 Technical Sales Road
Herndon, VA 20171

240-338-0050
engineeringsales@gmail.com

HIGHLIGHTS

Revenue-driven Technical Sales Consultant with diverse experience in IT, engineering, and scientific environments. Penetrated new markets and closed high-volume sales throughout North and South America and Europe. Presented and successfully negotiated million dollar, multi-year contracts with executives from Global 1000 companies. Skilled in conducting comprehensive needs analyses, defining technical requirements, mapping out strategic plans, and calculating ROI and financial benefits. Conduct business using fluency in French, Italian, and Spanish. B.S. degree in Mechanical Engineering.

EXPERIENCE

CHEM TECHNOLOGIES, INC., Reston, Virginia   2007 – Present
Provides system solutions for global regulatory compliance, landed cost management, and international transactions for companies in the high-tech, pharmaceutical, energy, chemical, and consumer packaged goods industries.

Senior Account Executive • Manager of Business Consulting

Sales:
- Penetrated and expanded new markets throughout a 10-state territory in the South East/South Central United States. Secured high-volume sales of engineering software and services that range from $250,000 to $1 million.
- Emerged as the #1 sales producer year-to-date with more than $5 million in the pipeline for sales in North and South America.
- Targeted and established ties with Global 1000 clients such as ColorCon and Ashland, Inc.
- Generated new business with such clients as Merck & Co., DSM, and British Petroleum.
- Negotiate and close multi-year contractual agreements that provide recurring revenue streams for as long as 5 years.
- Manage more than 30 active installed accounts. Foster long-term relationships and close sales on new products, services, and upgrades.

Business Consulting:
- Give detailed product demonstrations and comprehensive presentations to corporate executives on regulatory compliance management and global trade logistics software.
- Interview clients' executive staff to analyze financial, technical, and systemic needs as well as to map out business processes with technical solutions.
- Collaborated with the Vice President to spearhead a consulting program, which promoted value based sales and dramatically increased the closure rate from 30% to 80%.
- Prepare and present 100-page technical proposals that quantify clients' Net Present Value and ROI when incorporating Chem Technologies technical solutions. These proposals also detail business processes, performance measures, technology requirements, and competitive analyses.
- Evaluate customer requirements, map out current processes, and propose/modify new business systems.

Revenue Generation:
- Established the ColorCon account and closed $800,000 in sales of materials compliance solution software for worldwide application to support a $400 million company and 1,000 employees.
- Co-established the Ashland, Inc. account resulting in $1 million contract. Performed pre-sales consulting, which included analyses of business processes and development of value justifications.
- Increased revenues of the Merck account more than 20%.

205

PROCOM, Montreal, Canada   2005 – 2007

Designs, manufactures, and promotes HVAC products serving the commercial, marine, industrial, and institutional markets.

Regional Manager

Sales Management:
- Managed sales of industrial HVAC systems ranging in value from $50,000 to $2.2 million. Facilitated a 3-fold rise in gross annual corporate revenues from $10 million to $30 million.
- Generated more than $4 million in annual revenues, which was the highest volume in 4 territories and exceeded corporate quotas of as much as 50%.
- Supported 10 sales representatives, engineers, and contractors to develop business opportunities throughout 3 Canadian provinces and 10 U.S. states.

Technical Expertise:
- Developed engineering bids with detailed CAD drawings.
- Coordinated several multi-million dollar projects concurrently from bid through delivery.
- Oversaw the construction, delivery, and installation of HVAC equipment.
- Sized and selected research and development equipment for pilot manufacturing initiatives.

EISENBERG/CANADA, INC., Montreal, Canada   2003 – 2005

A major pharmaceutical company that researches, develops, manufacturers, and markets innovative medicines.

Junior Project Engineer

Engineering Experience:
- Supported 3 Senior Project Engineers in construction, renovation, and maintenance projects for 18 facilities on campus. Audited and redrafted blueprints for all campus buildings, which had not been updated since the 1950s.
- Collaborated with the lead Project Engineer in the design and construction of a new oral contraceptive manufacturing facility. Used CAD to design a $9 million construction project involving a sterile clean room with optimized air locks.
- Applied knowledge of fluid dynamics, reverse osmosis, and heat transfer/exchange for the development of a $200,000+ de-ionization system.
- Implemented CAD system for the Engineering Department.

SUPPLEMENT

    Education: **B.S. Degree**, Mechanical Engineering, 2002, Concordia University, Montreal, Canada
               Minor in Pharmaceutical Sciences

    Languages: Conducted business in Europe and throughout North and South America using fluency in   English, French, Italian, and Spanish.

    Systems: ERP, SAP, JD Edwards, Oracle, AutoCAD by AutoDesk, Adobe Acrobat, Visio, .Net Meeting, Lotus Notes, and MS Windows products.

    Affiliation: Member of the Quebec Order of Engineers

CORY SCHULMAN

26009 Territory Sales Circle
Rockville, Maryland 20850

240-338-0050
sales@gmail.com

HIGHLIGHTS

- *Sales Performance:* Profit-driven sales executive with extensive business experience, especially in penetrating new markets, expanding account bases, and achieving sales objectives. Exceeded sales goals for 8 consecutive years for three employers. Adept at giving persuasive in-person presentations with ability to convert objections into closed agreements.

- *Marketing:* Skilled in devising and implementing various marketing strategies, including cold calling, networking, advertising, and related promotional initiatives.

- *Leadership:* Managed grand opening of a multi-million establishment featured in *The Washingtonian* and *The Washington Post*. Recruited and developed strong sales and management teams.

EXPERIENCE

U.S. DISTRIBUTION SERVICE, Manassas, Virginia   2007 – Present
Territory Manager

- Exceeded corporate goals of $1.75 million per annum by opening and managing commercial accounts in the restaurant, hotel, and institutional sectors throughout the Washington Metropolitan region.
- Increased territory sales four-fold and doubled the account base within first year.
- Sustained the territory's #1 ranking and improved gross profit per customer about 25%.
- Applied bilingual skills to penetrate Spanish-speaking communities and increase market share.
- Pre-qualify prospective accounts, take applications, and submit information to the credit department.
- Give persuasive presentations and negotiate contracts, involving agreements on price, quality, and delivery issues.
- Conduct cost analyses to identify transaction options.
- Ensure productive relationships resulting in customer retention and referral business.

WASHINGTON PRINTING, Washington, DC   2001 – 2007
Sales Manager

- Earned Rookie-of-the-Year in 2001 for outstanding sales performance, and exceeded projected gross annual sales volume for 6 consecutive years.
- Established the Outside Sales Division which increased business 75% and expanded account development among real estate agencies, pharmaceutical manufacturers, law firms, financial management companies, and educational institutions.
- Secured new business through highly-polished in-person presentations and cold calls to prospective accounts.
- Conducted cost analyses of local/national vendors for the procurement of commercial equipment valued in excess of $175,000. Negotiated reduction in cost of goods.
- Devised and implemented successful marketing campaigns involving special promotions, mass mailings, social media, and advertising blitzes.

SUPPLEMENT

Education:	University of Maryland, College Park, Maryland B.S. in Criminal Justice, 2000
Applications:	Use various applications to track, analyze, and report sales.
Languages:	Fluent in Spanish. Lived in Venezuela for 6 years. Traveled to Peru.

CORY SCHULMAN

20001 Security Lane
Rockville, Maryland 20850
240-338-0050
security@gmail.com

Chief Executive Officer

Business Development:

- Tripled multi-million dollar revenues by transitioning a small security business into an internationally recognized firm that provides worldwide consulting, protective services, and risk mitigation.

- Negotiated $20 million contracts.

- Established international accounts with corporations, federal governments, and high net worth individuals.

Media Relations:

- Frequent guest speaker as a Special Warfare/Intelligence Operations and Counterterrorism Expert on the O'Reilly Factor, ABC/CBS/NBC/FOX news, and other network, cable, and radio media.

Infrastructure:

- Industry Consultant on risk management, crisis management, contingency planning, intelligence acquisition, investigations, and technical solutions. Experienced in acquisitions, due diligence, organizational design, and integration.

Security Expertise:

- Knowledgeable of chemical, biological, and nuclear material weaponization and deployment methodologies. Former U.S. Marine with 15 years consulting experience on all aspects of worldwide protective services; law enforcement; special warfare operations; counterterrorism; civil, criminal, personal, and corporate investigations; and computer/network security and data protection.

OBJECTIVE

To drive corporate growth and industry-leading profits in a CEO, COO, or related executive position.

EXPERIENCE

SECURE ASSOCIATES, Rockville, Maryland	2006 – Present

Originally recruited by Bender Strategies International LLC trading as Secure Associates, Inc. to conduct surveillance operations. Promoted to Section Division Manager, then to President. Purchased this full-service Risk Management, Security Consulting, and Intelligence Acquisition firm in 2002.

President, 2011 – Present

Executive Management:

- Visionary CEO of a security firm specializing in worldwide counter terrorism, crisis/risk management, and intelligence operations for the United States and foreign governments, international conglomerates, and high net worth/high-profile individuals.
- Adept in conducting large-scale and complex needs assessments; customizing and presenting client solutions; and negotiating contracts as large as $20 million with corporate executives and international officials.
- Applied expertise in organizational design, revenue generation, personnel recruitment, media relations, brand building, alliance development, change management, and business continuity planning.

Infrastructure Re-engineering: Business Development

- Reinvented the company from a small domestic business to an internationally recognized firm providing covert/overt security worldwide.
- Tripled gross annual revenues from $3 million to $9 million within 2½ years, and positioned the company to entertain contracts valued up to $20 million.
- Acquired a New Zealand firm that contributed highly qualified specialists who added capabilities in special warfare operations, intelligence, and law enforcement, which generated an additional $1.3 million in gross annual revenues.
- Established an Indonesian office, which has poised the company to secure larger multi-million dollar contracts, and introduced a presence in Asia, including the hostile Malacca straits and Summatra.
- Grew the company's bottom line roughly 30% within the first year while cutting operational costs. Liquidated unprofitable satellite offices and terminated unproductive staff. Upgraded LAN with 10+ servers running on Windows.

Personnel Management:

- Identified, recruited, trained, and supervised tier one special operations staff comprising former CIA, FBI, Secret Service, and Delta Force Operatives; Seal Team 4/6s; Air Force Night Stalkers; and Navy Special Boat Squadron professionals.

Communications: Media, International Council Meetings, and Public Talks

- Gained international acclaim through extensive media exposure as a vocal industry leader and guest speaker on network television, cable, and radio programs: The O'Reilly Factor, Fox News Live, NBC/CBS News, Washington Public Eye, and National Public Radio (NPR).
- Negotiated multi-million dollar contracts with such clients as governments; international corporations; and high net worth/high profile individuals, celebrities, and political dignitaries.
- Participated in overseas Security Advisory Council meetings to exchange intelligence on security threats.
- Gave public talks on corporate security in Iraq before 250 attendees in Washington, DC.

Operations Management:

- Secure engagements involving the deployment of staff for security and risk management operations. Develop and execute crisis management and extraction planning; safeguard residential compounds, food, and supply convoys; and escort VIPs through hostile areas.
- Provide specialists with military and law enforcement training to protect persons and property during natural disasters, civil disturbances, public demonstrations, labor disputes, plant downsizing, workplace violence, and large-scale corporate events.
- Authorize contingency planning for broad ranging issues: evacuations, kidnappings/extortions, malicious tampering, and catastrophic incidents.
- Manage technical security countermeasures (TSCM) and related computer experts who identify and monitor perpetrators of electronic crime. Conduct covert mobile video surveillances and electronic sweeps of secure and suspected compromised areas.
- Ensure continuous business functionality, protect data/e-commerce, prevent breaches in information security, and address internal/external threats against complex network environments.
- Oversee aircrew, maritime, and on-premises staff training programs: force protection, counter-terrorism, terror tactics recognition, firearm usage, self-defense, survival, fire safety, executive protection, etc.
- Devise branding strategies and marketing campaigns that enable market dominance.

Writing Skills:

- Prepare risk assessment and post action reports; kidnap/extortion response plans; and ISPS code compliant maritime security plans (up to 1,000 pages) for large sea vessels.

Technical Skills:

- Ensure privacy, data integrity, and continuous business functionality across secure networks, servers, and desktops. Incorporate and use cutting-edge LAN specializing in secure communications, forensic examinations, disaster recovery, and data analysis. Trained in using the Judicial Information System (JIS).

Acting President, 2010 (4 months)

- Appointed to temporarily lead the company until a new President could be hired after the critical departure of the incumbent President who had governed the company since 1972.
- Led rapid growth of the company from approximately $1.5 million to $2 million in gross annual revenue. Resigned as Acting President once the new President was hired, but was requested to return as President after 1 month.

Division Manager, 2008 – 2010
- Directed field operations and international strategies to provide surveillance operations, force protection, executive protection, and corporate investigative actions for industry leading software manufacturers, the United States and foreign governments, and high net worth individuals.
- Emerged as the #1 Division Manager leading the most profitable division in the company.
- Devised and implemented new business development strategies that secured new clients; negotiated contracts valued up to $300,000 per transaction.
- Enhanced the caliber of the staff by replacing unskilled personnel with experienced, degreed, and highly-networked professionals with security clearances.
- Provided comprehensive training in investigations, surveillance, risk management, and contingency planning.

TAYLOR, INC., Silver Spring, Maryland   2002 – 2006
International Consultant
- Established this investigative and security consulting firm that specialized in investigations, risk assessments, risk mitigation, international consulting, and manpower/resource utilization.
- Generated more than $1 million in gross annual revenues from start up.

FREELANCE CONSULTING, Rockville, Maryland   1999 – 2002
International Consultant
- Provided international consulting with peripheral roles in intelligence and law enforcement operations for 25 domestic and overseas projects.
- Participated in teams involved in reconnaissance planning and surveillance, asset recovery, and corporate intelligence operations.

SUPPLEMENT

Military:
- U.S. Marines, Camp Giegr, Jacksonville, North Carolina, 1995 – 1999
- Led surveillance and target acquisition team as a Platoon/Squad Leader, First Battalion.
- Member of the U.S. Marine Super Squad, 1996

Affiliations:
- Member of the Overseas Security Advisory Council (OSAC)
- Member of the National Association of Former Intelligence Officers
- Member of MENSA

CORY S. SCHULMAN, CPP

20004 Security Drive
Gaithersburg, Maryland 20882

240-338-0050
security@gmail.com

OBJECTIVE

To implement airport security plans for the protection of life, property, and information in a Federal Security position.

HIGHLIGHTS

Leadership:

- Lieutenant and Commander of Special Services Section for the Maryland National Capital Park Police and Board Certified in Security Management, Certified Protection Professional (CPP).
- Possess firearms, CPR, first responder, and MD State Trained Police Certifications.
- Twenty-six years law enforcement experience includes planning, implementing, and managing security plans for 350 parks, protests, sporting contests, international events, VIP details, and FEMA disaster scenarios.
- Manage law enforcement for 30,000+ acres of parkland and 10 million visitors per year.
- Direct more than 70 community crime-prevention programs.
- Coordinate as many as 170 personnel comprising sworn police officers and volunteers.
- Travel to police agencies throughout the United States to ensure compliance with standards of the Commission for Accreditation for Law Enforcement Agencies (CALEA).

Counter-Terrorism:

- Completed Airport Security and Screening training from Reagan National Airport and the Pentagon.
- Knowledgeable of domestic and international terrorism prevention, including behavioral profiling, and detection of weapons of mass destruction and biological/chemical explosives.
- Planned and coordinated the 1996 Olympic Security Detail to Atlanta, Georgia as the Special Operations Section Commander. Supervised the equestrian venue, which was recognized by ACOG as one of the safest of the Olympic Games. Participated in joint efforts with the FBI, CIA, Secret Service, ATF, U.S. Federal Marshals, and related local, state, and federal law enforcement.

Security Planning & Enforcement:

- Supervised preparation of security plan for the Persian-American Cultural Festival, which hosted 10,000 attendees. Bridged communications with non-English speaking permit holders.
- Co-planned VIP protection and security for a 60,000-seat stadium at the 1996 Atlanta Olympics.
- Led use of K-9s; bicycle, motorcycle, and horse mounted officers; boat patrols, and uniformed patrols.
- Performed special event analysis and planning, which included examining large group activity within the park system, determining security needs, and implementing appropriate security measures. Skilled in crowd control, executive protection, perimeter security, search & seizure, and screening.
- Adept at conducting investigations, collecting evidence, interviewing witnesses, and apprehending suspects.

Environmental Security & Equipment:

- Developed crisis management plans, including wide-spread emergency notification, response, evacuation, and communications with critical staff to assist the public at high-profile facilities: airports, arenas, stadiums, sports complexes, and community centers.
- Advised plan review committees (architects, engineers, master planners) in requirements for environmental designs that best deter criminal activity.

- Performed facility security assessments and proposed limits for public access, floor plan re-engineering construction, and other security measures, which were distributed to division chiefs and facility coordinators.
- Used various high-tech security devices, such as CCTV, digital video records, motion sensors, metal detectors, and the Proximity access control system

EXPERIENCE

MARYLAND NATIONAL CAPITAL PARK POLICE, Montgomery County Division   1995 – Present
Lieutenant, 2002 – Present
- Ensure security for 31,000 acres of parkland, multi-use athletic sports facilities, and 10 million visitors per year.
- Appointed by the Executive Director of the Park and Planning Commission (MNCPPC) to coordinate and oversee the Bi-County Emergency Preparedness Task Force. Provide security for 2,500 employees and 50 facilities, including sports arenas, community centers, and administrative buildings.
- Direct 5 officers and 150 volunteers to manage 70 crime prevention programs dealing with fraud, identity theft, substance abuse, and other crimes pertaining to youths, adults, and varying ethnic groups.
- Implemented the mentor program for new officers/recruits preparing for the police academy.
- Represented the Department on live TV, radio, and print media by relaying accurate information from crime scenes, accident localities, and large special events.
- Interfaced with alarm specialists, access control technicians, police officers, human resource professionals, health/safety risk managers, and security officers.

Acting Captain/Assistant Chief, 1997 – 2002
- Directed the Patrol Section which provided 24-hour security for the Montgomery County Park System.
- Deployed 86-sworn police officers and 21 civilians to protect 350 urban, rural, and regional parks with 40 miles of trails and 3 parkways. Reduced the number of reported rapes, sexual assaults, car thefts, DWIs, and vandalism cases.
- Oversaw criminal and employment background investigations.
- Coordinated security plan and controlled crowds without incident for a publicly provocative KKK rally which attracted 1,500 anti-Klan protesters.
- Established SOPs for four sections: Patrol, Special Operations, Community Services, and Investigations, which facilitated accreditation for 1999 Field Operations.

Commander of Special Operations, 1995 – 1997
- Led Special Operations entailing horse-mounted, motorcycle, and marine patrols to secure regional parks, stream valleys, trails, special events, and crowds.
- Appointed to Presidential detail, which involved dignitary protection, perimeter security, and escort services.
- Met with the Atlanta Committee of the 1996 Olympic Games and collaborated with the CIA, Secret Service, FBI, and related local, state, and federal law enforcement to facilitate the planning and coordination of security contingencies for 40 security personnel.
- Safeguarded the equestrian venue and the Georgia International Equestrian Stadium, which seated 60,000 people.
- Provided VIP protection to politicians and international dignitaries such as the King of Spain.

SUPPLEMENT

Bachelor of Science, 1994, Planning, University of Maryland, College Park, Maryland
Associate of Arts, 1992, Geography, Montgomery College, Rockville, Maryland

Award: Proclamation of Recognition from Senator John Hurson for 1996 Summer Olympics

CORY SCHULMAN
15004 Software Engineer Road
Frederick, Maryland 21703
C: 240-338-0050
Software@gmail.com

SUMMARY

Designed, developed, and supported various real-time UNIX and Microsoft Windows applications as a Software Developer.

Languages: C#, C++, C, Visual Basic, Java, Perl

Applications: Solaris Visual Workshop, Motif, Oracle Pro C, Sybase Pro C, Microsoft ODBC, Laserdata Imaging, TeamWork Document Handler Imaging, TMS Imaging SDK

EXPERIENCE

NETWORK SYSTEMS, INC., Lanham, Maryland   2014 – Present
Senior Software Engineer
- Promoted business development with major commercial/government contractors by writing satellite communication applications to decomputate telemetry using various algorithms and frame formats for 13 different satellites.
- Designed an unlimited redundancy/backup system that enabled synchronization among real-time operating systems with independent configurations.
- Used C++ and TCP/IP with socket connection and multi-threaded applications running on UNIX to enable distribution of 8,000 parameters to secondary systems, the first time the company achieved this capability in its 20-year history.
- Devised a process that filtered information from telemetry archive in accordance with U.S. Air Force security requirements.
- Wrote Device Handler used to measure power reading of ground antennas for commanding/receiving satellite telemetry.
- Maintained all Graphical User Interface (GUI) applications for Integral System Inc. EPOCH version III satellite ground control systems software using Motif and C/C++ under UNIX Sun Solaris.
- Developed and maintain custom real-time applications that extend functionality to meet customers' specific needs and enhance EPOCH ground monitoring and command software system.
- Developed C/C++ real-time process that monitors ground and spacecraft telemetry points for changes in order to synchronize and distribute change data throughout all EPOCH's Front End Processors (FEP).

EDUCATION

University of Maryland University College, College Park, Maryland
Bachelor of Science in Computer Science, 2014

CORY SCHULMAN

28001 Store Manager Way
Germantown, Maryland 20876
240-338-0050
storemanager@aol.com

OBJECTIVE

To maximize corporate profits, employee productivity, and customer satisfaction as a Store Manager of a big-box retailer.

EXPERIENCE

Q-MART, Montgomery County, Maryland   2007 – Present
Store Manager, Germantown, Maryland, 2011 – Present
- Revitalized management of a troubled store, comprising 360 employees and spanning 150,000 square feet, one of the largest Q-Mart stores in the 75-store Mid-Atlantic region.
- Increased gross annual revenues from $60 million to $67 million, which exceeded the corporate goal of $1 million and nearly doubled the net profit.
- Earned the #1 ranking year-to-date for sales increases in the district and maintained one of the highest net-profit increases in the region.
- Curtailed rampant employee turnover from 83% to 33%, which was half the allowable rate according to corporate guidelines.
- Increased the sales per labor hour approximately 19% while reducing wage percentage of sales 10%.
- Reduced shrinkage 45% saving the company roughly $600,000 and maintained shrinkage well below industry averages.
- Freed more than $500,000 in working capital by eliminating unnecessary physical inventory while improving turns 33%.
- Interfaced with 30 – 40 vendors for food & beverage, apparel, hardlines, and homelines.
- Developed and monitored an operating budget of $13.4 million.

General Merchandise Co-Manager, Scottsdale, Arizona, 2009 – 2011
- Participated in the hiring and training of the first 550 employees for the grand opening of a 208,000 square foot Supercenter that generated $72 million in FY 2011.
- Increased sales 42%, which led the company in sales improvement among all 2,700 stores nationwide.

International Transition Team, Store Planning, Germany, 2007 – 2009
- Collaborated with the Store Planning Division to install the SMART and POS systems in stores throughout Germany.
- Provided technical support by troubleshooting system glitches and facilitated the training of 1,200 associates.

EDUCATION

Bachelor of Science, Business Administration, 2006, University of Arizona, Tucson, Arizona
Reading Financial Statements, 2007, Dunn & Bradstreet, Scottsdale, Arizona

CORY SCHULMAN

28002 Store Manager Road
Rockville, Maryland 20851
240-338-0050
storemanager@gmail.com

EXPERIENCE

WILLIARDS, Maryland, Pennsylvania, New Hampshire   2010 – Present

Store Manager, District Store, Wheaton, Maryland

- Manage 40 departments, warehouse operations, and as many as 225 employees for a $22 million store, which serves as a showcase for a 13-store district.
- Increased gross annual revenues $1.3 million by revitalizing store operations.
- Revamped 60% of the staff and strengthened internal controls resulting in a dramatic turnaround in gross annual revenues from $1.2 million in losses to profitability within 1 year.
- Increased store ranking from #17 to #8 among 352 stores nationwide.
- Generated a 7.5% rise in annual sales despite declining sales throughout the chain.
- Devised and deployed an inventory tracking system, which curtailed shrinkage from more than 5% to nearly 1%, saving the company approximately $600,000.
- Implemented new grids, planograms, and prototype configurations as a District Store Manager. Participated in finalizing apparel configuration in three stores.

Store Manager, Greensburg, Pennsylvania

- Achieved annual revenues 15% above company-wide averages per unit within 19 months for a $17 million store.

Store Manager, Nashua, New Hampshire

- Increased store ranking for in-store performance from over #100 to #1 among 352 stores nationwide.
- Developed and led teams, increased employee productivity, reduced expenses, and raised quality of customer service standards.

SEASONS TOYS, Montgomery County, Maryland   2007 – 2010

Floor Manager

- Provided leadership in 10+ stores throughout the Montgomery County district.
- Directed as many as 27 support staff and scheduled up to 320 hours per week in accordance with budgeted labor and sales ratios.
- Trained store managers in inventory control, budget reporting, employee supervision, customer relations, report generation, and computer operations. Hired and mentored new hires, which resolved high employee turnover and chronic understaffing issues.
- Managed stores that doubled corporate sales projections and earned the highest Mystery Shopping scores for outstanding service and operational efficiency.
- Implemented promotional campaigns and devised employee incentive programs that resulted in the highest gross sales in the district. Exceeded projected goals for 3 consecutive years.

ADDITIONAL EXPERIENCE & EDUCATION

Store Manager in Training, Chyles Department Stores, Cuyahoga Falls, Ohio   2005 – 2006
Assistant Store Manager, Mattress Center, Akron, Ohio   2003 – 2004
Bachelor of Arts, Business Administration, Walsh University, Canton, Ohio   2002

CORY SCHULMAN

28004 Grocery Store Manager Lane
Frederick, Maryland 21703
240-338-0050
storemanager@gmail.com

OBJECTIVE

To maximize corporate profits in an Executive position within supermarket retail or wholesale distribution environments.

EXPERIENCE

GRUMER FOODS, INC., Rockville, Maryland	2013 – Present

Director, Meat-Deli-Seafood Operations

- ***Revenue Generation:*** Increased gross annual revenues of Meat Departments 30%, doubled sales in Deli Departments, and tripled volume in Seafood Departments within all 12 company stores, which generate approximately $160 million per annum. Improved aggregate departmental revenues from $15 million to $26 million per annum, which accounted for 73% of the corporation's rise in annual revenues. Doubled sales for a rotisserie product, which was rated #1 on a regional survey featured in *The Washington Post*.

- ***Marketing/Store Design:*** Reversed declining profit by introducing and launching new marketing campaigns, which included aggressive branding, pricing structures, and merchandising initiatives. Revamped product selections and store layouts, which entailed expansions, relocations, and new store openings. Designed layouts for Meat-Deli-Seafood Departments in two new units spanning 28,000 and 37,000 square feet. Remodeled departments and kitchens in 10 other stores.

- ***Strategic Analysis/Initiatives:*** Expanded Deli and Seafood Departments. Instituted on-site chefs and gourmet centers that provided full-service Deli Departments. Transitioned negotiations from the distributor to the packer level, resulting in reduced costs for higher product quality. Shifted procurement of seafood from local distributors to the primary seafood processor. Diversified product lines and negotiated 5% cost reductions for Meat/Deli products.

- ***Human Resources:*** Provide executive oversight for over 190+ employees. Overhauled management team and maintained their longevity for more than 3 years. Curtailed labor costs 10% while improving productivity approximately 25%.

FOOD MART COMPANIES, INC., Paramus, New Jersey	2001 – 2013

Vice President, Meat-Deli-Seafood Operations

- Achieved steady growth for 12 consecutive years raising gross profits from 22% to 27% for meat, from 35% to 42% for deli, and from 26% to 30% for seafood. Led expansion efforts from 12 to 21 stores and oversaw 300+ employees. Elected as one of seven members of Executive Meat-Deli-Seafood Committees for a 140 store co-op. Committee presided over purchasing, advertising, budgeting, and a 250,000 square foot warehouse distribution center.
- Emerged as one of the leaders in generating gross profit and sales per square foot among the co-op members.

SOUTHERN MEAT COMPANY, Empire Division, Waterford, New York	1998 – 2001

Meat Superintendent

- Managed the Empire Southern Division Meat and Store Operations, consisting of 110 stores in 3 states and generating approximately $100 million per annum, the #2 highest in the country and the most profitable division for Grand Union. Oversaw procurement, merchandising, and operations staff.

CORY SCHULMAN

28005 Store Manager Place
Montgomery Village, MD 20886
240-338-0050
storemanager@gmail.com

HIGHLIGHTS

Customer-focused and sales-driven Manager with decorated history of increasing sales, customer satisfaction, employee productivity, and operational efficiency of multi-million dollar establishments. Managed numerous stores concurrently and gained experience in preparing stores for grand openings as well as for final closings. Revitalized several retail operations by restaffing personnel, providing effective training, and instituting viable policies and internal controls.

- One of 30 managers among 950 company-wide store managers to win a sales contest sponsored by Nike Corporation.
- Led Athletic Center store to achieve the highest grossing sales volume in its district.
- Won Rookie-of-the-Year for improving sales, customer service, and employee morale.
- Inducted in the 1% Club for shrinkage control.

EXPERIENCE

ATHLETIC CENTER, Manhattan, New York   2014 – Present
Store Manager
- Earned four promotions as a Manager of multi-million dollar stores ranked as high as #2 within a district of 22 stores. Revamped operations as a Marquee Manager of the company's flagship store in New York City, improving the ranking from #18 to #6. Improved the ranking of the Valley Stream store from #11 to #3.
- Spearheaded improvements in sales, service, and operations for all stores managed. Reduced operating expenses, especially in labor, shrinkage, and inventory control. Enhanced employee productivity by developing teams, improving morale, and providing intensive training in sales and customer service.
- Overhauled the staff of 15 employees and instituted new internal controls, which reduced shrinkage from $140,000 to $22,000.
- Increased the customer satisfaction index from 20 to 89 based on outstanding mystery shopper scores.
- Served as a store trainer for new development managers.
- Recruited, trained, and managed 60 diverse employees in preparation for the grand opening of the Valley Stream store and led the store to generate $2.5 million per annum.
- Participated in quarterly management meetings to focus on marketing strategies, recruitment, and merchandise selection.

EDUCATION

Diploma, 2013, Leadership Skills, Non-Commissioned Officer School
Diploma, 2012, Business School

CORY SCHULMAN

28006 District Manager Drive
Germantown, MD 20874

240-338-0050
storemanager@gmail.com

OBJECTIVE

To apply experience in marketing, administration, or human resources in a managerial capacity.

EXPERIENCE

BENTEE STORES, INC., Bethesda, Maryland; Tyson's Corner, Virginia   11/2008 – Present

District Manager

- Manage a 13-store district that generates approximately $30 million per annum. Revitalized robust patronage and eliminated a 25% shortfall in revenues. Rectified chronic employee turnover throughout the Metro-Washington market.
- Hired more than 80 employees, including 33 new management personnel. Devised and led intensive training and instilled strong work ethics that have improved productivity, customer service, and employee longevity.
- Revamped 25 positions at the Tyson's Corner store and maintained a stable and productive sales force.
- Opened two new locations that are projected to represent 40% of the district revenues. Hired 50 sales and management personnel in preparation for soft opening.
- Co-coordinated three fashion shows and secured media coverage for the grand opening of the Wisconsin store.
- Cut excessive shrinkage roughly 45% by terminating 6 management staff and strengthening internal controls.
- Reversed declining sales among Bentee stores in close proximity to each other by resolving redundant merchandising themes.

BARNSTON STORES, INC., Chicago, Illinois; Washington, DC   3/2004 – 11/2008

Regional Manager, 1/2005 – 11/2008

- Managed 2 divisions across a 12-state territory, consisting of 62 stores that generate approximately $30 million per annum. Coordinated the opening of 11 new stores.
- Introduced and incorporated fresh ideas that enhanced operations, seized greater market share, opened communication channels, and improved personnel productivity.
- Increased sales in the 2 divisions 11% year-to-date and as much as 22% in prior years.
- Converted troubled units in North Carolina and Tennessee into profitable stores by spearheading a dramatic 40% – 50% rise in sales.
- Raised employees' hourly productivity in Tennessee from $60 to $90.
- Initiated a resurgence in profits by conducting fashion show infomercials on radio and television.
- Conducted employee training seminars that focused on time management and customer relations.
- Reduced employee turnover by strengthening recruitment and training effectiveness.

Divisional Manager, 3/2004 – 1/2005

- Promoted 3 times within the first year to manage 49 retail stores and 350 employees of the South East Division, which grossed more than $23 million per annum.
- Revitalized gross annual revenues of some units as much as 29%.
- Prevented the closure of troubled units by resolving operational deficiencies: revamped unproductive staffs, eliminated severe shrinkage, reorganized and remerchandised stock, cross trained personnel, and instilled customer service as the primary focus.
- Rebuilt loyal clientele for the entire eight-state region by aggressively networking among professional offices and government agencies.
- Introduced new product lines, which were successfully sold in 225 stores nationwide.
- Launched effective marketing campaigns by coordinating network advertising, tradeshows, fashion shows, and other promotional events that attracted up to 2,000 attendees.

CORY SCHULMAN

29001 Teacher Court • Frederick, Maryland 21703 • 240-338-0050 • teacher@gmail.com

OBJECTIVE

To promote students' academic, social, and emotional development as an experienced Math Teacher dedicated to strong classroom management.

EXPERIENCE

WINSTON CHURCHILL ELEMENTARY SCHOOL, Frederick, Maryland   2008 – Present

5th Grade Teacher

- *Instruction:* Teach all primary courses, which include Math A, to classes consisting of gifted and talented, on-level, 504 plan, and IEP students. Brought the majority of IEP students and low achievers from far below level to on-level within the first year. Developed a curriculum for summer Math A preparatory class. Implemented special projects: the Reading Incentive Program and Reading Across the USA, which incorporated math and graph reading skills. Proctored MSPAP, CRTS, MSAs, and other standardized tests.

- *Classroom Management:* Ensured a proper environment conducive for academic study by employing effective behavioral management strategies. Emphasized the development of effective study habits and academic skills, including organization, time management, and test taking strategies. Applied various methodologies such as whole group, cooperative learning, and peer study techniques.

- *Leadership:* Held weekly meetings as the Team Leader for 5th grade teachers and presided over academic requirements, students' needs, curriculum coordination, administrative policies, social events, and field trips. Brought the year book from conceptualization to publication on-time and within budget as the Year-Book Coordinator. Coordinated 5th grade trip to Philadelphia and led 100+ students throughout historical and downtown areas.

- *After-School Teaching Activities:* Tutored students in math A, B, C, IM, and Algebra. Devised and introduced creative activities that intrigued below-level students into performing math exercises. Participated in the American History Grant Program, which involved an intensive 6-day tour through the Smithsonian Institution and interaction with curators.

5th Grade Musical Coordinator

- Auditioned students for parts in such plays as Ben Franklin and Lewis & Clark; and co-directed after-school rehearsals.

CARL SANDBURG ELEMENTARY SCHOOL, Philadelphia, Pennsylvania   2003 – 2007

4th & 5th Grade Teacher

- Taught Intensive Academic Support Classes, which entailed restructuring academic/behavioral management plans and modifying curricula to address students with learning difficulties. Customized lessons to address diverse learning styles among At-Risk students resulting in the improvement of three grade levels.
- Improved students' attendance, class participation, homework, and test performance despite complete absence of parental involvement. Enhanced critical thinking skills by educating students on inferences, fact, and opinion; cause and effect; contextual clues; comparison and contrast; classifications; and sequencing.
- Established learning centers that focused on math, language arts, computer technology, and writing.
- Researched and presented resource information in lieu of text books due to severe budgetary limitations.

EDUCATION • CERTIFICATION • AFFILIATIONS

Master of Education, 2002, West Chester University, West Chester, Pennsylvania
Bachelor of Education, 2000, Kutztown University, Kutztown, Pennsylvania
Possess K – 8 Teaching Certifications from the State of Maryland and the State of Pennsylvania
Member, National Education Association (NEA); and the MD State Teachers' Association (MSTA)

CORY SCHULMAN

29002 Teacher Court
Rockville, MD 20854
240-338-0050
teacher@gmail.com

OBJECTIVE

To advance students' academic, emotional, and social development as an elementary or middle school teacher.

EXPERIENCE

MONTGOMERY COUNTY PUBLIC SCHOOL SYSTEM, Germantown, Maryland   2014 – Present
Second, Third, and Fourth Grade Teacher, Roberto Clemente Elementary School

TEMPLE BETH TIKVA, Kensington, Maryland   2012 – 2014
Fourth, Fifth, and Ninth Grade Teacher

HIGHLIGHTS

- Co-authored new social studies curriculum, which has been published and is currently used throughout Montgomery County schools.
- Developed creative curricula for all primary subjects, including math, science, and writing with special emphasis in cooperative learning.
- Completed the Maryland Collaborative for Teacher Mentor Training Seminar to mentor teachers in technology, math, science, Internet, graphics, and self-directed learning techniques.
- Conducted a seminar that trained student teachers in the primary elements for success in teaching.
- Created and developed the Teachers' Resource Center. Provided recommendations for the future of Student Teaching Program at the Professional Development Center.
- Prepared individualized, weekly reports on student behavior and academic progress.
- Collaborated with the County Police Department to promote Gang Resistance, Education, and Training (GREAT).
- Directed class plays: Sleeping Beauty and The Wizard of Oz.

Primary Attributes: Provide a warm and stimulating classroom environment with strong classroom and behavioral management skills. Inspire young minds to think independently and work cooperatively with special emphasis on critical thinking, problem resolution, and knowledge acquisition. Devise creative projects that intrigue students and promote their self-esteem, academic skills, and social development. Foster strong relations with parents through frequent student status reports and conferences.

EDUCATION

M.A. Degree, 2011, Education, Graduated with Distinction, American University
B.S. Degree, Elementary Education, 2009, University of Maryland
B.A. Degree, 2008, F.M.C.D. - Family Counseling, University of Maryland
Completed Maryland Collaborative for Teacher Mentor Training Seminar

CORY SCHULMAN

29003 Teacher Drive
Plainsboro, NJ 08536
240-338-0050
teacher@gmail.com

OBJECTIVE

To provide strong classroom leadership for advancing students' academic, behavioral, and emotional development as a Pre-School Teacher or a related position.

EXPERIENCE

PRE-SCHOOL LEARNING CENTER, Columbia, Maryland   2013 – Present
Teacher

- Led preschool classes by preparing and administering daily lessons and activities that complied with the curriculum.
- Focused on various subjects, including language development, mathematics, arts, crafts, and music. Prepared exercises to reinforce understanding of concepts such as shapes, colors, counting, and other preparatory requirements.
- Encouraged critical thinking through stimulating classroom question and answer routines.
- Honed children's skills by promoting their competencies in listening, recall, following directions, making observations, decision making; and identifying patterns, generalities, and specifics.
- Chaperoned field trips to museums, parks, restaurants, and cinemas.
- Held conferences with parents and school officials, including the school psychiatrist to address unusual student needs.
- Evaluated and documented students' progress and deficits; recommended individualized actions for each student.

MONTGOMERY ACADEMY EARLY LEARNING, Arlington, Virginia   2011 – 2013
Teacher

- Promoted academic, social, and behavioral development among class of pre-school students by effectively providing strong classroom management.
- Commanded attentiveness among students for demonstrations, and encouraged lively participation in group exercises.
- Focused on developing verbal communications, social interaction, motor skills, and fundamental knowledge of colors, numbers, the alphabet, and related early learning concepts.
- Implemented the school's curriculum and daily lessons. Evaluated students' progress and prepared semi-annual report cards. Administered tests for academic progress.
- Led dance classes in preparation for an after-school dance competition among other area schools. Led group singing and game sessions. Chaperoned class field trips to the zoo, park, pool, and farms.
- Conducted parent conferences to discuss strengths and weaknesses of their children's progress. Discussed potential learning disabilities or other signs of cognitive, emotional, and/or behavioral challenges.
- Participated in faculty meetings and updated sessions with the supervisor regarding academic programs and related issues.
- Earned an award for Best Class Decoration Project among five classes.

EDUCATION

Certificate of Completion, 2010, 90-hour program, Child Development Institute, Washington, DC
Certificate of Completion, 2010, Child Development Association, Rockville, Maryland

CORY SCHULMAN
29004 Music Teacher Road
Washington, DC 20012
240-338-0050
musicteacher@gmail.com

EXPERIENCE

ROBERTO CLEMENTE MIDDLE SCHOOL, Germantown, MD   August 2011 – Present
Instrumental Music Teacher (Grades 6 – 8 Band)
- Schedule and provide music instruction to 5 classes consisting of 150 total students who varied in talent and instrument forte.
- Create syllabi that encompass subject matter in compliance with state standards.
- Record, analyze, and evaluate students' concert performances and in-class rehearsals.
- Develop students' understanding and skill in reading sheet music; use of technique with woodwind, brass, and percussion instruments; and producing ensemble coordination.
- Focus on tone quality, intonation, rhythmic precision, dynamic contrast, phrasing, and balance/blend ensemble.
- Coordinate numerous class trips for students to observe and participate in off-site concerts. Plan itinerary and secure written permission from parents for student participation.
- Received excellent ratings based on groups' performance level at a county band festival.
- Increased the number of students selected as top performers from 35 to 45.
- Conduct parent/teacher conferences and represent the Music Department as a guest speaker before 100 parents of students entering the Music Department's 6th grade program.
- Draft and revise handbooks consisting of policies, procedures, and concert dates.
- Prepare general correspondence regarding concert events and student evaluations.
- Perform ancillary functions, which include ensuring the Music Department operates within budget and repairing instruments.
- Facilitate the registration process by collaborating with counselors in recommending placement of incoming students.

ROBERT FROST ELEMENTARY SCHOOL, Silver Spring, MD   January 2008 – August 2011
Student Teacher, Grades 3 – 5 Strings and Band
- Rehearsed symphonic band, concert band, orchestra, and jazz ensemble.
- Taught secondary dominants and modulation to the music theory class.
- Designed and implemented lesson plans that included students with special needs.
- Practiced effective music teaching methods such as Ti – Ri and 1e&a systems of rhythmic training; use of singing to improve intonation; and aural demonstration of concepts as a supplement to verbal explanation (dotted quarter note).
- Taught beginning violinists to use 4th finger on the G, D, and A strings.
- Discussed breathing techniques with beginning flute, trombone, and clarinet classes.
- Fostered ensemble listening activities in orchestra and band settings.
- Tuned string instruments daily.

EDUCATION

BS, Instrumental Music Education, GPA: 3.47, University of Maryland, College Park, MD

CORY SCHULMAN

29005 Special Education Drive
Olney, MD 20832
240-338-0050
teacher@gmail.com

OBJECTIVE

To inspire student's academic, emotional, and social development as an experienced Administrator, Classroom Teacher, or Special Education Leader.

EDUCATION

American University, Washington, DC
MA/MEQ in Psychology and Adolescent Education, 2007
BA in Psychology and Special Education, Cum Laude within 3 years, 2004
Certified in State of Maryland
Advanced Professional Certificate to Teach Special Education K- 12

HIGHLIGHTS

Special Education:
- Former MCPS Title I Teacher, Special Education Teacher for learning disabled and emotionally impaired adolescents since 2007.
- Possess extensive knowledge of federal, state, and local laws governing special education, including ARD, SARD, CARD, IDEA, PL94142, and the Education For All Individuals Act.
- Skilled in due-process and the appeal process in support of parents' rights.
- Wrote, developed, and implemented programs for multiply-handicapped students.
- Possess in-depth knowledge and servicing of 01 through 14 handicapping conditions.

EXPERIENCE

TEAM ADVOCACY, Rockville, Maryland, 2007 – Present
Special Education Advocate
- Travel to public schools throughout the Washington Metropolitan region to provide on-site advocacy for special education students and their parents.
- Interview parents and test students to assess needs and offer objective advice. Provide strong leadership for pursuing special education services in the least restrictive environment.
- Write assessments and develop action plans based on private testing, teacher/parent reports, classroom observation, and proposed special education needs.
- Pursued available services, voiced qualifications for program requirements, and ensured compliance with the application/appeal process.
- Won parent's interest to secure higher level of special education services in Montgomery, Howard, and Anne Arundel County Public School systems by presenting a successful defense before the Admission, Review, and Dismissal Committee.

Special Education Teacher
- Taught students ages 12 - 16 diagnosed with learning disabilities, language disabilities, emotional disturbances, attention deficit disorders, traumatic brain damage, and severely emotional disturbances in an intensity 05 setting.
- Developed and taught whole programs, interdisciplinary units, parallel curriculum units, lesson plans, learner verified text and novels, and manipulatives.
- Prepared audio-visual materials and taped text.
- Administered various standardized tests such as MSPAP, Woodcock Reading Mastery, Wiatt, Woodcock-Johnson, and Key Math tests.

CORY F. SCHULMAN, MT, CLS

300 Technologist Drive • Montgomery Village, Maryland 20886 • 240-338-0050 • technologist@gmail.com

EXPERIENCE

GREATER WASHINGTON COMMUNITY HOSPITAL, Washington, DC   2010 – Present
Medical Technologist
- Conduct pretransfusion testing, identification of alloantibodies to red cell antigens, direct antiglobulin tests, and elution studies.
- Select compatible blood and blood components, including plasma pheresis, platelets, cryoprecipitate, and Rh Immune Globulin.
- Administer routine hematological tests: CBCs, CFSs, and ESRs.
- Perform coagulation studies, including fibrinogen, PT/PTT, and factor assays.
- Manage the lab inventory to prevent blood product shortages.
- Train new medical technologists in techniques for pretransfusion tests, selecting compatible blood products, and operating the LIS and HIS terminals.
- Eliminated chronic complaints by dramatically improving accuracy and processing time, inventory control, and professional communications among hundreds of physicians and support staff.
- Coordinate actions to supply compatible donor units for concurrent emergencies among in-patients/out-patients throughout this 500-bed trauma care hospital.

ST. FRANCIS HOSPITAL, Washington, DC   2005 – 2010
Generalist, Immunology and Microbiology
- Performed plating, colony morphology, gram staining, pathogenic bacterial identification, and antimicrobial susceptibility tests. Prepared and sterilized media.
- Conducted immunological tests for hepatitis, HIV, RPR/FTA, and chlamydia.
- Trained newly hired medical technologists in bacteriological techniques and use of immunology and microbiology equipment.
- Performed emergency tests in numerous sections: Chemistry, Hematology, Urinalysis, Coagulation, and Microbiology/Immunology.

SHADY GROVE HOSPITAL, Rockville, Maryland   2001 – 2005
Generalist, Clinical Chemistry
- Analyzed patient samples and conducted various tests of the following: endocrine measurements, thyroid functions, electrolytes, hepatic functions, serum enzyme determinations, pancreatic disorders, cerebrospinal fluids, seminal fluids, sickle cell screening, and fetal hemoglobin.
- Prepared reagents and reference materials. Calibrated machines and ensured quality control.
- Performed therapeutic drug monitoring and detection of illicit drugs of patients.

HEALTH & WELLNESS FOUNDATION, Silver Spring, Maryland   1999 – 2001
Generalist
- Worked in all sections: Hematology, Coagulation, Blood Bank, Urinalysis, Chemistry, Phlebotomy, Microbiology, and Immunology.
- Conducted various specialized, manual, and automated diagnostic tests, which entailed evaluating, recording, and reporting results to physicians.
- Performed daily maintenance of equipment: Dade Dimension AR/IMT Clinical Chemistry System, Dupont ACA Star Discrete Clinical Analyzer, MLA-Electra 800 Automatic Coag, DyanMedix Gensys Plu LIS, Coulter Onyx Analyzer, and Baxter.

EDUCATION

Henson School of Science and Technology, Salisbury State University, Salisbury, Maryland
Bachelor of Science in Medical Technology, May 1998

CORY S. SCHULMAN, M.T. (ASCP)

30004 Lab Management Terrace
Montgomery Village, Maryland 20886
240-338-0050
labmanagement@gmail.com

PROFILE

- Extensive lab management and consulting experience in microbiology, chemistry, urinalysis, and hematology 30 - 40 hours per week. Enforced quality control, initiated quality assurance (QA), and standardized lab supplies and testing protocols. Developed new procedural methods. Ensure labs meet OSHA and CLIA requirements and pass inspections. Instituted external proficiency testing. Secured licensure for seven laboratories.

- Financial Management: Identified profitability of in-house procedures versus reference labs. Adhered to annual budgets; recommended revenue expense considerations for annual budgets. Maintained budgeted F.T.E.'s for lab personnel. Reduced operating costs and procurement expenses.

- Performed multi-functioned roles, including Laboratory Consultant, AIDS Coordinator, Lab Manager, Corporate Resource, and Representative. Served as a liaison to state officials concerning quality control and procedural changes. Organized community health fairs.

EXPERIENCE

HEALTH LABORATORIES, Gaithersburg, Maryland   2006 – Present
Lab Manager, 2011 – Present
- Manage five internal labs and an outside pediatric office. Coordinate QA procedures between five urgent care labs and five hospitals.
- Oversee accurate collection of hundreds of corporate and federally mandated drug screens per month.
- Orient, train, and supervise up to 70 lab technicians per year in hematology, microbiology, chemistry, urinalysis, and body fluid examinations (KOH, web preps, gram stains).
- Standardized diagnostic tests, machinery, and procedures for microbiology, hematology, and chemistry.
- Reduced operating costs 20-30% per year by consolidating usage of lab supplies.
- Improved documentation of controls and instituted QA program.
- Spearheaded the development of pre/post HIV tests in 2008.
- Upgraded labs to comply with OSHA and CLIA standards resulting in 25 flawless inspections since 2011.

Staff Medical Technologist, Health Max Medical Care, 2006 – 2011

Additional Technical Experience:
Staff Technologist, ATF Health Institute, 2004 – 2006
Staff Technologist, Wilson Hope Laboratory, 2002 – 2004
Staff Medical Technologist, University of Phoenix, 2000 – 2002

EDUCATION

Medical Technologist, 2000, Licensed by The American Society of Clinical Pathologists
CPR Certified
B.A. (Biology), 1999, Thiel College, Greenville, Pennsylvania

CORY SCHULMAN

30005 Autoclave Terrace
Montgomery Village, Maryland 20886
240-338-0050
autoclave@gmail.com

OBJECTIVE

To maximize quality control, productivity, and system integrity as a dedicated Technician.

EXPERIENCE

BIO-MEDS, Gaithersburg, Maryland   June 2009 – Present

Autoclave Technician

- Recognized as one of the fastest and most accurate technicians in the company for repairing bio-medical equipment such as autoclaves (sterilizers).
- Inspect, diagnose, and repair malfunctions such as pressure leaks and electronic damage; replace worn parts; calibrate pressure and temperature of sterilizing chambers.
- Achieved approximately 40% more repairs than the average technician in the unit.
- Doubled repair time efficiency by developing strategies and techniques to streamline repair operations.
- Participated in the construction of a national autoclave repair center, the largest dental sterilizer repair facility in the world. Assembled work benches and wired repair/test stations.
- Manage inventory valued at hundreds of thousands of dollars. Order supplies, parts, and tools from a national vendor.
- Maintain positive client relationships by providing effective technical support.
- Use diagnostic equipment, including power supplies, oscilloscopes, digital volt meters, pressure sensors, thermocouples, etc.
- Possess broad ranging knowledge of fasteners such as nuts, bolts, glues, epoxies, adhesives, compression fittings, tubing, rivets, etc.
- Train new technicians in diagnostics, troubleshooting, and repair or autoclaves.

SUPPLEMENT

Education: Catholic University, Washington, DC, Economics, 2006 – 2009

Corporate Training: Dale Carnegie, Human Relations, 2008

Volunteerism: Montgomery County Road Runners; Nature Conservancy; and Adirondack Mountain Club

CORY SCHULMAN

31001 Television Producer Terrace
Montgomery Village, Maryland 20886

240-338-0050
producer@gmail.com

OBJECTIVE

To execute the highest quality broadcasts as a Producer or a related career opportunity in local or network television.

HIGHLIGHTS

Award-winning Producer for WTNT TV-31 News with 7 years' experience coordinating accurate and timely live newscasts. Covered the era's most salient stories: the first stem-cell assisted recovery from paraplegia, ISIS in Syria, the commercial Antares rocket explosion, Nelson Mandela's death, national/local campaigns and elections, and many others. Led teams to produce highly accurate and visually appealing newscasts and news specials.

Awards:
- 2015 Capitol Region Emmy Award, News Specials: Program, "Katherine Graham: A Washington Legend."
- 2014 Regional Edward R. Murrow Award, Best Newscast, coverage of the Rise of ISIS.
- Nomination for Capitol Region Emmy Award, Producer, 9 News at 11 pm, coverage of 12/31/13 celebration.
- Nomination for Capitol Region Emmy Award, Producer, Capitol Hill Shooting Special, 7/27/10.

Production Software:
- Station System Manager, INews/Avstar software. Editor, Avid Newscutter software.

EXPERIENCE

WTNT TV-31 NEWS, NW Washington, DC   2008 – Present

Producer, 2010 – Present (Currently 11 pm newscast)
- Produce up to two long-form, live newscasts per day with energetic and quality conscious leadership resulting in a two point ratings increase and several industry awards.
- Enhanced the overall freshness of the 11 pm newscast by selecting stories that appeal to a broader audience; increasing the number of new and updated stories; incorporating greater use of anchor packages (PKGs), natural sounds (NATs), sound on tapes (SOTs), voice overs (VOs), video opens, montages, and dynamic graphics; and achieving a greater mix of interviews from both key officials and the public.
- Improved the caliber and performance of the staff, comprising reporters, graphic designers, writers, editors, and anchors. Collaborate with reporters to establish visions for the presentation of the show and segments. Achieved seamless transitions and overall flowing content. Work with the Director to ensure technical capability of special production elements of the show.
- Provide instruction to the assignment editor regarding outside logistics.
- Map program elements such as Chyron formatting by using Station System Manager INews Avstar software. Edit VOs and SOTs using Avid Newscutter software.

Nightside Executive Producer, 2008 – 2010
- Directed producers, reporters, and editors/writers for the 5, 6, and 11 pm newscasts to ensure appropriate story selection, technical operability, and split-second decisions to cover breaking news.

EDUCATION

A.A. in Television/Radio, 2008, Montgomery College, Rockville, Maryland
Major: Communications, 2004 – 2006, University of Delaware, Newark, Delaware

CORY SCHULMAN

31002 Television Producer Terrace
Montgomery Village, Maryland 20886

240-338-0050
producer@gmail.com

HIGHLIGHTS

- Edited and produced features, documentary segments, and hard news for major market news organizations, including CNN, ABC, BBC, ITN, and APTV.

- Directed production teams for live shoots and features. Traveled to Eastern Europe, the Middle East, Japan, and other remote locations throughout world to cover breaking news events. Interviewed high-profile dignitaries, entertainers, and victims of crises.

- Adept at applying linear and nonlinear editing to produce live and taped programming. Proficient in script writing, camera operations, lighting, and audio.

- Won an Emmy Award for coverage of the Syrian civil war as a Producer and Editor.

EXPERIENCE

FREELANCE PRODUCTION, Washington, DC   2015 – Present
Writer, Editor, & Producer
- Produced a 6 minute film for CNN on a village in Cyprus as well as feature stories on Yemen and Dubai, which entailed writing, filming, and editing.
- Produced and edited features and news stories on crises within the Baltic region, Soviet Union, and the Middle East.
- Filmed documentaries on the history of the British Royals. Conducted undercover investigative reports on the spread of Russian corruption to East Germany.
- Covered the Israeli Palestinian peace talks, which included interviews with Syrian President Assad and Jordan's King Hussein. Produced features on the coup attempt in Moscow, West Bank riots, Somalian police force, Kurdish refugees in Turkey, war torn Serbia/Croatia, and the effects of pollution on Egyptian pyramids.

CBS NEWS, London, United Kingdom   2013 – 2015
Tape Producer/Editor
- Coordinate elements for News One stories, including Northern Ireland, Iraq, heat pumps, and national celebrations.

WORLD VOICE, Berlin, Germany; Tokyo, Japan   2011 – 2013
Producer/Editor
- Coordinated stories, covered breaking news, and produced features. Traveled to breaking stories in Europe and the Middle East.
- Produced 8 minute features on arts and entertainment for "Inside Germany," a half hour program (2012).

EDUCATION

B.A. in Broadcast Production, 2011, University of Colorado School of Journalism

CORY SCHULMAN
16005 Transportation Place
N. Potomac, MD 20878
240-338-0050
transportation@gmail.com

OBJECTIVE

To apply expertise in transportation management, hazardous material regulations, Class 8 equipment specifications, and accident prevention as a Director of Safety and Compliance.

EXPERIENCE

THE CMV CORPORATION, Capitol Heights, Maryland   2007 – Present

Transportation Manager, 2010 – Present
- Manage operation and maintenance of approximately 270 commercial motor vehicles (CMVs) and company cars for a $120 million construction company.
- Spec out and purchase up to $500,000 worth of CMVs and trucks per annum in support of private and government construction projects.
- Saved the company roughly $800,000 by right-sizing the vehicular fleet without compromising operational efficiency.
- Devise routes and obtain the necessary permits for 5,200 hauls per year of heavy equipment and excavated earth along the East Coast.
- Recruit and test drive new drivers. Curtailed accidents by implementing an effective training program. Ensure compliance pertaining to driver qualification files.
- Cut the number of overweight violations 75% by developing a program in Excel to determine proper weight distribution.
- Reduced downtime from trucks out-of-service by strengthening spec requirements and enforcing strict preventive maintenance programs.
- Give presentations on the state of the company's Trucking Division, including operational improvements, cost savings, manpower, regulatory compliance, and safety issues.

Maintenance Director, 2007 – 2010
- Supervised a 60,000 square foot facility, 20 employees, and the maintenance of a 230 unit vehicular fleet.
- Maintained 100+ pieces of heavy construction equipment and commercial motor vehicles.

DELAVAL TURBINE, INC., Oakland, California   2004 – 2007

Power Plant Foreman
- Oversaw repairs and erection of diesel engines with up to 13,500 HP capability. Managed construction of two power plants in Saudi Arabia. Coordinated emergency engine repair on 25,000 SWT oil tankers for the Military Sealift Command in both Hawaii and Trinidad.

SUPPLEMENT

Education:
Diploma, Diesel Engine Technology, 2004, Engine City Technical Institute, Union, New Jersey
Diploma, Automotive Technology, 2003, Franklin Institute of Boston, Boston, Massachusetts

Affiliations:
President, Washington DC Area Fleet Maintenance Council, 2000 – 2003
Member of Board of Directors, Maryland Motor Truck Association, 2010 – Present

CORY SCHULMAN

31005 Video Terrace
Montgomery Village, Maryland 20886

240-338-0050
video@gmail.com

OBJECTIVE

To achieve dynamic, informative, and revealing footage as a Video Coordinator or a related position within the entertainment/media field.

HIGHLIGHTS

Video Experience:
- Filmed and edited video highlights of NFL and championship university teams for scouting purposes and game analysis during the preseason through the playoffs and bowl contests. Achieved sharp resolution during all climate and lighting conditions. Provided managerial, administrative, and technical support to video departments. Served an instrumental role helping the Video Coordinator earn the Big East Video Coordinator of the Year Award, 2011 and 2012.

Education:
- **Master of Science,** Sports Administration, University of Miami, Coral Gables, Florida, 2008
- **Bachelor of Arts**, Political Science, Howard University, Washington, DC, May 2006

Technical Skills:
- Used Avid/Pinnacle Sports Pro (MAC/PC), Avid DV Express Editor, Scorpion, Sports-Tech Editor Lexicom, Avid non-linear editor, simple linear tape editing.

EXPERIENCE

UNIVERSITY OF FLORIDA, Coral Gables, Florida   Fall 2013 – Present
Assistant Video Coordinator
- Coordinate daily operations of the video department for the football team and other NCAA sports.
- Provide technical and administrative support to football coaches, which entails filming/editing video, budgeting, customer relations, and employee supervision.
- Videotape practices, the regular season, and bowl games (Nokia Sugar Bowl, FedEx Orange Bowl, Rose Bowl, and Tostitos' Fiesta Bowl).
- Assist the offense staff and special teams by building cutups of opponents and self-scout film.
- Coordinate game film and highlights for pro-scout and player reviews.

Video Production:
- Create promotional highlights broadcast on network television (ESPN, MTV, and ABC) and used for pregame motivational purposes as well as end-of-the-year banquets.
- Assist with the video functions during official recruiting weekends and annual coaches' clinics.

OAKLAND RAIDERS, Oakland, California   Spring/Summer 2013
Intern
- Facilitated scouting duties by filming practices and creating highlight film in preparation for the annual NFL draft.
- Assisted with operating the Video Department, which included maintaining the video inventory.

UNIVERSITY OF MARYLAND, Adelphi, Maryland   Fall 2012
Student Video Coordinator
- Cut, edited, and copied all incoming and out-going game film for coaches' review.
- Videotaped wide and tight copies of all games and practices. Set up film for NFL scout reviews.

CORY SCHULMAN
15003 Web Development Road
Gaithersburg, MD 20879
240-338-0050
webdevelopment@gmail.com

OBJECTIVE

To develop applications as an experienced Web Developer using .NET technology and Microsoft related languages.

TECHNICAL SKILLS

Programming Languages:

Perl	Visual Basic	Java, Java Servlets	ColdFusion
JavaScript	XML/XSL	SQL and PL/SQL	Xerces
ASP and VBScript	C++, C#	HTML/DHTML	JDOM

Application Development Tools:

Visual Studio .NET	Macromedia Dreamweaver	TOAD
Allaire HomeSite	Oracle8 with SQL*Plus	Allaire Kawa

Servers:

SilverStream	Microsoft IIS	Java Web Server
Apache/Tomcat	Microsoft SQL Server	Resin

Operating Environments:

Microsoft 9x/NT/2000/XP/2010	Novell	Fedora Core

Web Browsers:

Microsoft Internet Explorer	Chrome	Safari

Databases and Additional Applications:

Oracle 8I	SQL 6.5/7	Paint Shop Pro	GifBuilder
Adobe Photoshop	Java Webrazor	Image Builder	Netstudio

EXPERIENCE

Web Developer, IT World Corporation, Bethesda, Maryland, 2012 – Present

On-line Education:
- Used cutting-edge .NET technology and various design pattern techniques to co-develop a multi-million dollar online educational application that is being installed in major hospitals and universities to facilitate nursing certifications. Designed the framework using C#.
- Led team project that used Visual Studio .NET and C# to develop 80% of a backend ingestion engine, which transitioned data from PowerPoint documents to the database. Developed .NET Windows Forms to interface this engine.
- Coordinated three teams and enforced milestones as Configuration Manager to update and rollout the latest versions of video streaming and intelligent tutoring systems.
- Optimized performance of the EDE application, which involved technical support for coding and hardware/software configuration.
- Created original data design using SQL to store PowerPoint information.
- Developed low-level interface tools combining XML/XSL and Visual Basic in Visual Studio .NET to produce HTML output from database.
- Used SQL explicit queries and stored procedures to return XML from database.
- Created installation CD using Visual Studio's Setup and Deployment Projects.

System Development Specialist, FCG, Vienna, Virginia, 2010 – 2012

Healthcare Industry:
- Designed, developed, and administrated Web applications for clients in the healthcare industry to facilitate business to business and business to consumer systems.
- Developed proprietary programs enabling automated insurance validation and address verification procedures for a major hospital in Indiana. Used First Logic and RealMed as well as integrated FCG applications. Gained knowledge in healthcare standards 270/271 transaction processing.
- Co-developed a multi-million dollar FCG application that maintained a centralized database containing details on doctors, hospitals, and insurance information from 52 centers nationwide. Completed this 15-month project on time and under budget.
- Devised Java custom software for complex queries to access databases and enable 100+ employees to secure detailed information on doctors nationwide. Developed XML-based error files. Wrote Java modules for error handling. Administered SilverStream application server in the development environment. Performed code management, which involved changes in HTML, JavaScript, XML/XSL, and Java.

Technology & Dot.com Companies:
- Administered a website for a startup firm that develops and prices health and disability products for online Internet purchases by businesses and consumers. Interfaced with client to provide technical consultation on website upgrades. Modified code to enhance text, links, transactional programming, and graphics.
- Re-developed Employee Administration application on intranet using HTML, ASP, and SQL.
- Revamped codes, updated, and maintained website for major educational organization. Used HTML, DHTML, JavaScript, and Cascading Style Sheets.

PC Support Specialist, Technical Office Solutions, McLean, Virginia, 2008 – 2010
- Provided tier 1, tier 2, and tier 3 technical support to troubleshoot a variety of problems such as hardware failures, fire wall malfunctions, application glitches, programming errors, software/hardware conflicts, viruses, etc.
- Supported three branches as a network administrator in support of a 250-node LAN with 12 servers.
- Served as a Telecom Administrator: performed cellular phone and page administration, voice and modem line management, voice mail account administration, and batch program development.
- Provided website construction and maintenance support.

CERTIFICATIONS

- Microsoft Certified Professional (MCP)
- Microsoft Certified Systems Engineer (MCSE)
- Certified Netware Administration (CNA)
- A+

EDUCATION

Major: Computer Engineering, August 2003 – January 2007, Old Dominion University
Computer Networking, July 2002, Montgomery College
Network Essentials, 2008, Orange Systems
Windows NT Workstation 4, May 2008, Attronica
Windows NT Server Enterprise 4, August 2008 Attronica
TCP/IP, October 2008, IKON Office Solutions

233

CORY SCHULMAN
30001 Writer's Circle
Germantown, Maryland 20874
240-338-0050
writer@gmail.com

EXPERIENCE

QCI INFORMATION SYSTEMS/ALTA IT SERVICES, Washington, DC, 2008 – Present
A $470 million ISO 9001:2000–certified company with 100 locations worldwide. QCI staffs approximately 2,500 employees and provides full lifecycle IT services to the Federal Government.

Technical Writer with Public Trust Clearance
Served QCI as a Contractor for 3 months through Alta IT Services. Hired by QCI full time to write and maintain technical documents in support of QCI's contract with the U.S. Housing and Urban Development Office of the Inspector General (HUD-OIG).

- Documented a suite of integrated programs that supported HUD OIG's mission. Wrote User's Manuals for the Case Management Information Subsystem (CMISS), the Employee Database Subsystem (EDSS), the Hotline Information Subsystem (HISS), and a SharePoint Portal. Manuals ranged in length from 100 pages to 450 pages. Interviewed developers, analyzed and described functionality of more than 13 modules, cropped screenshots, documented caveats, and identified system anomalies.
- Appointed as a Requirements Analyst for the SharePoint customization project, which was deployed to HUD OIG, impacting all of its Departments: Investigations, Audit, OMAP, and Legal. Took minutes for envisioning meetings with stakeholders. Interfaced with the primary developer to gather requirements and develop the Requirements Traceability Matrix. Wrote portions of the Functional Requirements Document.
- Wrote the requirements for an integration between the CMISS and HISS subsystems.
- Supported the development of the EDSS Functional Requirements Document, Requirements Traceability Matrix, Deployment Plan, Systems Subsystems manual, and the Program Specifications document.
- Conducted regression testing of CMISS and wrote defect reports. Presented findings in daily review meetings. Devised an elaborate matrix to track more than 20 variables used in the reporting function of CMISS. Used Quality Center (Formerly Test Director) to catalog procedures for generating reports.
- Produced Visio flow charts for system architecture, defect reporting processes, quality assurance plans, sub-systems, various modules of CMISS, and business logic and data access layers representations.
- Appointed by the Program Manager to draft a proposal on using SharePoint 2007 to centralize and organize a HUD-OIG compliant documentation repository.
- Coordinated the development of three Operations and Maintenance manuals.

TECHNOLOGIES FIRST, INC., Rockville, Maryland, 2007 – 2008
A small business specializing in IT solutions and employing 150 professionals.

Proposal Writer
Facilitated proposal development in response to Request for Proposals (RFPs) from various government agencies. Tailored content to RFP sections C, L, and M for proposals to the U.S. Department of Commerce, U.S. Department of Agriculture, U.S. Department of Labor, and U.S. Department of Health and Human Services, National Institutes of Health, U.S. Department of Defense, the Overseas Private Investment Corporation, and other recipients.

- Interviewed primary personnel and wrote content used in a winning recompete proposal for the U.S. Department of Commerce.
- Researched and identified business opportunities using on-line databases such as Fedbizops, Input, and ebuy.

CACI, INC., Washington, DC/Alexandria, Virginia, 2004 – 2006
A $1.6 billion global corporation with approximately 10,000 employees providing Automated Litigation Support (ALS) and IT solutions to the Federal Government and private industry.

Technical Writer with NACI Security Clearance
Wrote and edited technical documents at internal facilities and Federal client sites, including the U.S. Department of Energy, the Environment and Natural Resources Division, and the U.S. Department of Justice. Produced diverse documentation, such as user manuals, specifications, procedural references, style guides, memoranda, marketing material, storyboards, and compliance assessment interview summaries.

Knowledge Based Solutions (KBS) Operations Facility
- Developed storyboards and graphics in support of the Mega 3 contract proposal.
- Identified documentary needs and drafted manuals on proprietary applications based on interviews with subject matter experts (system engineers, programmers, developers, and section supervisors).
- Tested and modified procedures for scanning, coding, quality control, and quality assurance.

Department of Energy (DOE)
- Documented DOE processes and procedures in support of licensing certification requirements for the Yucca Mountain project, a multi-billion dollar proposal to build a geologic repository for high-level radioactive waste.
- Wrote narrative summaries of compliance assessment interviews used to brief the Mega 2 Civil Division Director on issues adversely impacting the certification process.
- Interviewed IT personnel and wrote marketing literature on CACI applications that showcased CACI ingenuity to produce proprietary software.
- Revised a style manual by modifying numerous sections, including punctuation and grammar, multi-layered lists, page numbering, headers/footers, headings, table of contents, saving styles, and cover page elements.
- Reported on automated container tracking systems, multi-document interfacing, JSP Web-based and Java server programs, an error-detection capability, a suite of Delphi/Oracle applications, image transformation, data import, reporting, and image information loader applications.

Environment and Natural Resources Division (ENRD)
- Revamped two user manuals on CACI proprietary software programs, such as the Supplemental Application for Financial Analysis and Reporting of Information.
- Consulted with programmers on technical elements, such as system architecture, topography, source codes, properties, configuration, maintenance, security, and documentation.
- Interviewed Security Manager on security elements pertaining to the Department of Justice network.

Department of Justice (DOJ), Civil Division, Tobacco Facility
- Produced technical documents in support of the company's most prestigious automated litigation support contract for the largest Federal case in U.S. history.
- Interviewed IT personnel and wrote procedural guides for complex networks, software programs, and hardware, including workstations, servers, scanners, and industrial photocopiers. Wrote an article for the Tobacco Website. Initiated a reference guide to research legal cases on Westlaw application. Summarized U.S. Federal Court decisions for an attorney.
- Drafted reference guides on help desk functions, such as imaging PC, mapping drives, canceling print jobs on the Heidelberg, disabling Web services on the M-1 server, installing Network Oracle on workstations, allocating user's administrative rights to the C: Drive, taking meter readings on 8500/2400/600 series printers, and other associated procedures.

EDUCATION

Bachelor of Arts Degree, 2004, Salisbury State College, Salisbury, Maryland

CORY SCHULMAN
30002 Writer's Circle
Germantown, Maryland 20874
240-338-0050
writer@gmail.com

RESUME CENTER, Gaithersburg/Germantown, Maryland, 2001 – Present

A writing service specializing in employment and business documentation. Provided services to the public and private industry.

Technical Writer, Business Manager
Provided general writing services to satisfy governmental, private sector, and individual client requirements. Interviewed clients and produced diverse writing projects, including business plans, Federal applications, narratives, correspondence, speeches, resumes, books, marketing literature, and biographies. Addressed all occupational fields, especially IT, business, healthcare, administration, management, sales, service, and education.

Publications:
- Authored *Resumes for Higher Paying Positions*, a 187-page, oversized paperback book that sold in major bookstore chains through nationwide distributors. Also available through Amazon.com.
- Wrote articles for a local newspaper, the *Montgomery Sentinel*, as a Special Correspondent.

Communications:
- Conducted 90-minute lectures to promote publication at Borders Bookshops, the Chubb Institute, the Department of Energy, and the Lion's Club.
- Served as a guest speaker to promote biography services at a Sheraton Hotel for Medallion Financial Group.
- Led class segments for English 100 as an Assistant to a Professor at the University of Maryland, University College.
- Interviewed thousands of professionals to gain insights into diverse occupations and productivity.

Business Management:
- Increased annual revenues for 15 consecutive years during national recessions and robust economic conditions.
- Researched and coordinated contracts for office space, merchant systems, advertisers, suppliers, professional services, and computer equipment.
- Presented services, analyzed client needs, recommended solutions, and closed transactions ranging from $75 to $3,500.
- Developed and implemented policies for quality control, pricing structures, public relations/telephone scripts, and other business protocols.
- Established alliances with corporations, which generated referrals for resume and biography services.

EDUCATION

HTML Programming in C#, VB.NET, and Java Courses, 2005, Montgomery College
Manager in a Technological Society, 2000, Graduate Credits, University of Maryland
Bachelor of Arts Degree, 1999, Salisbury State College
Technical Writing Certificate, 1997, one-year program, Montgomery College